ART PSYCHOTHERAPY

ART
PSYCHOTHERAPY

HARRIET WADESON
University of Houston

A WILEY–INTERSCIENCE PUBLICATION

JOHN WILEY & SONS
New York • Chichester • Brisbane • Toronto • Singapore

Library of Congress Cataloging in Publication Data

Wadeson, Harriet, 1931-
    Art psychotherapy.

"A Wiley-Interscience publication."
Includes bibliographical references and index.
1. Art Therapy.   I. Title.

RC489.A7W32   616.8'916'5   79-21440
ISBN 0-471-06383-5
ISBN 0-471-62904-9 (paper)

Printed in the United States of America

21 20 19 18 17

To my children, Lisa, Eric, and Keith
with appreciation for the creative challenges, enrichment, joy, and love
they have brought to my life.

Preface

Art psychotherapy begins with an expressed image, and so shall this book begin. I have selected as an introduction to this field a drawing by Craig, a young man diagnosed paranoid schizophrenic, because his images are eloquent. By expressing himself in them, he probably averted further decompensation. Through his pictures he divulged his "secrets" to me, overcoming his fears and building trust by sharing his images. On the next page is his picture of The Mother of the Universe, with Craig as the tiny person sitting in her hand. It was the many experiences of a deep involvement with people through their images, such as my journey into Craig's inner world (described more fully later) that pushed this book into being.

The book developed out of a double need—an internal push, and an external pull. The push from within has been the wish to draw together what I consider a breadth and depth of experience available to few art therapists and to share the observations and ideas that have evolved over my 18 years in art therapy. This push had nothing to do with decision. It felt more like destiny. My professional and personal growth, as it intertwined with the budding of the profession of art therapy during the 1960s and 1970s, had about it many of the "happy accidents" the artist experiences. A drip of paint or an accidental smudge directs the composition in a new and exciting way. An experienced artist learns to recognize and maximize these happy accidents.

My career as an art therapist has profited by such fortuitous events. I discovered art therapy at the National Institutes of Health almost by chance, at a time when budgeting was generous and I could find employment there as an art therapist despite a lack of experience and training. In this rarefied atmosphere I felt I was witnessing (and later participating in) the leading edge of psychiatric research. I entered art therapy when it was all but unknown and ripe for pioneering. As a result, I have been fortunate in having the opportunity to innovate and to have my work published in journals that are read throughout the world.

The surge of the Human Potential Movement with its valuation of creativity and direct experience found me in the right place at the right time and opened opportunities for me beyond the psychiatric world to which I had been introduced at NIH. Subsequently, the increasing professionalization of art therapy has led to challenging opportunities for the training of students and for developing my thinking about what constitutes high-quality training for art therapists.

Figure 1. *Mother of the Universe,* a delusion by Craig, diagnosed paranoid schizophrenic. He believed he was the keeper of Mother Nature's secrets.

The external pull has come from a strong need I have recognized in the training of art therapists and other professionals in more recent years. I have not had a comprehensive book to recommend to students and other professionals interested in the field. As time passed, it became clearer and clearer to me that the book I wanted I would have to write myself.

This double need was of such significance to me that for a long time I staggered under its import. The task seemed monumental. Once I overcame that obstacle, the words fairly flew onto the pages. It was as though the book was almost written in my head and had only to flow down my arm and out my pen.

Obviously this book is not, nor is it intended to be, the last word on art psychotherapy. The profession is young and energetic, with much growth still to come. But this book *is* intended to provide philosophy, principles, practice, abundant variety of case material, and research. It is written from a highly personal perspective. It is clear to me that the therapist is a large part of the process, and to have written a book devoid of my personal beliefs and reactions would have made it an empty shell. I have tried to make my biases explicit. Basically, I would describe my approach as humanistic, existential, and phenomenological. I see psychotherapy as primarily an educational process to help people with problems in living rather than as a treatment for a disease. The educational process is not the traditional cognitive model, but rather an affectually oriented facilitation of emotional growth. I make no pretense of speaking for the entire profession; rather, I am expressing my view and experience of it.

The title, *Art Psychotherapy,* reflects my way of practicing art therapy. The field is a broad one with much variety among the approaches of different practitioners. Some place emphasis on the art, some on the therapy, and many on both. Some art therapists consider themselves psychotherapists using art expression as a therapeutic modality. Their work is art psychotherapy, and they are comfortable with both primary therapeutic responsibility and working as part of a treatment team. Art psychotherapists distinguish themselves from others with less training and experience who work in an adjunctive capacity only.

The first part of the book furnishes a foundation: philosophy, history, application, training. These discussions inform the case material that follows in succeeding sections. It is possible to proceed directly to the case material in any order desired; that is, the book can be approached in its totality as a text, or be used as a reference for specific information. To develop each chapter so that it can stand alone, a small amount of repetition has been necessary. The basic approach is described in the first section, then illustrated in the following sections which form the major portion of the book. My intention has been to discuss and illustrate art therapy conducted with the primary psychiatric populations more extensively than has been heretofore published in book form. A final chapter explores art therapy research.

Despite the aim of this work to be a comprehensive book, there are some deliberate omissions. Since the focus of the book is emotional disturbance, organic brain syndromes are not included. There is minimal material about work with children. Most art therapy books published to date have dealt exclusively with children. Many are excellent. In contrast, there is presently very little published in book form on art psychotherapy with adults. Since my experience has been primarily in this realm, and need for information in this area is so much greater, I have not tried to overextend myself into child art therapy.

Another significant omission is the use of art expression for diagnosis. I considered writing a chapter titled "Diagnosis and Misdiagnosis," but felt that the point was made sufficiently in Chapter 15, "Comparison of Art Expression in Schizophrenia, Depression, and Manic-Depressive Psychosis."

Related to this decision is the whole issue of psychiatric labeling. I struggled with this one for some time. When art expression (or any other form of data) is used to gain a fuller understanding of the client or patient, a diagnostic term can be a useful sort of shorthand. On the other hand, when a diagnostic label is used as a means of classification without an attempt to comprehend the individual's uniqueness, then the shorthand becomes a shortcut, circumventing the more demanding process of dealing with the individual humanly. There are other abuses perpetrated through psychiatric classification—such as stigmatization, and facilitation of distancing between therapist and patient, with each of them viewing the former as "well" and the latter as "sick." These are crucial issues in the field of psychotherapy.

Despite the problems surrounding diagnosis, and my own personal distaste for applying a diagnostic label, I have divided the case material into chapters according to diagnostic categories. There are two reasons for this. First, as stated earlier, I believe that to some extent these classifications are valid. Second, and perhaps more important, it is necessary that students and mental health professionals understand these categories as they form the framework of our present understanding of those undergoing psychotherapy. As used here, however, I hope it is clear that diagnosis is never implemented to pigeonhole, but rather as a means of organizing the material presented to differentiate the kinds of problems the art therapist encounters with various populations.

Since the material in this book spans a number of years of work, there are certain variations in approach as my professional activities evolved and developed over time—for example, my early work was focused much more on the patient than on our relationship, and the case material reported from my early years in art therapy reflects that focus. The rough chronology of the work is as follows: I began working with adolescents; then successively with depressive and manic depressive psychotics, families, and schizophrenics; and lastly with neurotics and alcoholics. (Naturally, there was some overlap.) My research interests and approaches also changed over the years and, although not detailed in this book, to the extent that they are introduced, a fair amount of variety may be seen.

Selection of the illustrations was based on applicability, presentational qualities, intrinsic interest, and photographic reproducibility. The choice was sometimes difficult, because there were often many excellent examples to illustrate a particular point. In a few instances pictures have not been supplied becuase the available examples did not reproduce well or required too lengthy an explanation.

Finally, it is my hope that this work conveys some of my own gratification from the creative opportunities afforded me in the young and exciting profession of art therapy. Because the field is a dynamic one, this book is intended to be thought-provoking rather than conclusive.

HARRIET WADESON

Houston, Texas
September 1979

Acknowledgments

I wish to express my appreciation first to Lyman Wynne, M.D., Ph.D., for his support and inspiration throughout my art therapy career. It was Lyman who gave me my first art therapy job, who has provided me challenging professional opportunities since, and who has enthusiastically supported art therapy from its early days when it was an unrecognized therapeutic modality. Lyman's work and being have been a source of inspiration to me throughout our years of personal friendship and professional association. I am grateful, as well, for his careful reading of this manuscript and his valuable suggestions.

Next I would like to acknowledge Hanna Yaxa Kwiatkowska, my first art therapy mentor, who, in a sense, gave me a profession that has provided me with abundant gratification and challenging opportunities. Similarly, I would like to thank William Bunney, M.D., and Will Carpenter, M.D., for their support and supervision of my work at NIH. Both provided me with learning and opportunity for research through art therapy.

To Roy Fairfield, Ph.D., Richard Gillespie, Ph.D., Joyce Cohen, Ph.D., Marcia Hart, M.A., ATR, and Nancy White, M.A., go my thanks for reading this manuscript and offering some excellent suggestions. I am particularly indebted to Roy for responding to some of the case material in poetry, a beautiful way of letting me know he understood what I was trying to say.

I give my thanks to my mother, Sophie Weisman, who typed many rough drafts as a labor of love, to Al Jankowitz and Frank Riley for assistance in duplication, and to Rose Allinder for proofing and indexing.

Finally, my profoundest gratitude is for the clients, patients, and students who are the life of this book.

H. W.

Contents

**PART ONE—PHILOSOPHY, PRINCIPLES,
AND APPLICATION**

1 **CREATIVE PROCESS IN LIFE**   3

Nature of the Creative Experience, 5
Creativity in Art Therapy, 6

2 **ADVANTAGES OF ART THERAPY**   8

Imagery, 8
Decreased Defenses, 9
Objectification, 10
Permanence, 10
Spatial Matrix, 11
Creative and Physical Energy, 11

3 **HISTORY AND APPLICATION OF ART THERAPY**   13

Application of Art Therapy, 14
Physical Environment, 15
Session Structure, 16
Art Media, 18

4 **INSTITUTIONAL POLITICS**   19

Staff Relations, 20
Art Therapist as Advocate, 21

5 **ART THERAPY TRAINING**   23

A Student's Self-Exploration, 24
My Own Art Therapy Education, 28

6 **THERAPEUTIC RELATIONSHIP**   32

General Considerations, 32
Particular Considerations in Art Therapy, 38

Confidentiality, 41
Ownership, 42
Art Therapist's Participation in Art, 42

PART TWO—AFFECTIVE DISORDERS

7   DEPRESSION   **46**

Therapeutic Relationship, 47
Case Study, 49
Characteristics of Art Expression in Depression, 61

8   MANIC-DEPRESSIVE PSYCHOSIS   **68**

Case Study, 68
Further Examples, 75
Therapeutic Relationship, 79
Characteristics of Art Expression in Bipolar Depression, 80

9   SUICIDE   **82**

Therapeutic Relationship, 83
Hospitalized Patients, 84
Suicide Messages, 85
Anger, 88
Feelings of Harmfulness to Others, 90
Self-Hate, 91
Hopelessness, 93
Communication or Isolation, 96
Spiral Symbol, 98
Conclusion, 101

10   COMBINING EXPRESSIVE THERAPIES IN AN EFFORT TO SURVIVE ON A DEPRESSION WARD   **102**

Structure, 103
Movement to Music, 104
Relaxation, 105
Mural Making, 107
Dramatic Expression, 107
Fantasy, 108
Results, 108

PART THREE—SCHIZOPHRENIA

11 GENERAL CHARACTERISTICS AND CLINICAL
CONSIDERATIONS IN SCHIZOPHRENIA   112

Therapeutic Relationship and the Meaning of Meaning, 114

12 PHENOMENOLOGY OF SCHIZOPHRENIA
EXPRESSED IN ART   117

Subjective Experience of Schizophrenia, 118
Hallucinations and Delusions, 131
Prevalence of Recurrent Motifs in Psychotic Delusions, 141
Case Study, 152

13 INSTITUTIONAL IMPACT   163

Impact of The Seclusion Room Experience, 163
TV: Programming Delusions, 170

14 ART EXPRESSION AND RECOVERY STYLE IN
ACUTE SCHIZOPHRENIA   176

Examples, 178
Discussion, 185

15 COMPARISON OF ART EXPRESSION IN
SCHIZOPHRENIA, DEPRESSION, AND
MANIC-DEPRESSIVE PSYCHOSIS   188

Unipolar Depressives, 190
Bipolar Manic-Depressives, 191
Schizophrenics, 191
Organization, 193
Age-Matched Groups, 196
Discussion, 197

PART FOUR—NEUROSIS AND ADDICTION

16 JUST PLAIN FOLKS   200

Case Study, 201

17 DREAMS   210

Examples, 211

18 ALCOHOL ABUSE   220

Evaluations of Alcoholic Families, 224

PART FIVE—GROUP AND FAMILY ART THERAPY

19 GROUP ART THERAPY   236

Structure, 237
Time, 238
Shared Images, 239
Role of the Art Therapist in the Group, 239
Examples from Art Therapy Groups, 241
Hospitalized Adolescent Groups, 241
Private Practice Groups of Well-Functioning Adults, 256

20 FAMILY ART THERAPY   280

Therapeutic Relationship, 282
Couple Art Therapy Techniques, 283
Couple Art Techniques in Manic-Depressive Research, 299
Multi-Family Art Therapy, 308

PART SIX—RESEARCH

21 PROBLEMS IN ART THERAPY RESEARCH   318

Overview of Types of Research, 319
Examples, 321
Problems Intrinsic to Art Therapy Research, 328
Applying Methodologic Rigor, 329
Comment, 330

CONCLUDING REMARKS   332
APPENDIX   334
REFERENCES   337
SUBJECT INDEX   341
AUTHOR INDEX   347

Foreword

The concepts and the practices of art psychotherapy have evolved both within and outside the sphere of psychotherapy. In the 1940s, under the pioneering leadership of Margaret Naumburg, the initial framework was psychoanalytic. By studying clinical cases in detail, with artistic expression as the springboard for the patient's associations and the therapist's interpretations, Naumburg established an invaluable tradition that continues as one component of present-day art psychotherapy.

Other psychoanalytically oriented pioneers, such as Edith Kramer, gave greater emphasis to the healing potentialities of the psychological processes activated in the creative act itself. Still others, such as Hanna Yaxa Kwiatkowska, began some 20 years ago to expand the scope of art psychotherapy into the interpersonal field of families.

At about that time, innovations quite suddenly proliferated not only with fresh concepts and methods, but also with newly defined professional roles for art therapists in private practice and in a great array of clinical settings and academic and research institutions. It was my good fortune to be in a position in the Intramural Program of the National Institute of Mental Health, where I could readily be aware of these exciting developments, especially in Washington and Philadelphia, and to facilitate, more explicitly, the creative work of Hanna Kwiatkowska and Harriet Wadeson at NIMH.

Over the subsequent years Harriet Wadeson has continued to add to her clinical, research, and artistic experience. On the one hand, she has published numerous research papers in leading psychiatric journals; on the other hand, she has thoroughly familiarized herself with developments in existential psychology and the Human Potential Movement, making use not only of graphic arts but also of other modalities of expressive therapies.

This book, then, has become a personalized statement arising from her highly diversified professional background. She shows how this personal philosophy can be successfully adapted for use with a variety of people, ranging from those with major and minor psychiatric symptoms to those who wish to enhance their growth in dealing with the problems of living.

As an ingredient of the professionlization of art psychotherapy, Harriet Wadeson discusses forthrightly many of the special problems that art therapists, especially when working in insitutional settings, have had while establishing their status and identity. Earlier, art therapists often worked as psychodiagnosticians, and their therapy was defined as adjunctive to the primary therapy of someone else. Wadeson asserts that "art therapists should be psychotherapists plus," that is, psychotherapists who are qualified to work alone or in a team of colleagues and who also are trained in the theory and practice of art therapy, have technical expertise in art, and are experienced in using art for self-expression. Surely, this professional identity is a far cry from "messing around" and "killing time" with art materials in activities programs. In my view, psychiatrists and psychologists even today have failed to understand how much they can learn from skilled art psychotherapists. Interdisciplinary acknowledgment clearly needs to be reciprocal; the gains then are mutual.

On the other hand, I must express a personal hope—indeed recognized in this volume—that a sophisticated approach to art psychotherapy will not neglect those deeply impaired individuals whose creactivity becomes manifest through developing simple but often surprising and personally meaningful "artistic" skills. Also, certain patients can benefit from art therapy that begins stepwise, helping patients to extend their attention span, develop the ability to integrate parts into a whole, improve their motor control, and gain better ability to focus or perceive. Such approaches are quite compatible with a comprehensive approach that also has been enriched by the incorporation of a humanistic tradition concerned with helping all persons, including "normal" clients, to improve authenticity, individuality, and self-actualization. In varying degrees, all approaches to art therapy require a transfer from the realm of materials to the realms of individual creative processes and interpersonal relationships.

Harriet Wadeson's many years as an art therapist have engendered thoughtful and quite detailed guidelines here for dealing with a multiplicity of patients and situations. She devotes an entire chapter or more to each of the following: mania, depression, suicide, schizophrenia, neurosis, alcoholism, families, and hospitalized and "normal" groups. A most important chapter explains the hypothesis that the recovery style of schizophrenics (either "integrating" or "sealing-over") can be determined and assessed by the quality of the patient's pictorial expression. These findings are documented by collaborative research which suggests that the patient's recovery style can be elucidated by the quality and expressiveness of his or hers pictorial representation. The recovery style can then be a determining factor in planning the best type of treatment by all the staff and in deciding whether drug therapy or other approaches are indicated.

The book as a whole makes it clear that Dr. Wadeson especially enjoys working with the "integrators," those persons who want to explore the meaning of disturbing experience to the totality of their lives. At the same time that this work delineates many details of technique and the examination of research hypotheses, she effectively models for the reader her interest in the therapist's use of self. She shares with us some of her life experiences, dreams, art productions, and even a poem or two. The chapter on research concludes with a statement that gives a clear picture of the author's professional goals: "It is my hope that the creativity which is the essence of the profession will be applied to new means of exploration of the human condition through the fertile expressiveness art therapists are trained to perceive."

Harriet Wadeson has waged a successful struggle to make a synthesis that does justice both to her personal viewpoint and to her profession. Grounded in artistic and psychodynamic traditions, she has absorbed and integrated diverse innovations with families and groups without surrendering her interest in personal meaning. She has worked in depth with psychotic inpatients as well as with dissatisfied "normals." Perhaps the most distinctive emphasis in her approach, and in my view the most difficult but most therapeutically valuable, is her concern with a creative therapeutic alliance. Within a framework of participant observation, in the reciprocal processes between therapist and client, lie the most powerful opportunities for personal growth and therapeutic change. Wadeson addresses both the potentialities and the pitfalls for client and therapist alike in such knotty issues as the extent of self-disclosure by the therapist. In art psychotherapy as in verbal therapies, the complexity of "countertransference" problems requires self-awareness. Further, she points out that as a therapist in a creative alliance, she does not abandon her own philosophy but is "receptive to the client's finding her own way" and thus enables the client to "experiment with new ways of being."

Lyman C. Wynne
Professor and former Chairman,
Director of the Division of Family Programs,
Department of Psychiatry,
University of Rochester School
of Medicine and Dentistry,
Rochester, New York

ART PSYCHOTHERAPY

PART ONE

Philosophy, Principles, and Application

CHAPTER 1

Creative Process In Life

Life. Meaning. Creativity. Art. In the largest sense, they are all one. In presenting Art Psychotherapy, the appropriate place to begin is in these larger realms which form the context for my profession. So I begin with meaning in life. Much of human striving, beyond mere survival needs, appears to me to be directed toward the creation of meaning in life. *Creation* of meaning, not discovery of meaning. Although an object or a process may have intrinsic characteristics, it is we who determine its import to us in the way we structure and integrate experience. For example, an intrinsic attribute of fire is its heat. The meaning we give it may be destructive force, weapon, necessity for warmth, useful tool, gift of the gods, magic power, and so forth.

An important part of the acculturation and socialization process in human development is the learning of shared meaning. Some beliefs are widely shared in our culture, such as a germ theory of disease. Others are prevalent but less universal, such as concepts of a divine being. And others may be peculiar to a small subculture, such as belief in reincarnation. It is evident that each of these examples has wide implications for how people choose to live their lives. The issue of belief and meaning is a complex one and much more subtle than these obvious examples illustrate. The evolution of a culture's myths reflect human-kind's ongoing search for meaning and the importance of these myths in directing the individual lives within the culture. Popular writings such as those by Carlos Castenada (1972) and Ram Dass (1974) point to the whole structure of meaning as merely an illusion. From such perspective, one may step back and look at the meanings we create rather than to assume that meaning is intrinsic.

The meaning of meaning is central to art and psychotherapy. To limit ourselves for the moment to the graphic arts, the art products are visual productions related to other visual perceptions. Visual perceptions themselves are nothing more than shapes of color we integrate into visually meaningful experiences. Optical illusions demonstrate the tricks that can be played on our integrating ability. This ability is so significant that we can even have visual experiences without use of our visual perceptors. We can close our eyes and "see with the mind's eye," and "see" involuntarily in our dreams.

3

The image that is produced in graphic art is created to be seen. It does not duplicate the natural world, although it may bear a strong resemblance to objects in it. The artist has created an illusion, a separate "reality," a personal vision that through transformation into an art object may be shared with others. It is the compelling nature of this communication that gives art its power.

Much has been written about what distinguishes great art from other comparable expressions which don't achieve greatness. I won't attempt to hazard the complexities of the field of aesthetics, nevertheless, there are a few points which appear obvious to me. Art that is considered great must communicate at a significant level of meaning. Expressions in art which are purely idiosyncratic do not achieve this end. Secondly, it seems to me that art which comes to be considered great does not merely reflect the status of the times, but in some way advances consciousness in the human view of the universe. Present meaning becomes transcended, and new forms emerge.

The relation of meaning to psychotherapy is both obvious and subtle. Troubled people who seek psychotherapy are obviously not giving their lives the meaning they want. They're depressed, unhappy with themselves, confused, angry, or disappointed. Others are sent into treatment because someone is unhappy with them. They may not ascribe to the consensual meaning endorsed by the culture, as illustrated by some of the schizophrenics described in this book. (One of these people believed he could control the weather; several were visited by the devil.) When the behavior predicated on such beliefs is threatening to others, these people are likely to be incarcerated. For example, a woman was hospitalized by her husband because she kept jumping out of their moving car to obey God's commandments to her. Thomas Szasz (1970) has written eloquently of society's measures for dealing with deviancy through institutionalization in mental hospitals. Phyllis Chesler (1972) also has spoken out about the incidences of women hospitalized for not successfully succumbing to the role society imposed upon them.

The more subtle issues of meaning emerge in the actual therapeutic work. Many values and doctrines of meaning are conveyed in the therapist's and institution's reaction to their clientele. These aspects of meaning are discussed further in Chapter 6 and Chapter 4.

Creativity is not the same as art. Not everyone is capable of becoming a great artist. But all are creative, no matter how limited. Frank Barron (1968a) writes:

> Because we are capable of reflecting upon ourselves, we are committed, willy-nilly, to an artistic enterprise in the creation of our own personality.

Consciously and unconsciously we use the multifarious influences which have played upon our lives to create meaning, to make choices, to fashion our behavior. Throughout our lives, we are engaged in an ongoing creative enterprise, in the broadest sense.

The field of the art therapist is one in which clients use the particular creative medium of art expression to advance the larger creativity of making meaningful their own lives. Reciprocally, art therapists create meaning in *their* own lives through their particular expertise in encouraging and relating to the meaning others create in their art expressions.

NATURE OF THE CREATIVE EXPERIENCE— A PERSONAL ACCOUNT

Creativity is difficult to discuss. No one seems to know exactly what it is or why some people are more creative, imaginative, original than others. A number of psychoanalytic theorists have written on the subject (Kris, 1952; Weissman, 1967; Arieti, 1976, to name a few). Barron (1968b) has conducted studies on it, and Koestler (1964) has described the process. I will not struggle through the maze of whys and wherefores but will instead say a few words about my own creative experience.

Many of my most deeply satisfying moments have been spent in the act of creative expression. For me this experience is an important part of my life. For others it has been even more—the mainspring of their existence. What makes personal artistic endeavors so compelling?

I believe my early relationship to art was an important influence and that the direction of my professional life has been a logical consequence of my childhood and adolescence. My mother used to boast: "Harriet painted before it was stylish, before everyone was doing it." Art expression has been an important outlet for as long as I can remember. I used to make up stories and tell them through a series of pictures before I could write. Artistic expression was reinforced further by the acclaim of classmates and teachers as well as the many uses I found to which it could be put. For example, when my brother and I believed my mother had instigated a campaign of discipline and, to us, harshness, I hung posters around the house depicting her as a gestapo agent. I remember as a small child spending hours in our attic looking over prints of the paintings of old masters. What musings they prompted, I don't remember. Even today, there are pictures at the National Gallery I view fondly as old friends— friends from whom I have grown away but who have a special place in my affection because of our history together.

I never considered art as a career, however. For one thing, I didn't think I was good enough. But perhaps even more significant, at the time of career choosing and most of the time since, I very much wanted involvement with others. For me art expression is a solitary experience. At times I have found it a necessary one in the development and exploration of my own individual relationship to myself and my world, but it is a journey into myself rather than an engagement with others.

I don't believe I can articulate how an amorphous mass of clay in my hands comes to take the form of a mother and child lying together in a way that says much to me about myself as both mother and child, as well as pleasing me aesthetically in relationships of shapes, mass, space, texture, and material. The message is one of image—beyond and before words. Usually I give myself over to the material and am surprised at what emerges. The element of surprise is certainly one of the delights. Sometimes, of course, nothing much happens and the result is disappointing.

A significant question for me is what is it that makes the creative experience so satisfying? I believe that it is a particular sort of paradox. On the one hand, there is a getting out of oneself, the sort of transcendence Koestler discusses in *The Act of Creation* (1964), a feeling of touching and being part of a more universal experience than the unique conditions of one's own life. For me, there is illumination and possible alleviation of pain in this sort of occurrence. On the other hand, the stuff of which the creation is made is deeply personal, often putting one more profoundly in touch with oneself. It is here that understanding is achieved. Integration is probably the result of the interface of the personal and the universal. Finally, there is the pleasure. I as creator can look at my creation and admire it, and realize that I am looking at myself.

I do not believe that the process is a magic one, but rather a flowering of germanating images and techniques. In this sense each work of art takes a lifetime to produce.

CREATIVITY IN ART THERAPY

Therapy conceived as an art form is created in the same manner. Each therapeutic intervention (like each brush stroke), each therapeutic case (like each work of art) is the result of the therapist's (artist's) training and experience. Both artist and therapist develop their sensibility so that their efforts flow from the heightened awareness of long discipline and reflection.

What is the place of creativity in the client's expeience in art therapy? There are some who believe that the quality of the art product is indicative of the degree of sublimation achieved (Edith Kramer, 1971). Followers of this school of thought propose that it is the synthesizing effect of the creative force that produces art therapy's beneficial effect. I do not hold with this belief. Although I have worked with many people who achieved clarity and direction seemingly unconsciously and almost mysteriously through their art expression, I have worked with many others whose art expression was minimal or undeveloped, who achieved important insights and changes in themselves through reflecting on their images. In either case, there is creativity involved, but not necessarily only the narrow artistic sublimation Kramer suggests.

The client's creativity, as well as the therapist's, encompasses the entire art psychotherapeutic process. Such is the case in any form of therapy. In art therapy, however, the medium of expression is an art form, thereby encouraging a more focused creativity than otherwise. Since expression in visual imagery encourages production of fantasy material (as discussed in the next chapter), there is stimulation of some of the deeper layers of consciousness, bringing to bear on the creative processes richer resources than may be ordinarily available.

CHAPTER 2

Advantages of Art Therapy

Why art therapy? What does it have to offer? If I am giving a presentation to familiarize mental health professionals with art therapy, I usually conduct an experiential session so that they can discover for themselves. I try to explain that art therapy is a "doing" sort of therapy and that to try to describe it is like trying to explain the flavor of chocolate to one who has never tasted it. Because needs and perspectives differ, those experiencing art therapy for the first time may not all discover the same things.

Despite the limitations inherent in presenting art therapy in the abstract, there are some unique advantages which art expression contributes to the psychotherapy process that may be helpful in reflecting on the illustrative material in this book:

IMAGERY

We think in images. We thought in images before we had words. We could recognize mother before we could say "mama." No doubt other senses played a part too, such as touch and smell, but it is evident that in the second half of the first year of life, babies come to recognize their mothers by sight. Although some of us develop to become more visually oriented than others (for example, those with photographic memories are an extreme), in all of us much of our preverbal thinking took the form of images. Primary process is the psychoanalytic term used to denote primitive, id-related experience. It would seem logical that much of this experience laid down early in life (primary) has a significant image component. We can say, therefore, that imagery probably plays a large part in early personality formation, the core experiences which influence subsequent layers of personality development. (Such a scheme of personality building in which each developmental stage is strongly influenced by its predecessors is found in many theories, but perhaps is most explicit in the concepts of Erikson [1950].)

In addition to imagery forming a base of experience in personality development, it is also recognized as a primary component of unconscious phenomena.

8

In writing about dreams, which he considered to be the "royal road" to the unconscious, Freud (1963, p.90) stated:

We experience it (a dream) predominantly in visual images; feelings may be present too, and thoughts interwoven in it as well; the other senses may also experience something, but nonetheless it is predominantly a question of images. Part of the difficulty of giving an account of dreams is due to our having to translate these images into words. "I could draw it," a dreamer often says to us, "but I don't know how to say it."

In art therapy the image of a dream, fantasy, or experience is depicted in image form rather than having to be translated into words, as in purely verbal therapy. Jungians have encouraged their clients to produce pictures of their dreams and, in many cases, the interpretations of the pictures serve as the prime modality of a Jungian analysis. (An example is the work of Perry [1976].) Obviously words may be used to elaborate and associate to the art expression, but the essential message is conveyed in image form.

In addition to the *reflection* of images, the art medium often stimulates the *production* of images, tapping into primary process material and enhancing the creative process, both narrowly in an artistic sense, and broadly in the creation of solutions in living.

DECREASED DEFENSES

This attribute is closely related to the importance of imagery, discussed above. Because verbalization is our primary mode of communication, we are more adept at manipulating it and more facile in saying what we want to say and refraining from saying what we don't want to say than through other communicative modes. Art is a less customary communicative vehicle for most people and therefore less amenable to control. Unexpected things may burst forth in a picture or sculpture, sometimes totally contrary to the intentions of its creator. This is one of the most exciting potentialities in art therapy. Unexpected recognitions often form the leading edge of insight, learning, and growth.

A common misconception about art therapy is that artistic ability is necessary for self exploration through art expression. On the contrary, an artist may be less prone to accidental "slips of the brush" due to a high degree of ability in manipulating the materials. Occasionally I have worked with such people. On the other hand, I have also conducted therapy with a number of art therapists who were both skillful artistically and sophisticated psychologically, yet who were sufficiently open to self examination to relax their controls and let their pictures speak to them.

OBJECTIFICATION

In addition to working in images, another unique attribute of art therapy is the production of a tangible product. There are many implications to this aspect of the therapy, some of which are discussed in Chapter 6. A particular advantage of there being a tangible object produced is that it is often easier for a resistant patient to relate to the picture than to the self. For example, a hospitalized depressed man initially spoke of the angry expression on the face in his picture. He hadn't intended it to look that way and didn't understand why it had come out like that because he did not feel angry himself, he said. Eventually he came to identify with the figure in his picture and recognized his own anger. In this way the art expression can form a bridge. I call this process ''objectification'' because feelings or ideas are at first externalized in an object (picture or sculpture). The art object allows the individual, while separating from the feelings, to recognize their existance. If all goes well, the feelings become owned and integrated as a part of the self. Often this happens within one session. For particularly resistant people, it may take longer. For example, an agitated depressed elderly man denied for many months that his pictures had any relationship to his feelings. He had been a draftsman and was adept at depicting tranquil scenes. Eventually he drew a large smoldering volcano and recognized that it represented himself.

PERMANENCE

Unique to art therapy is the permanence of the object produced. The advantage here is that the picture or sculpture is not subject to the distortions of memory. It remains the same and can be recalled intact months or years after its creation. I have found that reviewing the art productions with clients is extremely beneficial. Sometimes new insights develop. Particularly helpful is noticing emerging patterns which may not be apparent when the work is viewed singly. There have been times when clients have forgotten a piece of work and seeing it recalls the feelings that were present at its creation. In this way it is possible for both therapist and client to derive a sense of the ongoing development that occurs in the therapeutic process. Such awareness can be very encouraging to a client, who thereby comes to recognize his or her own progress. Although it might seem likely that therapeutic progress would be self-evident, it is striking how easily people tend to forget how things were and how they felt. A series of pictures can provide ample documentation of the significant issues and their affectual components.

Permanence of the tangible object provides other advantages besides therapeutic ones. This very personal record created by the patient is a potent source of research data (see Part VI). It also furnishes a vivid and dramatic statement from the patient which can be shared with others.* At staff meetings I have found that although material was presented about the patient by other staff members—psychiatrist, social worker, nurse, occupational therapist—describing history, symptoms, family, and treatment process, frequently it has been the pictures I have brought which captured the attention of the meeting in the discussion period. They are a direct statement by the patient rather than information that has been filtered by others. They are often evocative, stimulating an emotional reaction from the onlookers beyond just intellectual processing.

SPATIAL MATRIX

Verbalization is linear communication. First we say one thing, then another. Art expression need not obey the rules of language—grammar, syntax, or logic. It is spatial in nature. There is no time element. In art, relationships occur in space. Sometimes this form of expression more nearly duplicates experience. If I were to tell you about my family, I would tell you about my mother, *then* about my father, *then* about their relationship to each other, *then* about my brother and his relationship to each of them, *then* about each one's relationship to me. Obviously, I experience all of this at once. And in a picture I can portray it all at once. I can show closeness and distance, bonds and divisions, similarities and differences, feelings, particular attributes, context of family life, ad infinitum.

CREATIVE AND PHYSICAL ENERGY

For years I taught an evening art therapy course attended mostly by professionals. They had worked all day and were tired when they came to class. It was primarily an experiential course, but often there was discussion at the beginning. I was struck time and again by how sleepy we all were until we began the art work. Then everyone seemed to wake up, and the discussion following the picture-making was much livelier than the initial interchange.

There seems to be an enlivening quality to be found in engaging in art expression. I have noticed a comparable phenomenon in ongoing art therapy groups. In the discussion following the drawing period, group members are often more open, revealing, and receptive than in initial discussion, even though the former may have been quite intense and probing.

I don't know how to explain this observation, but I have experienced the change in energy level in myself over and over again as well, as I have become

---

*Naturally, the pictures express confidential material and are not shown and discussed outside staff meetings except for professional presentations, when the patient's identity is disguised.

"activated" in art activity. It may be simply a matter of physical movement, but I doubt it, since often the physical activity is not that much greater than talking. I am more inclined to believe that it is a release of creative energy and a more direct participation in experience than in talking, especially "talking about." At times the creative activity takes on the character of play, and art therapy becomes more like fun than like work. Even when playful, however, I take the art therapy seriously.

CHAPTER 3

History and Application of Art Therapy

The roots of the art therapy profession reach back to prehistoric eras when our remote predecessors expressed their relationship to their world in cave drawings and sought the meaning of existence in imagery. The beginnings of thought itself probably began with the process of symbolization (Greek *syn* "together" and *ballein* "to throw"). Thus meaning became established by the "throwing together" of the known and the unknown. The concrete image could stand for the unknown, the mysterious, the ineffable. For example, in 2500 B.C. a crude Greek stone carving with protuberances to indicate breasts served as a fertility goddess (Jung, 1964, p. 107).

Art therapy today has grown out of the current psychiatric movement, with particular indebtedness to Freud and Jung, both of whom placed great significance on symbolization. Freud developed the concept of an unconscious, expressed particularly vividly in the symbolic imagery of dreams. Jung postulated a universal unconscious with common symbols appearing among different cultures through various epochs. As a result, Jungians have been especially interested in the art of many cultures.

Art of "insane asylum" inmates had been of interest in the past, particularly in regard to its sometimes bizarre qualities. It became a focus of attention in itself in the Heidelberg Collection, formed by Hans Prinzhorn (1972) in 1922 from art gathered from many of Europe's insane asylums.

The use of art expression as a therapeutic modality did not come into its own until the 1940s through the pioneering efforts of Margaret Naumburg (1966). Relying heavily on psychoanalytic theory and practice, she encouraged clients to draw spontaneously and to free associate to their pictures. She entered the world of therapy through her contacts with psychoanalysts whose children were students of the progressive school she directed. She was followed in the 1950s by Edith Kramer (1971), who worked extensively with children. Her approach was different from Naumburg's, in that she emphasized the integrative and healing properties of the creative process itself, which does not require verbal reflection. This differentiation of emphasis continued in a polarity in the profession, with one extreme placing the emphasis on the art and the other on the therapy. In the former, the creative process of the client is stressed; in the latter, the art forms the basis for insight.

From its early psychoanalytic beginnings, the profession has branched out and diverged into existentialistic directions that hold the individual responsible and accountable, in contrast with the more deterministic forces proposed by psychoanalytic theory. The Human Potential Movement has had a strong influence, as has the resurgence of Jungian psychology. As a result, the present state of the art encompasses many frameworks and approaches.

In the 1960s art therapy became a recognized profession. Two events were significant in its development at that time: the creation of the *American Journal of Art Therapy* (published initially as The *Bulletin of Art Therapy* in 1962) and the establishment of the American Art Therapy Association. Though composed of only a handful of members initially, AATA has grown rapidly. Its annual meetings, beginning in 1970, are highly professional, and the organization has taken steps toward accrediting art therapy training programs and lobbying for the development of the profession.

APPLICATION OF ART THERAPY

The term ''art therapy'' is a huge umbrella, covering the use of art expression for many purposes in a great variety of settings. There are art therapists in private practice whose work with clients is insight-oriented on a long-term basis. Art therapy may be used for clarification purposes in a short-term crisis intervention center. Elderly residents in nursing homes may use art therapy as a life review which is so important for those who are nearing the end of their lives. Drug and alcohol addiction centers use art therapy to help addicts examine their lives. Art therapy is being used increasingly with physically and mentally handicapped people as well.

Art therapy is probably used most extensively in hospital psychiatric wards and psychiatric out-patient settings where patients may be seen individually or in groups. In the latter, the shared art expression becomes an important vehicle of communication (Sinrod, 1964). Patients may also participate in family art therapy, which was developed by Kwiatkowska (1962, 1967a, b) at the Clinical Center of the National Institute of Mental Health. In a family art therapy session, family members draw their perceptions of the family and make joint pictures to explore family dynamics. Individual and family art therapy procedures are used for diagnostic and evaluative purposes as well as for treatment.

Art therapy has expanded beyond clinical settings to educational institutions. There it is used in work with children who have problems, such as the retarded, learning disabled, and emotionally disturbed, as well as the socially disadvantaged, such as ghetto children. Gradually, however, as educators are becoming more attuned to the development of the whole person, art therapy is finding a place in the education of so-called "normal" children. In such settings the emphasis is on growth through personal expression rather than the alleviation of ills as the term "therapy" implies.

In this regard, adults, too, are pursuing avenues of personal growth involving both self-exploration and creativity. Art expression geared toward self-development has become an important activity in the personal growth workshops that have proliferated with the development of the Human Potential Movement. Used in this way, art expression differs from traditional art education in that the emphasis is placed on the process rather than on the product.

Although it would seem that art used in the domains of therapy, education, and personal growth would differ, in fact, the differences are mainly semantic. All good therapy leads to both education and growth. Good education also brings about growth in the individual. Therefore, the differences in the uses made of art therapy are primarily dictated by the present needs of the individual who is experiencing it and the approach of the art therapist.

The way in which art therapy is practiced is an interplay between the conditions imposed by the setting with its particular population and what the art therapist contributes in theoretical approach, technical competencies, and personal style. This chapter focuses on population and setting. Chapter 6, discusses the art therapist's approach.

Obviously, goals and structure vary considerably, depending on population and setting. To take extreme examples, the design for art therapy sessions would be very different in a school for retarded children from that in a hospital crisis intervention unit.

PHYSICAL ENVIRONMENT

Some aspects of structure should apply to all art therapy, regardless of type. These highlight the importance of the physical setting and material necessities, which are less important in most other forms of therapy. For art work there should be ample space, adequate lighting, suitable art materials, clean-up equipment, and a room that does not have to be protected from stains. Quiet and privacy, requisite for other forms of therapy, of course, are needed for art therapy. Sometimes art therapy programs in hospitals have been relegated to activity or social areas which are open to other patients and staff during the sessions. It is not likely that any information the patients wish to be kept confidential will be shared in such an environment.

The desired conditions represent the ideal; many art therapists are used to working in whatever environment is available. Particularly in the early days of the profession, art therapists felt lucky to be granted any space of their own. My first office at the National Institutes of Health Clinical Center was a small hydrotherapy room with a large tub in the middle which took up most of the floor space. I had a cover made for it so that the tub became a table.

Sometimes a patient cannot come to the art therapy room. If there is physical disability, the art therapist may have to visit the patient's room and bring the art supplies. I have held sessions in the seclusion room when a patient was confined there. Clearly, it is easier to be more mobile and flexible in arranging individual art therapy sessions than in working with a group.

Certain specific aspects of the physical environment have an impact on the nature of the art therapy experience. In a group setting, the physical distance among members both while engaged in the art work and in the discussion of it can influence the experience. Furniture makes a difference, too, such as sitting and drawing on the floor or using easels and chairs. The former usually creates a more informal environment. An important consideration in art therapy is the physical relationship between the art producer and the art product. Many art therapists have the pictures hung on the wall for discussion purposes. Sometimes patients may be describing their pictures from across the room. I usually like to encourage a close proximity between creator and creation. Most often in my groups participants hold their pictures or display them in front of themselves so that others can look at the producer and the product at the same time. Holding the picture emphasizes the connection between the two so that the art product is more readily experienced as an extension of the self. There may be occasions, however, when the art therapist may wish to encourage distance between patient and picture for the purpose of greater objectivity. At such time, the patient may be asked to step back from the picture.

The storing of the art products may pose a logistical problem. Ideally it is best to have all the previous art work handy in case a present picture or sculpture relates to a previous one. Sometimes space considerations make storing all the material impractical. Until recently, I have done so, but lately space limitation has caused me to ask members of my private practice groups to hold onto their own work. They used large pads of paper which they brought to each session so that they carried some of their pictures with them. Since the groups met weekly for several years, however, they could not carry all of them. Sometimes we wanted to refer to a picture that had been left at home.

SESSION STRUCTURE

Other aspects of session structure should be determined by the goals of the treatment. These include frequency and length of meetings, media used, particular activities, manner of referral, and decisions about ending. At the first session in private practice, I make an oral contract with the client, which includes my fee, arrangements for missed sessions, insurance matters, and so forth. Sometimes I may make recommendations too, but these are not a part of the contract. At the National Institutes of Health, at first I saw patients on referral from their psychiatrists. At a later time, art therapy was part of the program, and all patients participated throughout their hospitalization. At other times there I saw patients who were interested in participating in art therapy and for whom I felt it would be beneficial after an initial evaluation. And finally, I have seen patients for evaluation only.

It is important to recognize that the structure of the sessions influences what transpires. For example, an open-ended group will behave differently from a time-limited one. Groups where members come and go or are not expected to come to all the sessions will not likely achieve the cohesiveness of groups with consistent membership. Art therapy sessions that do not begin or end on time, or are interrupted, will not be taken as seriously as those with a consistent schedule.

Although I generally operate with a consistent schedule, there are sometimes reasons to make exceptions. For example, every time I scheduled a hospitalized manic woman for a session, she was in the seclusion room because of her disruptive behavior, and the nursing staff did not want me to see her there. My office was on the ward, and she would pop in to visit when the door was open. She would draw at the easel and talk for about ten minutes and leave. That was the length of her attention span at the time. This arrangement worked out fine, and we continued it until her mania subsided, at which time we resumed our regular weekly hour sessions. In this instance my goal was to maintain contact with her and offer her some support. Intensive psychotherapy was not possible until her mania decreased.

At other times my NIH office was off the ward. This brought about some unexpected results. I would pick patients up on the ward and escort them to my office. A few related to me as someone who was not a part of the unit and would make use of the art therapy sessions to express their anger and disappointment with various staff members.

The variety of goals, settings, and structure of art therapy sessions is extremely diverse, depending on many circumstances. The point I wish to emphasize is that the the art therapist sets goals based on the population and the conditions of the setting in which he or she works. The structure then is established to enhance these goals. If a goal is dealing with a family crisis, then all family members may participate and be requested to draw pictures related to the crisis situation. If long-term insight-oriented psychotherapy is intended, then an individual may be seen alone on an ongoing basis using spontaneous picture-making. If socialization is an objective, then group projects or at least group sharing about individual art expressions may be encouraged, and so forth. This book's illustrative material describing art therapy with various populations gives substance to the guidelines suggested.

ART MEDIA

The art therapist may use a variety of materials. As is the case with other elements of session structure, media should be selected purposefully. In a relatively loose studio set up, art supplies might be arranged for the patient's choosing, particularly in art therapy with the emphasis on the art activity. If the art work is a vehicle for free association or family or group communication, relatively fast media, such as pastels, crayons, or felt tip pens, would be most suitable. Material preparation and cleanup certainly are factors to be considered. Unless there is time for the patient or client to participate in these responsibilities, the art therapist might prefer media that require little preparation or cleaning up. Handicapped individuals, very young children, and some elderly people might need materials that are easily manipulated.

Two important considerations in the selection of media are the dimensions of facilitation and control. A sufficient variety of colors, adequate sizes of paper or canvas, and enough clay should be provided, along with adequate working space to facilitate spontaneity in the client or patient. An overabundance of media can be overwhelming. Since clients and patients differ in this regard, the art therapist must be sensitive to the individual's needs. Obviously, frustrating materials should be avoided, such as newsprint which tears easily if pressure is applied to it or chalks that have worn down so much they can hardly be grasped.

Different media are more easy to control than others. Pencils lend themselves to tight control. Water colors and clay are more difficult to control because there are technical problems in manipulating them. In this regard, as well, the art therapist must be sensitive to the client or patient's needs. The opportunity to smear might be enlivening for a severely inhibited individual or it might be extremely frightening, for example. Sometimes changing the medium can be facilitating for an individual who is in a rut. The point is that it is necessary for the art therapist to be famliar with what may be evoked by the different media, what advantages each offers and what limitations each has, so that media may be selected appropriately.

In much of my work the art product is a vehicle for psychological insight. Since I want to devote as much time as possible to processing the image and the experience of creating it, I prefer a quick and simple medium. Also, I usually like to combine the possibility of control with smearing. For these purposes I have found wide soft pastels in a variety of vivid colors to by my "happy medium"—neither too tight nor too loose. (They are easy to wash off hands and clothes as well.)

CHAPTER 4

Institutional Politics

Closely related to issues of structure is institutional politics. Unless one is working privately, institutional politics exert a heavy influence on the work.

Institutional politics cover wide ranging effects. The art therapist finds him or herself working in an establishment that gives some very significant messages to its clientele. An authoritarian institution that depends on medication and/or locked doors to keep patients in control gives the clear message that patients are unable to care for themselves. A more voluntary arrangement with patients included in treatment planning conveys a faith in the patients' ability to be responsible. Research projects may tend to foster feelings in patients of being valued only for the data they provide. A manic-depressed woman who cycled every twenty-four hours (an unusual case) remarked to the visiting scientist interviewing her: "So you've come to see the phenomenon." The urine collected from the patients at NIH was referred to by the staff as "liquid gold" since it contained the metabolites being studied. Patients "acted out" their anger at being research subjects by urinating in each others' containers, dumping them over, urinating in the toilet (or on the floor), throwing cigarette butts in the urine, and so forth. They managed to get the message across to the research staff: "Piss on you" became more than a euphemism.

The art therapist becomes a part of the institutional system in which he or she works and must come to some sort of terms with it. Optimally, one would work in a system he or she fully endorses. Since utopias are hard to find, a more realistic possibility is working in a place where the basic approach is consonant with one's own beliefs. To operate without institutional and personal soul-searching, I believe, is at best irresponsible, at worst unconscionable. Beginning practitioners may have a lot to learn in the realm of institutional politics, and find it necessary to do a great deal of processing in the course of developing their own ideas.

Politics determine the place of art therapy in the institution's program. If it is highly valued, there will be adequate space, scheduling, and supplies. More important even, the message conveyed to the patient by the staff in terms of scheduling, interest, and support for the program will be that art therapy is a significant part of the treatment. Many art therapists have had to work their way into a system, proving the value of their work before being fully accepted.

The context in which this occurs constitutes the personality of the particular institution. Like humans, an institutional personality is not static. The institutional structure may be highly formal; lines of communication and areas of responsibility may be very clear or they may shift subtly. There may be an informal network which does not correspond to the explicit structure. For example, a therapist who has the ear of the facility director may exert more influence than another therapist of similar rank.

Some institutions are more hierarchically organized than others. Often the art therapist's position in the hierarchy may be quite ambiguous. The usual trend is for them to start near the bottom. The consequences of working themselves up, however, may be a mixed blessing. This has been particularly evident to me in strictly medical model institutions where M.D.'s are in authority. In addition to this element of elitism, since most art therapists are women, they also face the additional burden that women have in proving their competence in the male-dominated health professions.

Much of what I have discussed is the negative aspect of the art therapist's struggles with the bureaucracy. I do not mean to imply that the picture is a totally dark one. Nevertheless, the experiences of many art therapists whom I have known over the years has been gratification in the work and hassle with the system.

STAFF RELATIONS

In presenting the influence that institutional policies exact upon the work, I do not intend to imply that the art therapist is passive and merely accepts the status quo. In fact, as suggested earlier, it is often necessary for the art therapist to prove him or herself in order to gain acceptance and respect. I have often told students that working with patients is easy compared to working with the staff. Although many staff members may be sensitive, interested, and supportive, some who are unfamiliar with art therapy may be suspicious of or even feel threatened by the art therapist. The more successful the art therapist is in working with the patients, the more threatened other staff members may be, particularly if they begin to feel less successful in contrast. In addition, art itself may be threatening to those who do not feel comfortable with this form of expression.

Staff resentment may take many forms. I have had nursing staff members schedule patients for other appointments at times they were supposed to see me. I recall a particularly hostile head nurse questioning patients about their art work in a very mocking way. If the resentment comes from above, then there may be problems in obtaining institutional support. In general it is the least secure staff people, those who feel most shaky about their power base, who are likely to feel threatened. As art therapy is gaining a stronger foothold, however, there is likely to be greater initial acceptance and respect for the enrichment it offers a treatment program.

On the more positive side, art therapists have a very valuable public relations advantage. The art work itself can go a long way in attracting interest. I have found that the best lubricant for easing staff relations has been to involve staff members in my work. They have usually become intrigued by the art work, and instead of being adversaries, they have become interested allies. By bringing the pictures to staff meetings, making appointments or having informal chats with individual staff people, staff become curious and feel valued for their reactions. If the art therapist creates opportunities to educate the staff about art therapy, he or she will find much more support for the work. I have given workshops for staff so they can *experience* what art therapy is. Often these have turned out to be both illuminating and enjoyable for them.

I began to get requests for workshops when there had been some staff turnover or I moved to a new ward. After a while groups with whom I did not work requested workshops. In time I came to be regarded as a resource person with access to other forms of therapy and was given funds to invite consultants to conduct workshops. I brought in a movement therapist, a psychodramatist, gestalt therapist, and an eminent family therapist. Finally the public relations potential of art therapy was considered sufficiently attractive that the National Institute of Mental Health had me interviewed on two radio programs, one local and one national, and made funds available for an exhibit of art therapy work which was displayed at the National Institute of Mental Health's twenty-fifth anniversary celebration.

ART THERAPIST AS ADVOCATE

Some believe advocacy is a moral responsibility, although it is certainly not everyone's cup of tea. Art therapists are often in uniquely advantageous positions for advocacy since they usually are not co-opted by the traditional psychiatric staff groups—psychiatrists, psychologists, nurses, aides, social workers. They can, therefore, more readily ally themselves with whom they will. At one time, for example, I felt the nurses were not being treated fairly and argued for their rights. More often, however, I was, as one ward administrator designated me, a gadfly championing patients' rights. In a hierarchal system such as the one in which I worked, patients were clearly on the very lowest rung of the ladder. Since the institution was designed for research, those objectives were met with such zeal by the researchers that sometimes they were not sufficiently sensitive to some treatment considerations. Often researchers had no clinical involvement with the patients. This situation brought distance between themselves and the human beings whom they were investigating. I do not mean to imply that researchers were callous regarding patients' clinical needs, only that there were moments requiring greater clinical scrutiny than the research protocols called for.

Students in field placements or internships often feel ignorant and incompetent among the professionals who are training them. But students can provide a very useful function in helping the institution's staff in examining itself. Students bring a fresh approach; they are not inured to the institution's policies. Their questions can provoke reflection on policies and practices otherwise taken for granted.

In an advocacy position, the art therapist need not simply succumb to the travesties of the less-than-perfect institution in which he or she works. There is the possibility for implementing change. Certainly the consciousness necessary for such action requires confidence in one's own professional contribution rather than an attitude of simply being grateful for having a job. Advocacy has significant staff-relationship import. An advocate usually makes enemies. Advocacy can also create support. An effective advocate is a power to be reckoned with.

CHAPTER 5

Art Therapy Training

The first training program to offer a master's degree in art therapy was developed at Hahnemann Hospital in Philadelphia in the late sixties. Previously, in the 1950's, art therapy courses were taught in New York City by Margaret Naumburg and at the Washington School of Psychiatry in Washington, D.C., but the Hahnemann program was the first to award a graduate degree in art therapy. This beginning was followed rapidly with M.A. programs proliferating throughout the country. Within seven years of the first relatively small American Art Therapy Association annual conference in 1970, twenty master's degree programs had been established, and more have started since. At the time of this writing, Ph.D. programs in art therapy are being developed as well.

I have been involved in art therapy training for many years, both for budding art therapists and other professionals. I have worked with students in many ways—in courses, supervision, apprentice relationships, program planning, and program direction. I have found this work to be immensely challenging. It has stimulated my own thinking in developing my ideas about what is essential and what is optimal in art therapy education.

First one must determine just what sort of professional is to be trained. What sort of responsibilities will the future art therapist carry? There is some difference of opinion within the profession as to whether art therapists should be primary therapists. I have strong feelings about this question. The profundity of art expression makes the profession, by its very nature, one which demands of the art therapist a deep and thorough knowledge of the human condition and the ability to relate to another human being with sensitivity and care. For this reason it is essential that art therapy education include all the background material that any psychotherapist must learn—human development, psychological theory, abnormal psychology, systems of psychotherapy, group and family dynamics. As in other health professions, extensive supervised field work or internship is also necessary. With such solid training there is no reason art therapists should not be capable of primary therapeutic responsibility. Art therapists should be psychotherapists plus. There must also be training in art therapy theory and practice and both technical expertise in art and experience in using art for self expression. The supervised field work must be practice in art therapy.

Presently, most art therapy training is conducted in university master's degree programs. Training a ''psychotherapist plus'' is a large undertaking for what is the equivalent of a two–year full–time course of study. At this time Ph.D. art therapy programs are beginning to be developed which will probably produce more advanced clinicians, researchers, and art therapy educators. Those who obtain no higher than a bachelor's degree in art therapy are generally considered to be para-professionals or art therapy aides.

In addition to these traditional areas of learning, I believe that art psychotherapy requires two other important ingredients. The first ingredient is training in learning to improvise. Although there are many techniques that have been developed by art therapists and form something of a standard repetiore, often the best approach is the one tailored for the particular situation at hand. The unexpected conditions the art therapist may meet in any particular session call for the utmost in creativity and resourcefulness. (The discussion of combining expressive therapies on a ward of psychotic manics and depressives, Chapter 10, illustrates this challenge.) Students often ask me to give them a list of techniques in art therapy. Although I present many that I and others have developed, I encourage them to develop their own techniques, because therapists need to think on their feet and, above all, be responsive to the immediate situation. This too, is one of the exciting aspects of work in art therapy. (See Appendix for a list of techniques.)

The other ingredient is most important: the development of self awareness. Since the tool of psychotherapy is one's own reactions, the self is the instrument of the therapist's work. This instrument must be kept in fine tune.

I believe that to enhance their sensitivity, all art therapy students should participate in art therapy themselves. Although other forms of psychotherapy might achieve this end, sensitivity to art expression is enhanced through one's own self exploration in this mode.

An additional benefit of art therapy for art therapy students is to get some feeling for what their clients might experience, from the other side of the drawing pad, so to speak. By participating in art therapy, students learn first hand how a more experienced art therapist practices. I have had clients who were art therapy students from programs other than those in which I was teaching. Although the goal was clearly therapy, not training, they could step back and look at their reactions to the way I handled various aspects of the work. They were able to experience a philosophy and style of therapy more directly than through reading and observation.

A STUDENT'S SELF-EXPLORATION

Because I believe the sort of self-exploration that may be obtained through reflective art expression is important for students in their development into professionals, I have included an example of one student's processing of a portion of her training: When June requested to do a semester of field work at a hospice, I suggested that she try to understand her motivations. As we talked about her wish to work with the dying, it seemed likely to be rooted at some level in her need to deal with her own eventual death and the terminal illness of a close friend whom she had nursed. She decided to explore feelings about death in a series of pictures and wrote her comments about them. In seven paintings she represented a variety of aspects. Figure 2 is her first painting. She wrote:

Figure 2.   "Death as the demon lover" by June, an art therapy student.

Death as the demon lover, but here he looks almost innocent. The ground seems glowing from beneath as if much of the force in this image comes from the earth, so it is in a sense a Great Mother image, as she who gives birth and takes back into death.

June's Jungian orientation is apparent, and is seen in her next picture as well, Figure 3:

This picture dealt with the elements omitted in the first painting. This is death as a cruel Kali witch figure. She has everyone totally in her grasp. They *are* her grasp and won't be able to escape. Everyone will die. It is very cold and bleak, the land of what the alchemists called the black sun. The tree of life is dead utterly. The insects which make up her robe are like thoughts of death, fears that come up out of the unconscious and can't be controlled or clearly seen and that seem alien, primitive. She has a bird on her head indicating spirit, cold predatory spirit.

Figure 3.   "Death as a cruel Kali witch figure" by June.

In her fifth painting, Figure 4, she came closer to immediate experience:

By this point I became aware that all I was painting was various parts of myself, so here I tried to paint a dying person, thinking of people I had seen in a nursing home where I worked, a friend who had died. I tried to think of what they would be seeing when they seem very far away, somewhere else. The image of a waterfall came to my mind, perhaps as a feeling of falling into space, into a deep chasm, a peaceful place but very lonely. The colors are in the inner images since the outer world is an object of indifference. Of course, once I had painted this I realized that once again I was picturing my own image of the death experience. This made me wish to be able to be there with someone, to understand them, but perhaps it is impossible. Death is a lonely chasm.

Figure 4.   A dying patient by June.

Her final picture, Figure 5:

This was done a week or so after the others as a result of a dream. A friendly green demon reached out a sinous arm and showed me a book with peculiar writing in it. The writing turned into pictures which demonstrated to me exactly what I was doing in my life. All of this related to death. I was aware of its presence during the whole dream. It was a very powerful dream and to me integrated the whole process I had been going through in preparing to work with the dying. The green demon was much stronger and clearer than the one in the first picture, here acting as a guide and psychological reflector for me. The little men flying out of the book are insights, but more, potencies.

Going through this process of confronting, through art, my own ideas, feelings, and intuitions about death has been valuable to me personally. Thinking about death makes one aware of what is important, puts things in perspective (what green demons are for). I hope that it will have given me a stronger basis to operate from when I am dealing with dying people. It is so easy to project or repress one's feelings in confronting what is the most frightening and mystifying unknowable of all.

Figure 5.   A dream of a "friendly green demon" guide in June's preparation for work with the dying.

After her semester's work with the dying, June recognized that the patients were different from what she had expected. Each had unique impact on her, and she was struck with the intensity of their imaginations. Her case notes reflected their pathos as well as her own courage and sensitivity in her work with them. About her own reactions, she wrote the following:

When I look back on my experience working with the sick and dying, the image which immediately comes is that of the Shrouder . . . death puts a veil of silence and stillness over their features which once were open to us. Although the people with whom I worked were still very much living, I found the process of shrouding already occurring in the sense that in seeking to understand them, I felt led into a place of mystery where regular modes of understanding were strangely ineffectual. . . . I would reach a point beyond which I felt myself stepping into a deep blankness. . . . This emptiness itself became an experience . . . that I too would age, get sick, die; then everday life with its . . . feelings of permanence and substantiality seemed like a ridiculous joke . . . yes I would die— this was inevitable—I would grow old and ugly, smell bad perhaps. But why was this necessarily an evil? It was natural. Was not the nursing home itself, benign as this one was, a bone hotel isolated from human life in its wholeness, which created the particular horror of the scene? . . . I have had a horror of these sick and dying people, wanted at times not to have to look at them, to run away, but finally what I feel toward them is love and, more than that, respect for the hard work they are doing and gratitude for what they have taught me.

Finally, art therapy training does not end with receipt of the degree. Formal training is only a beginning. Hopefully, the graduate will continue to seek new information, to process new experience, to reflect on previous experience, and to be ever attentive to his or her own personal and professional development. A good education program will pave the way in encouraging continuous growth.

MY OWN ART THERAPY EDUCATION

Like others who entered the art therapy profession before it became formalized, my own training has been unorthodox. I describe it here to give something of a historical perspective as well as to present some of the background which has strongly influenced my viewpoints. My own training has been a backwards version of the training which I recommend, in the sense that I became an art therapist first and a psychotherapist next.

My earliest intentions occurred as a teenager when I used to baby sit for my cousin. My uncle was a psychiatrist so after I put her to bed I would spend the evening exploring his library. In those days the culture was not so psychologically sophisticated so Freud's writings on dreams came as an amazing revelation to me.

I planned to become a psychotherapist through psychiatric social work, but marriage and children intervened, so some years elapsed before I entered graduate education. With small children to care for and little money I began taking one course at a time with the hope of eventually obtaining a Ph.D. in clinical psychology. It was then that I heard of art therapy. I met Hanna Yaxa Kwiatkowska, who was practicing art therapy at the National Institutes of Health Clinical Center in Bethesda, MD. I realized that this field was the marriage of my two major interests, art and psychotherapy. I asked Hanna how I might obtain training, and she offered to serve as my mentor. I became a ''guest worker'' at the National Institutes of Health and worked with her in the Adult Psychiatry Branch directed by Lyman Wynne, M.D., Ph.D., and after several months I was hired. I continued work with Hanna for about a year and then branched off to work in what became the Section on Psychiatry in the Laboratory of Clinical Science, directed by William Bunney, M.D.

I was enthralled with the opportunities I found for learning at the National Institutes of Health. Weekly conferences featured scientists from all over the world presenting what was then the leading edge of psychiatric research. There were other staff meetings as well which not only focused on patients' dynamics, but dealt with conceptual issues as well. All the while I was reading extensively in the psychiatric "classics" and attending courses at the Washington School of Psychiatry.

As important as all of this learning was for me, I believe my most significant teachers were the patients with whom I worked. I came to "know" through the accumulation of experience. Depression, for example, was not merely "aggression turned inward," "psychomotor retardation," and so forth. I understood the complexities of depression through my experience with over one hundred depressed patients with whom I had worked intimately, seeing their worlds in their pictures, hearing their hopes and hopelessness, their fears, their tears, their living deaths. I worked with suicidal people until I could "smell" suicide. I came to have confidence in recommending suicidal precautions when I sensed suicidal intent.

Gradually I moved from being a student to being a professional to becoming an expert in some areas. I began to write, and I began to publish. It has been enormously gratifying to hear from others who have become interested in my work through my writings.

The earlier more traditional psychoanalytic influences became augmented by existentialistic theory and the Human Potential Movement. I availed myself of experiences in other approaches, such as gestalt therapy and Bion-type group process, and I participated in workshops and eventually began to design and lead them. Not the least of the influences on my work has been my own psychoanalysis and subsequent humanistic psychotherapy. All of this continuing exposure to various ways of working has led me to a very eclectic approach in which I form new syntheses based on my experiences and beliefs.

Along the way I augmented my National Institutes of Health work with a private practice and began teaching art therapy, first to paraprofessionals, then to other professionals, and finally to art therapists in training. These opportunities enabled me to develop and implement my ideas of art therapy training. Eventually I came to direct art therapy training programs.

I say that my training has been backwards for several reasons. I began working with hospitalized psychiatric patients before I had studied psychopathology. This was probably an advantage in that I was not limited by preconceived ideas, but was more open to my own experience. With only a B.A. degree, I began conducting research, publishing in psychiatric journals, and training therapists. I started as an art therapist and have since become more of a generalist, treating some patients without utilizing art therapy at all in instances where it is contraindicated. It has been only after doing what is usually the work of professionals with advanced degrees that I have obtained two masters' degrees (one in psychology and art therapy, the other in social work) and a Ph.D. (psychology and art therapy).

I would certainly encourage others to proceed in a forward direction, completing their formal training as early as possible to provide them preparation and to increase the possibility of obtaining work in art therapy. The opportunities that were mine are now not so likely to be found for those without advanced training.

CHAPTER 6

Therapeutic Relationship

This chapter contains some of my most deeply held beliefs. It is within the therapeutic relationship that the therapy begins, develops, matures, and ends. To speak of therapy without taking into account the relationship between therapist and client is to ignore one of its most basic ingredients. What follows is my own personal view of the experience of the therapeutic relationship. Although my view is not a unique one, it promotes a very different way of relating to the client from what many therapists practice. Much of what is discussed here pertains to psychotherapy in general. Some is particular to art psychotherapy.

GENERAL CONSIDERATIONS

It seems logical to begin with names. I call the people with whom I work by their first names, and they call me by mine. Since we will come to know each other intimately, surnames and titles seem incongruous. I believe it is important to be on an equal footing, because I do not feel superior to the people with whom I work. Sometimes I feel rather humbled in the gratitude I experience for their allowing me into the hidden recesses of their lives. In a sense they invite me to participate with them for a portion of their life's journey. I am not a guide or a leader. I will never know them as well as they know themselves, so I try to encourage them to believe in themselves.

What do I call these people with whom I work? Throughout this book I use the term "client," or "patient" if the person is hospitalized. I do not like either term. "Client" is too formal, and "patient" is pejorative. I would prefer "participant," but since such a term is not recognized for people participating in psychotherapy, it might prove confusing in this book.

The core of my approach to the therapeutic relationship is the respect I feel for the person with whom I am working. My initial attitude is one of being open to learning a great deal about this complex human being I am meeting. I don't experience myself as a guru or savior or white-coated healer. I am another struggling human being who makes it her work to listen, look, and respond to some others who want assistance in living their lives.

I want to speak of the client without having to resort to the awkward "him or her," so I will refer to a hypothetical female client throughout this chapter, but it could as readily be a male. I will also refer to the art therapist as "she," but since I am female, it could not so readily refer to a male. In other words, although the client is hypothetical, the therapist is not.

First of all, I try to enter the client's world. I want to know what are the important issues for *her*. I come to experience her point of view, her structuring of experience, her symbolization, her thought patterns. At the same time that I try to grasp her experience, I also stand apart and reflect on what it must be like to be her. I notice how she cheats herself, how she rewards herself, how she hurts herself, how she gives herself pleasure. In relating to her, I try to meet her on her ground; I don't try to move her to another plane. I am as receptive as I can be and communicate to her my sense of what she is sharing with me without imposing my views, opinions, judgements. In other words, I try to pick up on what's going on and reflect it back, particularly the nuances of feeling. It is a double dance of empathy and reflection.

Contract

It is important to clarify the contract at the first meeting—schedule, confidentiality, fee (if in private practice), arrangements for missed sessions, and so forth. I do so verbally. The therapist must be clear about what she is and is not willing to negotiate. I try to structure the arrangements in such a way that there will be a commitment to the work on both our parts. If I need to miss a session, I announce it well in advance and try to reschedule it. I expect clients not to miss sessions unless absolutely necessary, to be punctual, and to pay promptly for private practice sessions. These are obvious areas for acting out resistance, and if that happens I encourage the client to take a look at what is going on rather than assuming the role of a scolding parent. This is a part of the therapeutic alliance we are forming—partners in understanding the client's life and moving it in directions she would like to see it go.

If there is a treatment team, these structural issues can be used to wreak havoc in staff relationships. A hostilely manipulative patient may try to play off one staff member against another through scheduling conflicts, for example. In these instances it is very important for staff members to maintain clear communication with one another. On the other hand, intra-staff hostility can get played out in similar scheduling conflicts, with the patient caught in the middle. If a patient is being helpless, she may contribute to the confusion. If all are acting responsibly, these entanglements are less likely to occur.

At times I have found myself in quasi-therapy situations such as workshops and experiential courses. An unacknowledged agenda of some of the participants is often a quest for therapy. Under such circumstances it is necessary for me to reiterate my contract from time to time—that is, that although I encourage participants to be as open to the experience of self-exploration as they feel comfortable to do, I will not assume therapeutic responsibility, because I am clear that my contract is to conduct a workshop or teach a course.

Goals

The next step has to do with goals. Why has the client come to therapy, and what does she hope to achieve? Her goals may be different from mine. Throughout the therapy it is important to be clear about this. I may state my hopes, but I always identify them as mine, recognizing that it is the client's life we are dealing with and that her goals take precedence. Mine are only suggestions. I tell clients my belief that most problems in living stem from people not feeling good about themselves so that they become depressed or try to find self-affirmation in seeking power, money, status. Therefore, in addition to trying to help the client achieve her stated goals, I have as a goal her increased self-acceptance and self-love.

A Nurturing Laboratory

Most people grow up in an atmosphere of nonacceptance. They have not learned to love themselves because they have not felt loved. The neurotics of our times have usually felt judged and come to judge themselves harshly. In this regard, the therapeutic relationship itself becomes a primary curative agent in supplying what the client may never have had—an accepting, nonjudgemental, understanding, and loving relationship. The client comes to experience a new way of being cared for. The therapist models a new way of being in relation to another. In this sort of supportive milieu the client becomes sufficiently trusting to try out new ways of being, to try on new perspectives as she might a new set of clothes, to see how they look and whether they fit. In this nonthreatening atmosphere, the therapy can become a laboratory to try out changes in which the client need not pay the consequences that would be exacted in other contexts. Much of this I put into words. I encourage clients to look on the therapy as a laboratory and feel free to experiment, assuring them that here there are no prices to be paid for failures, that, in fact, failures can provide instructive learning. For example, an individual who has stifled anger can let it loose here without untoward repercussions and with an opportunity to reflect on the experience. As the first tender shoots of change begin to emerge, the nurturance of the therapeutic relationship serves as an incubation for growth.

Where does the wisdom reside? Hopefully there's some in the therapist. The client hopes so, at any rate. But what most clients don't know is that the ultimate wisdom for their own lives resides within themselves. In helping clients to accept themselves, I encourage them to respect their own judgements. I encourage them to own their ultimate responsibility for themselves and to take the reins of their lives into their own hands. There is no one truth. If I disagree with a client, I tell her what I think and that it's only my opinion, not ultimate wisdom. She is the one to choose how to live her life. My ideas are not necessarily better than hers. Our major difference is one of role. We are exploring her life, and I may be able to suggest some perspectives she has not recognized before.

Nevertheless, clients still may value my views more than their own or fit themselves to my ideas in order to please me. The more nurturance I provide, the greater the fear of my disapproval may be. In this regard it is impossible to deal with the therapeutic relationship without taking a look at transference. The responsibility of the therapist is an awesome one because of the power our clients give us. It's not because we are especially wise or competent. It is dumped in our laps willy-nilly, because our clients are so needful and hopeful that we can save them, or because they are so downtrodden that they have come to fear those in a position of authority. I believe that psychotherapists must respect this power and responsibility that is given them and not abuse it. Some do and use their clients for their own ends in power-tripping or intimacy-tripping. The idealization that is accorded the therapist by the client is an ego trip to which the therapist can be vulnerable as well. On the other hand, I don't recommend that therapists shy away from using the responsibility they have. Hopefully, when the therapist gives reactions or makes suggestions and recommendations, the client has learned that it is okay to object, disagree, and express to the therapist feelings of not being understood through having tested the waters and having found the therapist receptive to these responses. When such a climate has been established, the therapist can feel free to react without fear of imposing a viewpoint on the client. It may take time, however, for this sort of two-way trust to develop.

Earlier on when the client is trying to win my approval, rather than either give it or withhold it, I try to help the client to look at what she's doing, why she's doing it, her hopes and fears, and how it feels. Eventually, she comes to realize that my approval coincides with her own—that as she becomes more pleased with herself, I become pleased for her and gratified with the progress we have made. It's sort of a paradox: the more she tries to please me, the less she succeeds; by not trying to please me, she often does.

Despite clients' attempts to structure our relationship otherwise (such as powerful, all-giving mother and helpless child), I try to achieve a therapeutic alliance of partners in a common quest. It never works out perfectly, because the old pulls are too strong, but usually it is possible to develop a relationship that feels reciprocal rather than either top- or bottom-heavy.

One aspect of the transference that I have found especially prominent has been the use clients have made of me as a model. Therapists come to learn, as do parents, that if they model honesty, openness, lovingness, receptivity, it is those attributes their clients will learn from them. With some clients there have been characteristics of my life circumstances as well that have been instructive. Some women have seen me as the sort of independent professional they would like to become. Some art therapist-clients have been especially observant of my career developments. Some clients have found in me attributes about which they have felt conflicted within themselves. For example, a sexually repressed woman considered me "sensuous," sometimes liking that quality and sometimes reprimanding me for it.

Closely related to these considerations are problems of envy. Often female clients who have wanted to be like me in some ways have suffered the pains of envy and feared the hostility which they projected on to me. This, too, can be looked at. I try to empathize with the pain of envy, telling clients that it's a feeling I have experienced out of my own bad feelings about myself. More difficult to deal with is the envy a therapist may feel toward a client. This and other countertransference phenomena require some soul searching and work on the self by the therapist.

Psychotherapists are familiar with "the right interpretation at the wrong time." Sometimes clients just aren't ready to move, or perhaps they recognize some of their maladaptive defenses but aren't ready to give them up. I believe these defenses are to be respected, and I communicate this to the client. Once again I try to foster self-acceptance instead of self-abnegation. I tell the client that she developed these defenses for very good reasons, that they were necessary for her to survive in her early life, and that they are worthy of respect. This acceptance first by me and then herself makes it easier for her to claim the freedom to choose to relinquish the defenses or not.

Although mostly my style is one of receptivity and empathy, there are times when I use a tougher approach. I may kid the client, exaggerate by presenting a situation in its extreme so the client can see its absurdity, or play the devil's advocate to enable the client to experience the opposite position. The timing must be right for such interventions. The client should be able to use them and not simply become offended and more defensive. Naturally, there are times when the mark is missed. It may or may not be useful for the therapist to explain. If the client is feeling abandoned, it's probably a good idea to explain. Sometimes, however, allowing the client to ponder enables her to process the therapist's remarks and her feelings fruitfully.

Of course, some therapists are more confrontative than others, and some use paradox or Zen-master-like tricks to increase awareness much more than I do. The development of trust and the feeling of being well cared for that so many people have never experienced, I believe, must be the soil from which the recognition grows. A therapist's brilliant dance of paradox is counterproductive for a client who is feeling mocked. Her attention is more likely to be caught up in her feelings than in the message the therapist is conveying so ingeniously.

Negative Feelings Toward a Client

A student I was supervising presented work in which she recognized that she disliked her patient and felt manipulated by her. In delving into the problem, several factors became apparent. First, the student felt like a failure, because the patient had shown signs of progress that did not then materialize. Second, the patient became very critical of the student. It seems to me that if the therapist is comfortable with herself personally and professionally, conditions such as these are not likely to lead to dislike of the client. The student was not yet confident of herself professionally and felt a need to prove herself with this patient. She had not yet learned that some people really don't want or are not yet ready to change despite the best of intentions and efforts on the therapist's part. Second, had she felt more comfortable as a professional, she probably would not have experienced the patient's criticism as an assault, but would have been able to use it as instructive feedback and to help the patient to get in touch with her feelings in the relationship. The manipulation tango takes two, and the therapist does not have to join the dance.

Therapists are most likely to have negative feelings toward clients who display attributes the therapists dislike in themselves. Obviously, this is a counter-transference problem. The therapist can either work it out or avoid such clients. A problem I have encountered more often is the client who gives little to the therapeutic effort. The work can get tiresome and frustrating when the client is overly stuck for an overly long period of time. I try to connect with such clients' fear and pain. When they do move the result is enormously gratifying, because the struggle has been so great. Sometimes the clients who initially are the most closed off, defended, and frustrating turn out to be the most gratifying because they move so far. Participating in transformations can be extremely rewarding for a therapist. Basic to these feelings is the investment we put in our work. The growth of our clients is the proof of our pudding. If significant change were seldom wrought from our therapeutic efforts, we would begin to wonder about our own competence and meaningfulness in our work. Since therapeutic gain on the part of our clients is the hallmark of our accomplishments, we must be wary not to insist on it from our clients. We must allow them to be free to stay as they are if they choose and not progress just to feed our egos. It's a rough therapeutic row to hoe.

Therapist's Self-Disclosure

An important aspect of the relationship is the extent of self-disclosure of the therapist. Therapists span the extremes on this issue. My purpose in self-revelation is to advance the therapy, so I may share my feeling about the client, my reactions to her, and tell her of experiences in my life that echo her own and feelings I have had similar to hers in order to share a common base of understanding. On occasions I disclose aspects of myself so that the client will get to know me better. The reciprocal trust the therapist demonstrates in sharing personal and sometimes painful experiences with the client is often extremely important to the client and may advance the therapy process considerably. I don't speak about myself to ventilate or to work on my own problems. I believe this to be exploitative, since the therapist is being paid to attend to the client's needs.

To summarize, the therapeutic relationship, as I see it, is a creative alliance in which the therapist accompanies the client on a portion of her life journey for the purpose of helping her to relinquish perceptual and behavioral attitudes that are causing her pain and to replace them with new ones that will increase her joy in living and promote feelings of self-acceptance, self-worth, and self-love. The therapeutic relationship is one of commitment, nurturance, and support, enabling the client to experiment with new ways of being. In a sense, the therapist is a follower rather than a guide, taking the lead from the client who points out the territory to be explored and the directions to be taken. Although one cannot abandon one's own philosophy of life, the therapist tries not to impose on the client but to be receptive to the client's finding her own way.

PARTICULAR CONSIDERATIONS IN ART THERAPY

In addition to all of the above considerations, art therapy imposes some special factors in the therapeutic relationship. Added to the relationship between two people (or among many, as in group therapy), there is each one's relation to the art product. As an expression of self it becomes an extension of the client and must be respected as such. Therefore, the manner in which the art therapist regards it, handles it, puts it away, and recalls it, becomes extremely important. Obviously, in recognizing the art creation as an extension of the client, the art therapist does not work on it. She may demonstrate technical assistance on another piece of paper, but respects the integrity of the client's expression by not interfering with it.

Even the most minimal drawing is an expression that has something to say. Many people with whom I have worked, particularly hospitalized, depressed patients, have been convinced on entering art therapy that their art work was meaningless and inadequate (which is how they saw themselves). As a result of my interest in their art expressions they soon became interested in them themselves.

To whom does the art work speak? To the therapist, to the client? Both, but differently. For the client it is self-revelation. As in her own life, so in her art expressions she is the ultimate authority. As she is responsible for her own life, so is she responsible for the interpretation of her own art expression. I don't interpret it for her. What I read in it is an echo of my own life experience. Many times my experience may connect with hers and augment her understanding. This is the stuff of which intuition is made. Too often, art therapists act as if they *know* what a picture is saying without any confirmation from the client. For example, I witnessed a presentation of mandalas by a therapist who never even told the client her interpretations, but pointed out to the audience the emergence of the devil (a small snowman), the father in the center (yellow color), and many equally absurd assumptions. People and art are both too complex for that sort of divination.

And yet an art therapist *does* come to know her clients through their art. She comes to understand their language of imagery, their style, their individual themes, their specific symbols so that explanations don't need to be redundant. Art expression is a language, but not a common one. It is unique and not immediately understood. The client is encouraged to tutor the art therapist in its meaning. Once this language of the individual's symbolic imagery is understood, it need not be explained over and over again—there can be immediate communication from client to art therapist through the image. For many people, the language of symbolic imagery is undeveloped. As a result, it is not a ready-made lanugage that becomes communicated, but a language in process, as the client explores and builds her own visual mode of expression.

Just as the art therapist responds to a client's facial expression or voice tone without a description of the feeling tone being necessary to convey it, so does she respond to the mood of a picture. She can tell if it's empty, lively, disorganized, rigidly organized, chaotic, tranquil, and so forth. But what it means to the client is for the client to say.

The Mamas and The Papas used to sing:

> Words of love, so soft and tender,
> Won't win a girl's heart anymore,
> If you love her, you must send her
> Somewhere where she's never been before.
> *(Farewell to the First Golden Era*
> The Mamas and the Papas,
> Dunhill Records, Inc., N.Y.)

Psychotherapy is like that. It's not what people already know that grabs them. It's the new places that challenge them. One of the joys of art psychotherapy is its potential for sending the client "somewhere where she's never been before." Although the art therapist doesn't offer cut-and-dried interpretations, she does encourage the client to explore the potentialities of the art. For example, if a client is engrossed in the old and familiar meaning of the pictorial objects, I may direct her attention to the mood of the picture. I try to make my queries open-ended, rather than suggestive of an answer in all cases. I don't want to lead the client. I want her to discover herself. So I'll ask, "What sort of mood does the picture have," rather than, "It looks bleak, doesn't it?" I won't assume about objects either. I'll ask, "What does that green shape represent?" rather than, "Is that a snake?"

To help clients explore further I'll suggest that they fantasize about their pictures. I might ask them to tell me a story about it, or if a person has been drawn I might ask what the person-in-the-picture is doing, thinking, feeling.

Steps in Processing the Art

I don't begin this way, however. After the picture (or sculpture) has been completed, I wait for the client to tell me about it. I may ask questions for clarification. I will start out questioning any unexplained objects in the picture so that I can be sure I understand what has been intended, rather than making assumptions. I'll follow the client's lead in what seems important to her to pursue in her associations to the picture. Sometimes I might respond to a particular issue because of some indication that this is an important area for the client. This may be based on material that has come up previously or something in the client's manner when it comes up, or just a hunch whose basis I can't identify. What is called intuition I think is developed out of a great deal of experience from which ideas come to the fore without awareness of all their antecedents. Often my intuition opens doors for the client. Sometimes it comes to nothing. But since I am not invested in the client's acceptance of my notions and I wish to model the experimentation I hope the client will develop, I offer my hunches, as such, to be discarded if they are not helpful at the time.

Usually, though, I don't intervene until the client appears finished with her own exploration, so as not to interrupt her train of thought. It is then I am most likely to follow my hunches and to try to take her further to "somewhere where she's never been before" through probing questions or encouragement to fantasy.

It is important that the art therapist open possibilities, not close them off. She must sense where the client is and be receptive to what comes forth. Frequently this is enough. At times she may wish to nudge her a little, but should also respect the client's unwillingness to pursue a picture further. It is not necessary to plumb any one art expression to its depths. Material in the picture that is significant will emerge again and again. The main thing is to encourage the client in her own self exploration so that this process may continue long after the therapy has ended.

Gifts for the Therapist

In the initial phase of art therapy some people with whom I've worked have felt they were making pictures for me. This was particularly true in the hospital where patients weren't seeking art therapy, but where it was part of the program.

When I was collecting data for research, their perceptions were accurate, and I did not suggest that the purpose of our sessions was therapy, although I was hopeful that they might prove beneficial for the patient as well as for me. When the goal was therapy, however, there were patients, particularly depressed individuals, who were so oriented to pleasing that they initially structured the sessions into making gifts for me. Eventually they came to realize that my interest was in the art work's meaning to them, and they began to make pictures for themselves.

For some patients, in addition to the picture's being viewed as a gift for me, the quality had to meet with my approval. If an art therapist truly wants her clients to orient their lives to satisfying themselves rather than constantly seeking the approval of others, she must be consistent in her reactions to the pictures. That is, she must not dole out praise or criticism on the basis of artistic merit, but rather reinforce the client's self-exploration through the art. When a relatively minimal picture leads a client to startling new insights, for example, the art therapist might remark on the importance of the picture to the client. I believe that the art therapist should be accepting and nonjudgmental of the art product as well as of the client, giving over the responsibility for art expression to her.

Although I would recommend such an approach to many aspects of the therapy, it is especially necessary in relating to the art work. Most people who are inexperienced in art are reminded of their early picture-making experience in school. They feel like children in relation to a teacher who is expecting an adequate performance. If a therapeutic alliance is to be established, it is important that the art therapist decline the client's overtures to relate in this manner and remain interested in the client's experience and help her to reflect on her expectations and feelings about the therapist's response.

Confidentiality

The mantle of confidentiality extends to art work as a visual form of privileged communication. Therefore, if the purpose of the art sessions is a form of psychotherapy, art exhibits of the work are not appropriate. In addition to a possible violation of confidentiality, they give the message that the goal is the creation of a product rather than a process. If the art work is to be shown to other staff members, the art therapist should make explicit to the client who sees it and under what circumstances. It is helpful for the art therapist to reassure the client that the pictures and related information are shared only with the staff involved in her treatment and are not randomly displayed. If the art is used for professional communication in publications, presentations, or exhibits, then, as with other case material, the identity of clients is disguised. In this book, for example, all names have been changed as well as any other details that might reveal identity.

Ownership

Underlying the professional use made of the art productions is the issue of ownership. Who owns the art work? Since I consider art expression as an extension of the self, then I hold that the creator owns it. Therefore, it is important that I either make clear at the outset that a condition of the work is that I will be keeping the art work to study and share with others, or I ask permission at some later date to use the art. An example of the former is the work I did at NIH. Patients did not pay for their hospitalization; treatment there was conditional on agreeing to participate in the research and releasing the data for professional communication. In private practice, on the other hand, clients kept their art work (unless they wanted me to retain it for them). As described in Chapter 19, when I wished to make use of some of the pictures made in a private group, I requested permission of the members.

Finally, if a client or patient wishes to tear up a picture or smash a sculpture, since it belongs to her, it is her perogative. I request that she consider what she is doing so that in this action, as in others, she is acting with awareness rather than being on automatic pilot.

Art Therapist's Participation in Art

There is the question of whether the art therapist participates in the art work. Usually I don't, for several reasons. First, the field of exploration is the client's life, not mine. It's a matter of role. Second, for those clients who feel inadequate in art, my more experienced drawing might prove intimidating. Third, as amplified in Chapter 19, the processing of my picture or sculpture would take up valuable therapy time. Nevertheless, there are times when I do art work with clients. This occurs more often in group art therapy, and the occasions for it are described in Chapter 19. Sometimes there is a particular reason for drawing in individual therapy as well. For example, a severely depressed man with whom I had worked became mute after a serious suicide attempt. I found that although a verbal interchange with him was impossible, we were able to communicate nonverbally by making several joint pictures together. In them I followed his lead, responding with color, form, or symbol to his graphic ideas as we took turns adding to the picture.

Of course, one of the problems faced by art therapists is the frustration they may experience in watching others dig into the art media when they would love to do so themselves. This problem highlights another personal reason why I refrain from art work in the sessions. I tend to become so absorbed in my own expression that I neglect the client. Since observing the manner in which a piece of art develops is often revealing and since clients may want to comment as they are working, it is important to be available to them rather than lost in one's own world as I tend to be when I'm immersed in art materials.

Before concluding this chapter and moving directly into the case material which illustrates the points I have made here, I would like to note that changes have evolved in my therapeutic style over the years. The following clinical vignettes are presented as I experienced the clients or patients at the time I saw them. Although my present views, as outlined in this chapter, do not run contrary to my therapeutic position at any previous time, there has been a change in emphasis and focus. Briefly, in more recent work I have been more aware of what transpires *between* the patient or client and myself. I am also more aware of my own reactions. In earlier work there was greater focus on the client alone. The following clinical material reflects these differences.

PART TWO

Affective Disorders

CHAPTER 7

Depression

Unlike some other psychiatric syndromes, depression is a condition most of us have experienced to some degree, at one time or another. We might question the difference between feelings of ordinary sadness or grief, on the one hand, and the diagnosis of depression as psychopathology, on the other. Some features which distinguish depression include self-dislike, feelings of worthlessness, loss of gratification, loss of attachments, hopelessness, lethargy, lack of motivation, guilt, and indecisiveness. With severe depression, these symptoms are more extreme, and there may be a vegetative state as well, characterized by psychomotor retardation, sleeplessness, and loss of appetite. Psychotic depression is most clearly distinguished from neurotic depression by the presence of delusions, particularly around being condemned, unworthy, or bodily altered. In my experience, patients with psychotic delusions often believed they had sinned, become impoverished, or that their bodies were decaying.

Reactive and endogenous depression are ususally differentiated by a precipitating event causing the former, such as loss of a loved one or loss of position, as in a career set-back. The division between the two forms of depression is unclear, however, and some investigators believe that all depressions are reactive, although the precipitating event may not be apparent.

There have been numerous biological studies of depression, covering a number of physiological functions, for example, studies from the project on which I worked on the relationship between steroid secretion and depression by William Bunney and co-workers (1965a, b, c). Although many positive findings have not been successfully replicated, current research appears to be honing in on some significant correlations between biochemical balance, mood states, and psychiatric condition. The effective use of pharmocological mood elevators in treatment has helped substantiate this position.

In contrast to biological studies, there is a relative dearth of systematic psychological and psychodynamic studies of depression. Where such studies exist, there has often been inadequate attention to diagnosis, control of extraneous variables, such as age, and insufficient replication. One interesting group of investigations, however, demonstrated that in test situations depressed patients are able to perform as effectively as matched controls (Beck, Aaron T.,

1967). Thus, the inertia in depression may be related more to a factor such as loss of motivation than to physiological inhibition. These findings are particularly relevant to art therapy and bear out my experience that depressed individuals are quite able to express themselves and derive benefit from art therapy, despite much initial resistance.

Theoretical constructs describing the etiology of depressive psychodynamics are beyond the scope of this book, but a discussion of depression would not be complete without at least a doff of the hat to its most influential theorists. Sigmund Freud (1925) compared melancholia to normal grief with self accusations and manifestations of hostility to the introjected lost love object; Karl Abraham (1927) related hostility to orality in depression; Melanie Klein (1934) believed that depression was rooted in the mother-child relationship in the first year of life. In general, the dynamic precursors of depression may be summarized as follows: The depressed individual suffered loss and/or abandonment by the mothering person on whom he or she was totally dependent in infancy. The resultant rage was repressed for fear of further rejection or retaliation.

I find Aaron Beck's (1967) use of a cognitive model in his theoretical basis of depression convincing. In brief, he states that during the developmental period the depression-prone individual develped negative attitudes toward the self, the world, and the future. Because of these attitudes the individual becomes sensitive to certain stresses, such as being deprived, thwarted, or rejected. He or she responds to such stresses disproportionately with ideas of personal deficiency, self-blame, and pessimism.

Particularly interesting in Beck's construct is his emphasis on resulting cognitive patterns (schemata) which influence the way the individual orients him or herself to a situation. These schemata consist of negative conceptions, which when evoked mold thought content in such a way as to lead to the typical depressive feelings of sadness, guilt, loneliness, and pessimism. Although the schemata may be inactive during asymptomatic periods, they become activated with the onset of depression and increasingly dominate cognition, so as to displace more appropriate schemata and disrupt cognitive processes involved in attaining self-objectivity and reality testing. The relative absence of experiencing anger is attributed to the displacement of schemata relevant to blaming others by schemata of self-blame.

THERAPEUTIC RELATIONSHIP

Depression is depressing. For nine years I worked on a ward for psychotic depressives at the NIH Clinical Center seeing all patients in twice-weekly individual art therapy sessions. These patients taught me much about feelings of hopelessness, worthlessness, guilt, and suppressed anger. Many of them suffered psychomotor retardation for some portion of their hospital stay. In such a condition, they found almost any activity overwhelmingly difficult, having little available energy for anything other than internal preoccupations.

As a result, the request for self-expression through picture making was often resisted. Many patients associated drawing with a childhood activity and felt embarrassed. The patients' feelings of self-worth were challenged by their expectations that whatever they would draw would show their childish inadequacies. The manner in which I presented art therapy to the patient initially, therefore, was of utmost importance. I stressed that the purpose was to provide another mode of expression in addition to words (rather than artistic accomplishment) and that I had no expectation that the patient have artistic talent or experience. Nevertheless, patients often protested that they didn't know how to draw. Such statements seemed both an expression of inadequacy feelings and a warning that I shouldn't expect anything. Although most were willing to try, some needed even more encouragement—fearing judgment of whatever production they would make. In such instances, I often suggested experimenting with the colors and not worrying about "making a picture."*

One elderly man was particularly resistant. He was diagnosed to be suffering from an agitated depression. He drew nothing the first session, spending the hour pacing around the room nervously, making many jerking movements. At the second session, he informed me that he had had art lessons when young and was a draftsman before his retirement, but that he had lost all his drawing abilities. After much encouragement he picked up a piece of charcoal, but instead of touching the paper set up on the easel, he began drawing on a corner of a piece of paper in a supply stack. He demonstrated to me the way he had been taught to draw a head in art school. At the next session, also on a corner of supply paper, he demonstrated the sort of landscapes he used to paint as a hobby. From this experimentation, he realized that he had not lost his abilities and began to work at the easel using the whole paper to make the sort of meticulous landscapes he had done in the past.

At the next opportunity he asked his wife to bring in some of his paintings. He became less preoccupied with his psychotic delusions of poverty and bodily decay and began to produce paintings outside our sessions. For several months he continued to paint and draw pleasant landscapes which revealed little of his feelings. He became more adventurous and made his first abstract picture which was as tight as his landscapes. Finally, however, he expressed some of his feelings in a clay "death mask" and a drawing of a volcano which was smoldering, about to erupt. He had come a long way toward recognizing his suppressed rage when he was able to identify with the volcano.

---

*Such an introduction to the art activity is appropriate in working with most individuals inexperienced in art.

In the initial difficulties in working with severely depressed patients, usually the objection to art production embodies a projective expectation—that my judgment of the patient will be as harsh as the patient's judgment of him or herself. As experience accrues and the patients see that I am genuinely interested in whatever they do, for its meaning to themselves, they begin to internalize my approach and leave off judging themselves. We form a therapeutic alliance in our interest in the patient's expressions. One depressed woman whom I saw for several months said at our last session prior to her discharge,

At first I thought art therapy was silly and childish, but I really got alot out of making these pictures even though I never did learn how to draw.

CASE STUDY

No patient is ever a typical representation of a psychiatric syndrome—the classical case is an abstraction—but Mary's trajectory through art expression exemplified many of the dynamics seen in a number of depressed individuals. As an intelligent woman in her late twenties with young children, she was more highly motivated and more open to therapeutic intervention than some of the older depressed patients who appeared beaten down by life and more hopeless in the long run.

Many of the hospitalized patients exhibited the characteristics of depression described above, but many others covered their depression with a facade of cheeriness. Mary appeared at her first art therapy session bright and smiling, relating to me in a pleasant, social sort of way. As was the case with others, this facade both masked negative feelings and replaced awareness of them. This was two days after her serious suicide attempt in which she had turned on the gas in her home precipitating her hospitalization.

Her first picture was superficial and empty—a colorless field where the patients had been taken to play baseball. She then drew Figure 6, *Spiral,* * also empty and colorless, but more meaningful. She said that each circle represented an argument with her husband and that the circles became smaller as her ''tolerance'' decreased. She felt that what they said to each other no longer had meaning and that they had both lost control. At the center she came to a ''dead stop'' and could ''no longer face another day'' and made a suicide attempt.

I continued to see Mary twice a week for the next five months of her hospitalization. At the second session she drew *Embrace,* also pale and colorless. She related the picture to missing sex with her husband which was the last thing that held meaning for them. She felt that even this had become ''mechanical''

---

*Spirals are characteristic of suicidal pictures; see Chapter 9.

Figure 6. *Spiral* symbol representing Mary's first suicide attempt.

because her husband no longer found her attractive due to her overweight. She felt ''embarrassed'' with him. She did not draw herself as heavy, however.

During the first several weeks of our meetings, her manner continued to be bright and cheery even though she was beginning to express some of her painful feelings. She drew pictures of various female family members who were presently influential (often overbearing) in her life. I then suggested she express pictorially her feelings about her mother. Her manner changed, and she became thoughtful, serious, and subdued. She spoke of her mother being ill with cancer when she was twelve years old and knowing that her mother would die—wanting it so that she wouldn't continue a life of suffering, and feeling relief at her actual death. She spoke of how she cared for her mother during the night when her father was exhausted and of her brother's anger with her when she didn't cry at hearing the news of her mother's death. She said that she/felt ''numb'' and wanted to cry but was unable to. She cried only at the funeral and observed that since then she has been able to withstand crises well, but falls apart over little things.

She said that she could think of these feelings only in terms of black and initially made a black patch on one side of the paper and a black streak on the other (Figure 7). She described this as loneliness in a crowd, the patch representing other people and the streak representing herself, with a big separation between them. She mentioned her large family and her lack of communication with them. She added a ''tunnel'' with an opening at the other end. She said that she felt then, and feels now, as though she is in a tunnel and everybody else is on the outside—that this serves as a symbol of her feelings of separation from them.

She continued to explore these feelings in another picture, *Small Shadow*. She said that as a child she was very mature for her age, being treated as a dependable, responsible person having to care for her dying mother a number of nights, but that she also felt very much like a child. She expressed this by drawing herself casting a small shadow. She drew the belt of her dress in such a way that it looks as though her arm is tied down. She said that she accepted her mother's death and her father's remarriage well but feels that in actuality she never really accepted these at all. Her father remarried soon after her mother's death, creating a double loss for her as she expeienced alienation from him and his new wife.

She used color for the first time two weeks later in drawing Figure 8, *Broken Window*. A brick shattering a window illustrates her feeling of being over-whelmed by powerful emotion the previous day. She felt that there were "cracks in the facade" of the wall which she had built to prevent herself from feeling particular pains. The brick going through a window was an actual event. In anger she had gone downtown to talk with her husband because they had had a fight and he refused to listen to her. She then threw bricks through two of the windows in the building he was renovating. This occurred when he walked away from her and wouldn't listen to her. She felt that this is what happens to her when people

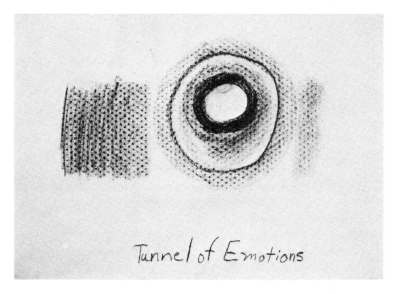

Figure 7. *Tunnel of Emotions* **illustrating Mary's feeling of separation from others.**

Figure 8.   *Broken Window* **representing Mary's rage.**

leave her. Her husband's response in this situation was to lie to her telling her that she had hurt someone with the brick and that he was taking that person to the hospital. In this way he "got the last word" which she said is what happened in many of their arguments. She felt that symbolically some of the glass had gone inside her. In this session she was beginning to deal with some of her overwhelming rage.

At the next session she let herself go more fully, drawing *The Sea* (Figure 9). She said she wanted to draw things breaking and thought of waves in a stormy, violent sea. When finished drawing, she saw power, conflict, and fury in her picture. She said she had been feeling fear, grief and hopelessness lately which she related to both her mother's death and the imminent departure of her psychiatrist from NIH. In this picture she covered almost the whole paper with color for the first time.

Her picture of the next session was the most colorful to date—a bright red rug (Figure 10). The paper was fully colored for the first time. She appeared much more involved in making it than any other previously, and it turned out to be livelier than any of the others. Nevertheless, her behavior was more depressed than heretofore. She explained the drawing as representing the rug being pulled out from under her by her doctor's termination with her—which left her feeling devastated and hopeless. She was experiencing a reenactment of her mother's death. Her bland superficiality had given way to recognition of her powerful emotions.

Figure 9. *The Sea*, Mary's fury.

Figure 10. Mary's feeling of the rug being pulled out from under her.

Two weeks later, Mary suffered another loss. Her roommate was discharged. She returned to colorlessness and her cheery, loquacious behavior in representing her feelings in *Dot's Side* (Figure 11), in which she depicted her roommate's empty side of the room. Dot was an older woman, whom Mary described as "constant." She was sort of motherly to Mary, and Mary stated that she was more disturbed by this separation than that with her doctor.

Mary found art expression a useful vehicle in continuing to explore her feelings toward her family, most particularly the anger which she had suppressed. She depicted her father's protection of her stepmother, drawing the "barbs" the pair fling at her. She felt her father had not protected her. Further pictures dealt with family pressures, guilt, and anger at feeling like an intruder when she wished to take care of her baby who was with her in-laws during her hospitalization. One picture of a vice represented her feelings around her family's expectations of her.

The next week, in making an abstract piece of sculpture (Figure 12), she became quite involved in her work, not talking as she often did. She saw it as herself. The portions that would be the face, guts, and a breast are gouged out. Her association was that she has "chopped away" at herself. She viewed it mainly in terms of uncovering portions of herself and saw the figure as leaning back, because she is still resistant to exploring her painful feelings. She spoke of having to "set aside" certain feelings which she did not recognize before, but had now uncovered.

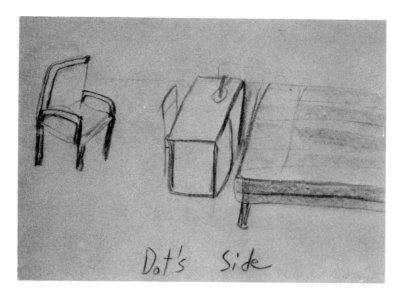

Figure 11. *Dot's Side*, Mary's loss of her roommate.

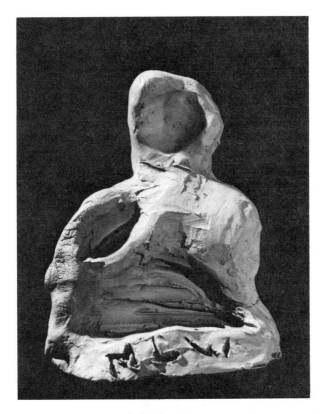

Figure 12.   Mary's sculpture with associations of her own and her mother's exploratory operations and fears of death.

This sculpture appeared to have meaning beyond being a metaphor dealing with feelings. Later, she related it to her own medical experiences which she connected with her mother's illness and death: She talked a great deal about her kidney removal four years earlier, saying that she had never expected to survive what was labeled an "exploratory operation." She remembered that her mother had also had an exploratory operation. She felt that things were "rotting" inside her, and that if her kidney had been "dead" for a long time without her knowing it, that other things inside her could have gone wrong too. Apparently the kidney suffered damage during her first two pregnancies. It was removed before her third pregnancy, but she felt that she would not live through the delivery of her third child and that the child would be deformed (further evidence of things being wrong inside her). I commented on the possibility that she felt, as a result of her first two pregnancies, that while something was growing inside her, that something was also dying inside her. She seemed quite taken by that idea. (This was so in the case of the cancer in her mother also.)

At the next session she drew *Fabric,* depicting herself as loosely woven fabric. She spoke of being pulled from either side, and wondered how she could withstand this. She said that she is not "very well put together," and when I mentioned something about being full of holes (as was her sculpture of herself) she agreed, saying that she doesn't know whether they are the result of emptiness which is not filled or holes that have been chopped away. She had been speaking of her difficulty in facing the return home and her decision not to be in the house all the time. She felt that she doesn't have very much to give, that she gives very little to herself and her family, and then there is nothing left, leaving her feeling depleted.

The theme of holes and being pulled (*Rug* and *Fabric*) continued in *Pulling,* a vivid painting of her husband and herself (Figure 13). She said she had felt like breaking dishes, throwing paint, or ripping something, but that because she could not do that, she ripped up herself instead. I encouraged her to put this in a picture. The red on the right represents herself and the blue on the left her husband. They are pulling at each other. In between are the things that are both of them—"pieces of things." She included among these, the children, experiences, and time. She noticed that these things aren't adhesive enough to connect them. She did not want to go home, particularly because she didn't want the

Figure 13.   *Pulling,* representing Mary and her husband pulling at each other.

Figure 14. *Parental Vigilence*, Mary's experience of hospitalization.

children to see any more of their "pulling" at each other. She chose red for herself because although she felt that her husband experienced as much anger as she did, hers was more "immediate." The allover impression is more of something which has been ripped apart than two things pulling at each other. The picture is vibrant and full of feeling.

During her last month of hospitalization, Mary went deeper into her feelings around her mother's death, her return to household responsibilities, and her separation from NIH. Regarding the former, she related a picture of herself juggling on a tight rope to feeling she had replaced her mother by "becoming her"—being the sort of person who was not satisfied and was striving for something more. She felt that her mother died unfulfilled. She spoke of an incident not long after her mother's death and her father's remarriage in which her father accused her of being a liar "just like your mother." This hurt her deeply because of her father's rejection of both herself and her mother. Her imagined feelings of rejection by her husband were rooted in her feelings that her father rejected both her and her mother (by remarriage very quickly), at the same time that her mother was lost to her. In describing her mother's early life, she noted that her mother left Russia and her roots to come to this country at precisely the same age that she, herself, lost her mother through her mother's death—a further identification with her dead, unfulfilled mother.

She drew many pictures of NIH in one form or another, such as Figure 14, *Parental Vigilance,* in which NIH looks like a large ghost (her mother?)

watching as she learns to build. In another, she drew a "prop" which she had intended as a lever lifting a boulder exposing the underside of a rock—the underside of herself. My notes on the day of the session included the following:

> The picture is really quite ominous, and she recognized this to an extent when she saw that the boulder could go the other way, in other words, back to the position from which it had been lifted, as well. From the way she has drawn it, it looks as though once the prop is pulled out, the boulder will go rolling down the hill and is perhaps predictive of a relapse for her.

My notes turned out to be predictive.

Much of the last month was spent in making arrangements. She took a job in order to escape from some of the pressure of her household and found a psychiatrist to continue outpatient treatment. Her pictures dealt with the transition she was making. She had dieted at NIH and had lost a great deal of weight. After a weekend at home during which she threw out maternity clothes and dresses that were now too big for her, she said she was burning her bridges behind her. She decided to put this idea into a picture and drew Figure 15, *Bridge*. When finished, she said she couldn't bring herself to add the fire and burn the bridge. She saw it as bridging the gap between NIH on the right and home on the left. The drop between them looks precipitous. Apparently, it was important to her that the bridge back to NIH remain intact.

Figure 15.   Mary's picture of the bridge between hospital and home.

Figure 16. *Morass*, Mary's dream of gore coming out of her son's abdominal incision and bars holding her down, after overdosing in her second suicide attempt.

At our session on her discharge day, Mary said that she would miss art therapy—she had found that she was able to express herself more directly in pictures than she often did in words, sometimes unintentionally so. I told her that I thought that she had made good use of these sessions, which was gratifying to me, and that I had come to like her and would miss her. She said she was very glad that I had said that. It gave her something to hold on to. She had wondered whether she would leave a sort of vacuum, as just another patient, or did she mean something as a person to anyone at NIH. She related a dream of the previous night which expressed her feelings that she was leaving something of herself at NIH.

Although Mary had made much progress in dealing with her feelings of loss, anger, and low self-esteem which contributed to her depression, she was not yet out of the woods. She managed her home life and job successfully for a year, but when confronted with additional stress, made another suicide attempt, although not a serious one this time. She was readmitted to NIH for several weeks. Her son had undergone abdominal surgery, and his incision had reopened after his return from the hospital. Her panic and fatigue from caring for him led her to an overdose of sleeping pills after a fight with her husband and a prediction from her mother-in-law that she would "crack up" under the strain. I saw her the day she was admitted. She said she just wanted to throw the paint and, in fact, had wished for art supplies while her son was in the hospital to relieve the tension, as she had in our art therapy sessions previously. She picked up her relationship with me much as she had left it a year earlier.

She painted *Morass* (Figure 16) with much gusto, filling the paper with vivid color, mostly red—quite a contrast to her first picture a year earlier after her first suicide attempt (Figure 6). She associated the picture to her dream after taking the overdose—the red in the picture was all the gore coming out of her son's incision. The blue streaks in the center "look like bars holding me down." For a week she had been thinking,

> I'm hurting everyone. They'd be better off without me . . . my being around was what was causing him to be ill, and no matter what I could do, he got worse. And this happened in my mother's case. I took care of her, I nursed her, and she got worse. And here was a kid sick, and my aunt said to me, "What is it you do to your kids?" . . . My pride has smothered him with attention or something which so weakens him that he's powerless, and he'd be better off without me around.

She was well in touch with her feelings this time—her anger and fear that her son would die, her expectation when the phone rang that it would be the doctor informing her of his death, her possessiveness in not wanting anyone else to care for him, coupled with the feeling quoted above that her care was poisonous.

Even after the catharsis experienced in painting and discussing *Morass,* Mary still had need for additional physical and emotional release, so I suggested that she work with clay. She punched a hole in a form she made and was reminded of her son's abdomen. I was reminded of her previous sculpture (Figure 12). She said its eviscerated apperance had been "a forecast." She commented that she knew there was something wrong with her in relation to her kidney operation and her mother's illness, but that it really got to her that something was wrong with her son as well.

During the several weeks of her hospitalization, Mary was eager to get back home and back to work, rather than being fearful as she had been during her previous hospitalization. She had gained much confidence. Her final picture pointed her in the direction she wished to go, and she was pleased with it. *Satisfaction* depicted her desk at work. She was especially pleased to be able to recall it in all its details. She was proud that she was able to function well at a demanding job in a fast-paced office.

When Mary first entered NIH, her art work was typical of the impoverished style characteristic of depression. Although she never developed much skill in artisitc expression, she was able to make good use of the process, both as a means of self-expression and release, as well as a tool for self-exploration. The problems she encountered regarding loss, death, suppressed anger, and feelings of harmfulness to others with resultant guilt are typical of depression. Art therapy was a useful process in her dealing with these problems and overcoming them sufficiently to live more satisfactorily.

CHARACTERISTICS OF ART EXPRESSION IN DEPRESSION

Although depression is a prevalent pathological clinical state, the literature contains few studies of the pictorial expressions of depressed patients, as compared with an abundance of material on schizophrenic art. As I read what there was, I was surprised to find that the observations of others differed in many respects from my own. Some authors noted commonality of content, whereas content has been so varied among over one hundred depressed patients with whom I have worked, that it would be impossible to point out common themes. Dax (1953) noted signs of death, immobile figures, and starless nights. Plokker (1965) observed depictions of torture or suicide, delusions of sin, poverty, and hypochondria. Enachescu (1971) found depressive themes, and Naumburg (1966) saw grief and mourning in the pictures. Related to content is Reitman's (1950c) observation of poverty of ideas.

I was surprised, too, by the descriptions of depressive style found in the literature. Dax (1953), Enachescu (1971), Plokker (1965), and Reitman (1950) all observed dark or somber colors as characteristic of depressives' pictures. Dax (1953) also noted bareness and lack of detail. Enachescu (1971) found the pictures dull and simple; Lehman and Risques (1953) saw evidence in the pictures of low energy; and Schube and Cowel (1939) found indications of restraint. Some of these observations were similar to my own impressions; others differed.

Most of these observations were simply that, observations, rather than results of systematic investigation. As discussed in Part VI (Research) many assumptions are made about patient art work without benefit of either the systematic investigation necessary to define characteristics of a large population, as is the case here, or the corroboration from the patient necessary to understand an individual piece of art expression.

As a result of both the dearth of reports on art expression in depression and the discrepancy between my observations and those reports that did exist, I decided to undertake a systematic study of characteristics of art expression in depression.*

To test characteristics of depressive art expression, pictures produced during increased depression were compared with pictures made when depression was diminished. The sample was comprised of pairs of pictures made by ten different patients (five male and five female). One picture was produced on a day when the patient was highly depressed and one picture from a day when depression was low. The determinations of the severity of depression were made independently by a nursing team trained in psychiatric research. The team rated depression in

---

*This study appeared in Wadeson, Harriet: Characteristics of Art Expression in Depression. *The Journal of Nervous and Mental Disease*, 153 (1971): 197–204.

each patient daily on a 15-point scale, with 15 the score for the most depression ever seen and one indicating an absence of depression. The selection of patients was determined by there being a wide range of ratings on days when the patients participated in art therapy.

The purpose of having each patient serve as his or her own control in this manner was to eliminate variables of intelligence, socio-economic background, artistic experience and ability, age, hand-eye coordination, and so on. Experience in art therapy was not a consistent variable, in that in some cases the picture in the sample produced on the more depressed day was made prior to the picture on the less depressed day, and in other cases, produced at a later date.

Each patient's pair of pictures was selected for the sample on the basis of the highest and the lowest depression ratings received on the days when he or she participated in art therapy.

Prior to the selection of the sample, I formulated pictorial characteristics descriptive of the predominance of pictures made during severe depression. This formulation resulted from general impressions over six years of work with depressed patients, as well as careful scrutiny of many pictures produced by a large number of patients, including quantification of color used in all pictures made by six patients.

I hypothesized that during higher depression, patients' pictures would exhibit the following characteristics to a greater degree than when they were less depressed.

1. Less color
2. More empty space
3. More constriction
4. More disorganization
5. Less investment of effort or less completeness
6. Less meaningfulness
   Either:
7. More depressive affect
   Or
8. Less affect

Five independent raters (psychiatrists) were asked to compare the two pictures made by each patient, determining which characteristics applied more to one picture than the other.

After the rating procedure, the raters were told that the characteristics listed previously were associated with depression and instructed to determine which picture in each pair was produced during greater depression on the basis of which exhibited more of these characteristics. The ratings indicated that during increased depression, patients' pictures revealed, at a statistically significant level, less color used, more empty space, less investment of effort or less completeness, more depressive affect or less affect, and a trend toward being more constricted and less meaningful than when less depressed. The hypothesis that they would also be more disorganized was not supported.

Examples

The following are examples of the pairs of pictures rated. (The raters were not given the background information presented here.)

Figure 17 was drawn in black by Joyce, a thirty-five year-old woman, the day after a suicide attempt. She looked and sounded depressed as she drew and talked about the picture. She clearly drew the injuries she had inflicted on her neck and wrists in her effort to kill herself, and the expression on the face is very forlorn. She was concerned about her children seeing her that way. Her depression was rated 12 by the nursing staff (15 is the highest possible rating).

Two months later she drew Figure 18 depicting herself at home with her family. The clothing and greenery are brightly colored. She was outgoing and animated during the session and saw her picture as looking "pleasant." Her depression rating was 4.

All five raters judged the more depressed picture (Figure 17) to have less color, more empty space, to be more disorganized, to have less investment of effort or be less complete, and have more depressive affect than Figure 18. Four raters judged it more constricted.

Figure 19 was painted in blue by Bob, a fifty-five year-old man. He was depressed and agitated during the session with little communication possible due to his constant preoccupation with delusions of physical malfunctioning, about which he complained. He resisted making a picture, but eventually did so without associating to it. His depression rating on that day was 10.

A year later, he drew Figure 20. He used mostly blue with some red and orange. He was outgoing and talkative, discussing nostalgically the details of the drawing. He speculated that if he hadn't left the area pictured here, he might not have become depressed. He was rated 4 in depression by the nursing staff.

All five raters considered the picture made on the more depressed day (Figure 19) to have more empty space, to be more constricted, to have less investment of effort or be less complete. Four of the five raters judged it to have less color, to be less meaningful, and show more depressive affect.

Discussion

Some of the formal characteristics commented upon by other authors bear a resemblance to those studied here. "Bareness" and "lack of detail," reported by Dax (1953), and "paucity of ideas," by Reitman (1950), are similar to the

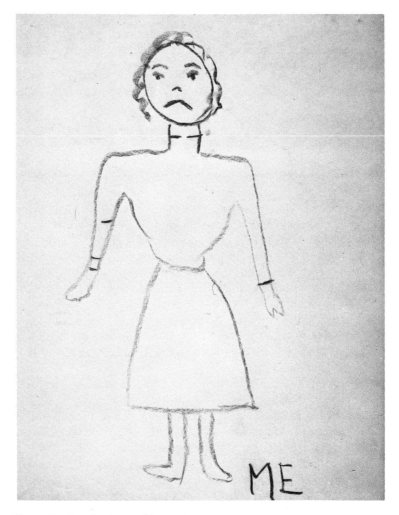

Figure 17.   Joyce's picture without color, drawn during severe depression, showing neck and wrist wounds from a suicide attempt the previous day.

classification of ''empty space'' and ''less investment of effort or less complete'' presented here. The most prominent difference concerned color. Four authors observed dark or sombre colors in the pictures of depressed patients, and Dax (1953) and Plokker (1965) noted that the upper half of the picture is often darker than the lower. Neither of these observations apply to most of the depression pictures here reviewed. Rather, the salient characteristic concerning color of the thousands of depressed pictures I have collected as illustrated in the present sample, is its lack. Plokker states that color becomes lighter as depression abates,

Figure 18.   A colorful picture by Joyce when severe depression had lifted.

whereas the finding here is that color returns when depression diminishes.

Why, then, is there a difference between some of the findings in this study and those of others? The answer appears to lie in the composition of the samples. Dax, Reitman and Plokker note that many depressed patients do not make pictures at all due to the inhibitory effect of the illness and psychomotor retardation. Therefore, it would seem that their populations were composed of patients motivated to draw. Dax states that the ''extensive'' terms describing depression ''are mostly capable of simple, concise and powerful translation to the field of painting'' (1965). Nevertheless, in order to find twleve examples of depressive pictures suitable for reproduction and discussion, he had to examine over 50,000 paintings by patients. His explanation of this phenomenon is that depressed patients' ''retardation, lack of drive and paucity of ideas make it difficult for them to register their symptoms at the time when they are most depressed'' (1953). Therefore, it is likely that the pictures he observed were produced by patients who wished to express themselves graphically, thus representing a skewed sample.

The depressed patients in my study, on the other hand, were scheduled for individual art therapy sessions on a regular basis and strongly encouraged to produce a picture. Many were resistant, but eventually did so. It was highly unusual for a patient to refuse altogether. The result is probably both a larger and more representative sample from which the ten patients studied here were selected.

Conclusions

The graphic characteristics associated with increased depression are of a piece: less color, more empty space, less investment of effort or less complete, more depressive affect or less affect, more constricted and less meaningful (the latter two not statistically significant but indicating a trend). These characteristics, particularly in combination, are the result of a paucity of pictorial development. (A possible exception might be depressive affect.) This paucity in picture making is congruent with the total image presented by the severely depressed individual: psychomotor retardation, general inhibition of expressiveness (for example, flattened affect), lack of productivity, and impoverished interpersonal communication sometimes to the extent of being mute. The total impact of depressed patients' pictures is frequently one of a pervading emptiness.

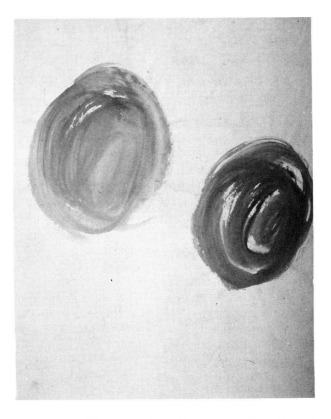

Figure 19. Bob's picture drawn during severe depression and agitation.

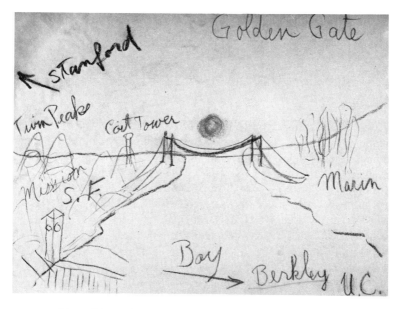

Figure 20.   A picture drawn by Bob when depression had lifted.

CHAPTER 8

Manic-Depressive Psychosis

My experience with manic-depressive patients has often been exciting, taxing, full of surprises, and frequently has kept me on the edge of my seat. The characteristics which both typify mania and make the manic patient so difficult to deal with are the high energy, totally unrealistic grandiosity, elation which goes far beyond pleasant feeling into skyrocketing euphoria, or a caustic anger. In many ways the manic phase of manic-depressive psychosis, or bipolar depression, as it has come to be labeled more recently, manifests itself in symptoms that are the direct opposite of those of depression. The condition is cyclic, with alternating phases of mania and depression, usually punctuated by periods of "normal" mood in between. The moods are usually of several months duration but, of course, may vary in intensity and time.

Like depression, mania-depression is considered a mood disorder. According to some nosologies, mania is a sub-category of depression. In others, bipolar depression is defined as a separate illness from unipolar depression. Recent genetic and biochemical studies appear to support this view. On the other hand, there is much clinical material which suggests that mania may be a defense against a core depression. As such, its prime mechanism is denial.

Since full-blown mania is a relatively rare condition, many experienced workers in psychiatric facilities have never encountered a manic episode. Therefore, I will introduce you to Rachel, forthwith, to give you a flavor of art therapy with a manic-depressive.

CASE STUDY

Although atypical in that her mood swings occurred every twenty-four hours, Rachel is a good example of the contrasting moods seen in mania-depression. Her art work expressed her contrasting point of view and feeling tone when "low" and "high."

Rachel was a forty year-old white female, tall and dark, with a relatively undistinguished appearance. For approximately two years she maintained a predictable forty-eight-hour cycle in which she was manic one day and depressed the next, manic the following day, and so forth. Upon entering the ward on any given day it was immediately apparent whether this was a ''high'' or ''low'' day for her, even if she was nowhere in sight. On manic days there was a tension noticeable in the staff, a sort of ''what-will-she-do-next'' air of expectancy. Often she was heard before she was seen—screaming from the seclusion room, arguing loudly, or talking excitedly and enthusiastically. When she came into view, she moved rapidly, darting from place to place, frequently moving furniture or smaller objects and actively engaging those around her, particularly visitors to the ward whom she practically accosted. This initial impact left one wishing to escape.

''Low'' or depressed days were conspicuous by the absence of such behavior. She slept a great deal and moved slowly, deliberately, and quietly. She did little to engage herself with her environment. She expressed guilt and remorse over her manic behavior and self-reproach for being unable to get herself moving. If asked about her feelings or condition, she usually repeated the question and often replied ''that's a good question'' but practically never came up with an answer.

On both manic and depressed days, it was almost impossible to have a meaningful interchange of ideas with her; on the former she seemed unable to hear and on the latter unable to speak.

History

Rachel was the older of two children, having a sister six years younger. As a child she had had severe temper tantrums until her sister was born. Throughout her school years she performed well academically. She was married to a professional man and was the mother of five adolescent children. For many years she held a full time editorial job, engaged in various hobbies, was active in her community, and after her fifth child was born, obtained a master's degree. Her life had had a hypomanic flavor, but at times this gave way to feelings of depression at the end of the day which she dissipated by going to sleep. Her illness was manifested approximately two years prior to admission at which time she noticed she was unable to work effectively every other day due to depression. For a year she remained fairly normal on the alternate days, but gradually during the following year established a pattern of depression one day and mania the next. This unusual forty-eight hour cycle continued with unrelenting regularity for two years.

Her illness appeared to be related to several factors: Her children were growing older and leaving home; her physician recommended that she have a hysterectomy; the family had recently moved from a neighborhood in which she was a leader to one which she felt was ''too rich for my blood;'' and with this move she changed jobs, disagreed with her new boss, and was eventually fired.

Description of Art Therapy Sessions

Rachel participated in 45-minute art therapy sessions twice a week. She was seen individually and told that the purpose was self-expression rather than the production of works of art. Nevertheless, when manic, she saw the two of us as kindred spirits who were artists. Her behavior in our sessions varied according to her mood. A few times when manic, she deliberately spilled the materials, ran out of the room, or talked so much that she never got around to doing art work. Sometimes when depressed, she dozed off in the middle of making a picture and had to be awakened. On such occasions she usually became sleepier as the session progressed. Most of the time, however, she enjoyed the sessions and tried to cooperate, in contrast with her behavior on the ward, which was withdrawn when she was depressed and often combative, or at best unreasonable, when she was manic.

Her relationship with me became concretized in a piece of sculpture on which she worked for several weeks. Two women, one younger and one older, stood together with arms around each other. She explained that the older one was offering affectionate guidance to the younger one. As she worked she posed me as her model, first in the position of one then the other, with her arm around me or mine around her. Lovingly she spanked the clay with a modelling tool. In fact, she was older than I, but as therapist I was in the mothering role in relation to her. The clay piece and her treatment of it coalesced much of her experience of our relationship.

Pictorial Themes

Since Rachel's explicit communication was minimal, her art expression was particularly important in conveying her experience. Like other manics, her insight was also minimal, but the art sessions provided her a significant avenue of catharsis and relationship. Although I called her attention to recurrent themes and variations in her pictures, she did not sustain continuity in integrating them meaningfully. These themes, however, provided a useful comprehension to me and the rest of the staff.*

The most frequent identifiable theme in Rachel's pictures was the representation of incarceration and death in the forms of prisons, cages, tombs, and coffins. This theme appeared during both mania and depression but in a markedly different way.

*The following material was reported in Wadeson, Harriet, and Bunney, William: Manic-depressive Art. *The Journal of Nervous and Mental Disease,* 150 (1970): 215–231.

Figure 21 is an example of the expression of this theme during depression. As she was verbalizing discouragement and despair, I suggested that she try to express these feeling in a picture. She made a central shape of dark blue with bar-like lines over it which she described as a "dark mood" and another barred form in brown on the far right. She designated the former a "tombstone" and the latter a "cage." She said, "I am afraid of these depressed feelings and try to run away from them." She then added some lighter, brighter color below and titled the picture *Dejection*.

Figure 22 provides a further example of this theme's appearance during depression. She began the picture with green vertical lines across the middle of the paper which she said was "very high grass." Beneath it she painted pod-shaped forms and stopped, saying she could not go on. After awhile, however, she resumed and filled in the shapes with brown and added dark colors above the grass. She titled the picture *Mumbo-Jumbo* because she said her thoughts were confused while she painted it. She became sleepy, but eventually said that the picture reminded her of death and the shapes under the grass were coffins.

Although the theme of incarceration appeared during mania, Rachel's associations were quite different from those during depression. When manic, she frequently called the hospital her prison. She made pictures of the hospital

Figure 21.   Tombs and cages by Rachel during depression.

Figure 22. Buried coffins by Rachel during depression.

building entitled *Prison* and vehemently drew barred structures as she angrily accused the staff of mistreating her. Her own recognition of the differing meaning this theme had for her was expressed in the following way. While depressed, in reference to a picture of prison bars she had made when manic to represent anger, she said that the idea still held true for her except that the feeling would now be fear—her fear that she would not get well. She said, ''In the past (when manic) I used the bars to represent external problems, but now I realize that the problems are inside.'' Since Rachel retained little continuity from manic to depressed days, the tangible art products provided a useful bridge for her to relate the experience of one to the other.

When manic, in addition to seeing her prision as something outside herself, such as the hospital, she produced images of bursting out. For example, on a slightly manic day she made a pattern of heavy black criss-crossing lines on brown paper, titling it in red, *Do Bars a Prison Make?* She said it was good to get out her frustrations. Her next picture was a blue barred structure on red paper, similar to the preceding one. This time, however, yellow streaks burst out of it. She titled it *The Bursting*. The next day her mania was increased. After drawing a picture of the hospital titled *Prison Perspective* (Figure 23), she drew a picture similar to *The Bursting,* but more disorganized. She named it *The Opening*. This theme of bursting out did not appear during depression.

My impression was that during depression, she frequently felt trapped in her own hopeless feelings as represented by her pictures of cages, tombs, and coffins. Although she attempted to escape these painful thoughts through what she called "positive thinking," she seemed unable to do so and could avoid them only through sleep.* When she was manic, however, it seemed that the causes of entrapment were often projected outward, and she perceived the hospital as her jail and the staff as her jailers. In addition, some of her efforts when manic appeared to be directed toward "bursting out" of the trap of depression.

Symbols

Similar to the enclosed shapes associated with cages, coffins, and tombs was a configuration of concentrically organized forms within forms which appeared frequently during depression.

Figure 23.   The hospital seen as a prison by Rachel during mania.

---

*On depressed days, in addition to taking frequent naps, she often fell asleep during the art therapy sessions, sometimes while standing before the easel. When this occurred, she usually became more sleepy as the session progressed. As Lewin (1950) states: " . . . sleep may become a defensive measure employed by the ego in an attempt to shut out excessive or qualitatively disturbing stimuli. In this sense, sleep is the deepest form of 'denial' of the environment."

Although Rachel said little to reveal what this configuration meant to her, it is interesting to note that two of the representations were connected with female reproductive anatomy. One with a red center drawn during depression was entitled *Uterus*. Another painted when she was highly manic was titled *Virgin* (Figure 24). Its red splotches look like blood. When I questioned the title, saying *"Virgin?"* she responded, "There is nothing vaginal about it." Since the threatened hysterectomy was the most clearly defined precipitating event leading to the psychosis, it seems possible that Rachel's pictures of wombs and female genitalia may have been associated with it. There may have been related fears of loss expressed through the symbol as well. For example, on the depressed day she painted *Uterus,* she cried over her husband's refusal to allow her to come home on weekends because of her recent uncontrolled behavior. Shortly prior to this, he had threatened divorce as well.

The most frequent manic symbol was a spiral (Figure 25). It was usually bounded by straight horizontal lines. These coils often filled the paper and gave the appearance of much motion. She did not draw spirals when depressed, with one exception.

Usually when she drew spirals there was so much flight of ideas and distractability that it was impossible to determine what this image meant to her. The rapid manner in which she made them suggested in part that they reflected

Figure 24.   *Virgin* **by Rachel during mania.**

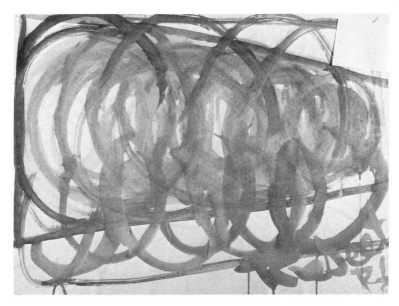

Figure 25.   Spiral figure by Rachel during mania.

her manic energy. Frequently, she expressed a great deal of anger as she produced them, and in this connection it is interesting to note that the spiral symbol is associated with anger in a previous study by Naumburg as well (1959). One of her obese women who often felt depressed entitled her picture of spirals *Rage*.

The one time Rachel drew a spiral when depressed, the symbol appeared in her final picture of the session and was accompanied by a marked change in mood from sobbing to a forced optimism which seemed, at least in part, produced by denial of her realistic difficulties. This particular spiral was small and tight compared to the larger, expansive ones produced in mania.*

Relationship Among Themes and Symbols

It is interesting to note a certain similarity between some of the themes and symbols in regard to their pictorial imagery as well as their possible meaning. The representations of wombs and closed forms associated with incarceration drawn during depression, are depicted by rather static looking enclosed shapes. The manic spiral symbol and "bursting out" streaks are linear in nature and expressive of movement. The concentric forms of the uterus and the closed

---

*Rachel's spirals were different from those made by suicidal patients described in Chapter 9. In the latter, the spiralling form became smaller as it progressed, whereas Rachel's expanded.

shapes of incarceration may be representative of depressive entrapment. One component of mania as an effort to break out of depressive suffering is suggested by the "bursting" streaks and spiralling motion of this manic theme and symbol, respectively.

FURTHER EXAMPLES

A few pictorial examples from other patients illustrate the relationship between mania and depression. Janet, at thirty-six, had a long history of manic-depressive psychosis beginning with depression in her early teens and continuing in recurring cycles of depression, mania, and "normality," roughly associated with the seasons of the year. She was depressed when she drew Figure 26. Her

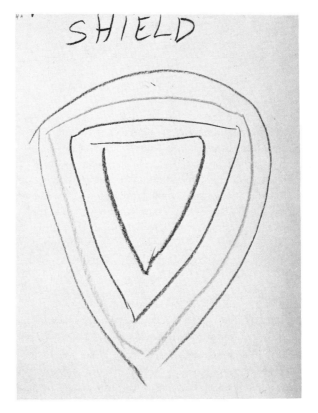

Figure 26.   Janet's shield against the world drawn during depression.

Figure 27. Janet's colorful *Energy Explosion*, predictive of her mania.

appearance was bedraggled, and she looked very anxious. She initially resisted making a picture because she feared it would look childish. Nevertheless, she picked up the green, blue and brown and made a design which she saw as a shield. She said that she needs a shield against the world since she can't live in it because she is different. She spoke a good deal about her history, particularly in regard to having always felt different. Studies of family backgrounds of manics indicate that these families had felt "different" (Cohen et al., 1954).

Six months later, she drew Figure 27 in vivid tones of red, fuchsia, yellow and orange. She was attractively dressed, smiling, and pleasant initially, but became angry toward the end of the session. She titled the picture *Energy Explosion* and said that although she is bored on the ward, she feels "excited inside." It seemed that she was possibly becoming manic. Nevertheless, she remained in good control for a month (despite some evidences of grandiosity and poor judgement), was discharged, shortly became manic, and had to be rehospitalized. The mood change had appeared more blatantly in her picture before being manifested in her behavior.

In recent years, mania has been treated with lithium carbonate, a drug which prevents manic episodes. An elderly woman who had had recurring manic attacks for most of her adult life drew a picture of her experience on lithium. She made layers of light blue and under them a layer of red and titled the picture, *Buried Fire*.

The effect of lithium on a very argumentative middle-aged man was to make him amenable to therapy. He frequently pontificated and would never listen to anyone, a posture which caused him to be intensely disliked on the ward and which led to many fights. At one art therapy session as he was pontificating away on the primary colors—in his "lecture" about them he referred to "red, yellow, and *green.*" I stopped myself short as I was about to correct him and instead reflected aloud, puzzling about why I might want to correct him when I really didn't care whether he knew what the primary colors were or not. Instead of arguing with me, he paused too and observed that his fights on the ward often began with someone challenging him. On this occasion, however, rather than arguing, we both stepped back to look at what was going on between us. I suggested that any time I was aware of a wish to correct him or put him down that I would tell him and we would try to understand what stimulated this response to him in me. Thus, we were able to establish the beginning of a therapeutic alliance, a significant departure from the pre-lithium, self-righteous authoritative lectures which made contact with him other than through argumentation impossible.

THERAPEUTIC RELATIONSHIP

This example points up an important factor in dealing with manics. Their behavior is often so outrageous in their attempts to test the therapist's limits, that the temptation is often to try to control them. Such a response usually leads to a power struggle which ends only after the therapist has summoned aides to drag the patient off to the seclusion room.

Since manic manipulation which is so offensive, is often directed toward securing attention, giving the patient as much attention and support as possible from the outset often decreases the patient's need to act out. Also, if in reaction to one's own anger, the therapist doesn't push the patient into a corner, the patient isn't called upon to fight, as in the case of the argumentative man just described. As a result of giving patients plenty of emotional room and support, I found that during my sessions with them they were relatively cooperative. There were occasions when patients came into my office screaming from battles on the ward, settled down with me, and a few minutes after returning to the ward resumed screaming in order to get total attention and control again.

The building of a therapeutic relationship with a manic patient often required much flexibility on my part. For example, as described in Chapter 3, one patient was confined to the seclusion room every time I had her scheduled for an art therapy session because her behavior was so wild that the staff kept her there most of the time. Since they did not want me to see her in seclusion, I had to make some other arrangement to work with her. My office was on the ward so I simply left my door open any time I was available to see her. She would breeze in, draw a quick picture, tell me what it meant to her, and breeze out, usually staying about ten minutes in all. That was about as much as she could handle at the time. It was important to allow her to monitor her own time limit and not force her to maintain controls she did not have at that time. Eventually her mania subsided and we were able to work more concertedly in regularly scheduled hour-long sessions.

Although some of the manic patients were combative, I did not suffer any injuries from them, nor was there ever an occasion where I feared violence. I believe this was the result of avoiding power struggles in trying to control the patients. On one occassion when I was concerned that Rachel (described previously) would escape, she was actually trying to help me. She was highly manic that day and had run off the ward (which was locked at that time). After her return I took her to my office which was then off the ward and near a staircase. During the session I dropped a metal sculpture stand on my foot, breaking my toe, and couldn't walk. She dashed out the door. I feared she would run down the stairs and out of the hospital. I couldn't chase her. I called her, and she came back into the room explaining that she was looking for help for me. I asked her to remain with me and told her that I would phone for help. While we waited for someone to come, she made wet compresses and applied them to my foot. Had our relationship been the usual antagonistic sort that manics generally instigate, she probably would have used the occasion to escape.

CHARACTERISTICS OF ART EXPRESSION IN BIPOLAR DEPRESSION

As is the case in unipolar depression, characteristics of art in bipolar depression have not been studied systematically. Descriptions in the literature are generally congruent with the disorganized hyperactivity of manic behavior. Content described includes sexual symbols (Zimmerman and Garfinkle, 1942), and euphoric themes (Enachescu, 1971), whatever that means. Style is described as having wild, vivid, or hot colors (Dax, 1953; Enachescu, 1971; Plokker, 1965; Reitman, 1954) as well as lack of color variety (Dax, 1953). Other stylistic characteristics are deterioration in composition (Plokker, 1965), carelessness (Dax, 1953), disordered lines (Reitman, 1954), scant detail and excitement (Zimmerman and Garfinkle, 1942), and indications of activity (Schube and Cowell, 1939).

Although I did not attempt to delineate characteristics of manic art, as I had done in depression, I did apply a systematic investigation to the art work of one patient, Rachel, to discern the difference between her pictures on manic and depressed days.* Raters blind to the hypotheses of the study confirmed the following characteristics of Rachel's art when manic and when depressed:

Depression	*Mania*
Color	Color
Pale	Vivid
Linear style	Linear style
Static	Full of motion
Tentative	Free
	Bold lines
Configurations	Configurations
Closed forms	Busy
Leaves areas barren	Fills paper
Organization	Organization
Tight	Confused and/or fragmented
	Loose but with attempts
	to control
	Very organized
Affect	Affect
Listless—less affect	Angry
Attempt at pleasantness	Gay
Hopeless emptiness	Sensuous
Enclosed, trapped feeling	Ebullient
	Wild

*Material from this study was reported in Wadeson, Harriet and Bunney, William: Manic-depressive Art. *The Journal of Nervous and Mental Disease*, 150 (1970): 215–231.

Finally, I will challenge Plokker's statement that art work of manic-depressives offers only "fairly monotonous products" and "that we find in the psychoses of the manic-depressive type virtually the same picture of the world in the case of all sufferers" (1965). My experience in art therapy has taught me that each individual is unique. Manic-depressives are no exception.

CHAPTER 9

Suicide

The threat of suicide forces the therapist to face significant existential questions of value in life and responsibility for another. At times a client's longing for the end of a life of suffering may resound in the therapist's own feelings of despair. More so than ordinarily, the therapist's sensitivity to the client is challenged. The feelings of therapeutic failure are seldom more acute than those of a therapist after the suicide of a client unsuspected of suicide intent.

The treatment of suicidal individuals raises profound questions. Is the therapist responsible for the patient's life? Does an individual have the right to take his or her life? What about the patient's family? Should they be spared the patient's death? Is the suicidal intent a fully considered act by a responsible person, the preoccupation of one who is no longer a responsible adult, or an act of impulse? Some therapists believe that death should be prevented at any cost. Some believe that a well-functioning individual should not be locked up to prevent suicide. Most recognize that often suicidal wishes evidence ambivalence, and, therefore, they work on behalf of the patient's life.

Many suicidal patients with whom I have worked held ambivalent feelings even at their most suicidal moments. Some who had made serious suicide attempts were later glad to have failed. The few who were resolutely determined eventually killed themselves. There were many others who acted out of a desperate impulse but had never been determined to die. Sometimes, the desperation evident in their communication was sufficient to gain the help they needed and which they felt they could get no other way. There's nothing like a suicide attempt to cause family members to sit up and take notice.

Although suicide is most often associated with depression, it is not confined to depression. For example, suicide can result from schizophrenic delusions or from a fear of a return of schizophrenic psychosis. It occurs among manic-depressives and those not diagnosed as psychiatrically ill. Some consider alcohol and drug abuse to be forms of suicide. For the most part those with whom I have worked, however, were depressed. Therefore, many of the examples presented here fall into that category.

A major problem in the treatment of potentially suicidal individuals is lack of communication of suicidal feelings. Often this is deliberate when suicide intent is strong, the rationale being that were the intent known, steps would be taken to prevent the act. In some cases, the feelings of isolation and hopelessness which are a part of the death wish lead to the belief that it is impossible to communicate meaningfully with others. Ambivalence about killing oneself frequently leads to an impaired or disguised message of suicide intent, sometimes accompanied by the fantasy that if the important "other" really cared, he or she would understand the message. That important "other" might be a family member. Sometimes it is the therapist.

THERAPEUTIC RELATIONSHIP

The therapeutic relationship with potentially suicidal individuals is especially complex and consequential. It is most important that the therapist be attuned to the patient. The following are examples from private practice in which I found myself in difficult positions vis-à-vis clients with suicidal histories.

Jean was a young woman beleaguered with too many small children and an overbearing husband. She was a timid person with few contacts outside her home. From time to time when she became particularly despairing, she threatened suicide. I saw her in a private-practice couples group with her husband. Although the group was quite gentle with Jean, on occasion she would clam up, withdraw, and physically shrink back into a corner. At those times her face reminded me of a death mask, hiding what I suspected were terror and rage. The expression on her face really frightened me. When I saw it, I immediately started worrying about suicide. I imagined this was what her husband felt, too. At these times Jean was unapproachable. Although she felt helpless in relation to her husband and life situation, she could gain some measure of control over her life by choosing to end it, and she could control us through our fear of that consequence.

It is moments such as this that the therapeutic relationship hangs in a delicate balance. I could be of little help to Jean if I dealt with her only through fear. I waited for a moment when she was receptive and told her my reaction to the death mask look on her face. She said that she withdrew when she felt pushed by the group but recognized that she really needed and wanted the pushing. I proposed a contract with her: that I would push her but that I would rely on her to let me know when she had enough or had gone as far as she was willing to go at that time. She readily agreed. In this manner she took control, became less fearful, and at the same time released me of the anxiety of not knowing what would push her into withdrawal.

She still retreated from time to time, but instead of remaining in chilling isolation, she would return to interact with the group. She formed alliances within the group, particularly with another member who was also rather closed.

As she became more responsive to others in the group, her voice would ring out, "I can't buy that" whenever she suspected fudging. She had emerged from her timidity to become a vibrant, self-assertive woman.

Carol had been hospitalized briefly as a result of a suicide attempt several years before beginning therapy with me privately. Her decision to undertake therapy resulted from a return of suicidal wishes. Her life was an isolated one in which she had no friends, lived alone, and was supported by her parents. Her only contacts were her parental family with whom she related in hostile dependency. They put value in appearances and refused to speak of feelings or anything "not nice." Her only other significant relationship had been with a husband who had abandoned her. Her relationship with me was the only fairly trusting and open one she had ever had. I was perplexed as to how to handle her disclosure to me that she kept a bottle of pills stashed away "just in case" and that I was the only one who knew about it. I decided to trust her and our relationship, lest she deceive me as she had done her parents during adolescence and her doctors during her previous hospitalization. She agreed to inform me of all medication she was taking and to call me if she felt desperate. I continued to work with her for several years during which she became more fully aware of her feelings and less negative in her relation to the world. She kept her "security bottle," but never took any of the pills.

HOSPITALIZED PATIENTS

Most of the suicidal people with whom I have worked were individuals hospitalized for psychotic depression at the Clinical Center of NIH on wards of the National Institute of Mental Health. I saw these patients in individual art therapy sessions either for evaluation or on a regular weekly schedule. Many had been referred for hospitalization as a result of a suicide attempt or threat. Frequently, their graphic representations of suicidal feelings produced greater clarity and related insights than words alone. Such is often the case among depressed patients with difficulty in verbalizing feelings. There were occasions where the first indication of death wishes appeared in a picture.

Of the ninety-three patients I saw in art therapy during eight years I worked on wards for the affective psychoses, twenty-four (twenty-six percent) made pictures associated with suicidal ideation. Of these, sixteen (two-thirds) had made suicide attempts or gestures from which five had almost died, and four others eventually killed themselves (two shortly after the picture was made and two following a lengthy interval subsequent to discharge from the hospital). Most of the patients were discharged after suicidal risk was over to continue in outpatient treatment. A few were transferred to other hospitals where longer hospitalization was available.

From these patients I formed a collection of suicidal art work consisting of fifty-six pictures and two works of clay.* It is comprised only of those works designated by the patient to be associated with suicidal ideation or made just prior to a suicide attempt, and does not include those where there is suspicion of suicidal preoccupation with no confirmation by the patient. The pictures and the patients' comments about them illustrate many of the ingredients of suicidal wishes.

The material is organized in the following categories: Suicide Messages, Anger, Feelings of Harmfulness to Others, Self Hate, Hopelessness, Communication or Isolation, and Spiral Symbol.

SUICIDE MESSAGES

My introduction to suicide was dramatic, unfortunate, and instructive. I had just begun working on the depression ward as a novice art therapist. I felt privileged to be included in weekly clinical-research sessions where the chief psychiatrist would interview a patient while the other psychiatrists, social worker, and I observed behind a one-way mirror. Afterwards we would all rate the patient and discuss our ratings with a particular focus on suicide potential. At one of the first such sessions I attended, Mr. Dunn, a middle-aged man, was interviewed. (Back in those days we were more formal and called patients by surnames.) No one considered Mr. Dunn suicidal, and he was given a weekend pass to go home.

During the next week I saw him in art therapy twice. At the first session he was more uncommunicative and withdrawn than usual. He said he did not feel well and had had a bad weekend. He painted Figure 28 covering over his original loop-shapes with red. My immediate association was nooses, but I kept my thoughts to myself, rather than impose my own "idiosyncratic" ideas on the patient. Two days later he picked a conventional subject for his drawing—a view from the window, Figure 29. The choice of an innocuous subject was typical of his reluctance to express his feelings directly. He drew the trees in the lower portion of the picture from left to right and seemed to let himself go a little more with each one, until the last was made with very rapid, forceful strokes. I suggested that a picture was a safe place for ventilating the anger he might be feeling, and in response he went over and over the road, bearing down heavily on the pencil. Afterwards, he seemed exhausted and crumpled into a fetal-like position in a chair in the corner, completely withdrawing into himself.

*Reports on this material, including some of the examples which follow, were presented in a scientific exhibit entitled *Portraits of Suicide* at the American Psychiatric Assoc. Annual Meeting 1971 (Bronze Medal Award), at the NIMH 25th Anniversary Celebration and published in Wadeson, Harriet: Suicide: Expression in Images. *American Journal of Art Therapy, 14 (1975): 75–82.*

Figure 28.   Loop-shaped forms predictive of Mr. Dunn's suicide by hanging.

Figure 29.   Mr. Dunn's release of feeling in the pencil strokes of trees and road.

Two days later he went home on a weekend pass and hung himself. He had purchased the rope and had hammered nails into beams for securing the rope the previous weekend.

Because I was a novice, because he had been evaluated by professionals with more training and experience than I, because he was observed and rated daily, I did not trust my own intuition. I did not even pay any attention to it. Mr. Dunn had not revealed his intentions to anyone. But they had surfaced in the art work.

I stated that my first experience with suicide had been instructive. I had become wiser when I worked with Frances, an angry, strident middle-aged woman who had made several serious suicide attempts. At one session she drew pictures of very grandiose and unrealistic dreams. When asked to compare them with reality, she became angry, tore them up and drew *Finale*, Figure 30. She said, "You eat and you defecate, and that's all there is to life." Her anger had been mounting, particularly in relation to her psychiatrist whom she felt did not value her. This time I expressed my concern to the rest of the staff, and she was put on suicide precaution. I had come to trust my gut reaction. Frequently, the pictures were the most complete communication of suicide feelings.

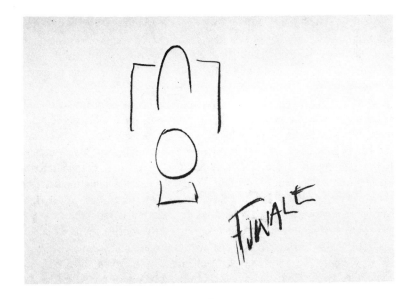

Figure 30.   *Finale*, **anger and hopelessness of Frances, indicating suicide risk.**

ANGER

As is evident in the pictures of Mr. Dunn and Frances, anger is an important component of suicidal feelings. In our population of manic and depressed patients, anger was expressed more frequently by those who were suicidal than by those who weren't. In fact, individuals who are severely depressed are often less in danger of suicide than those who are less depressed. Extremely severe depression may produce sufficient psychomotor retardation to impede the effort required to commit suicide. Therefore, many patients are in greatest jeopardy of suicide as they appear to be rallying from severe depression. Sometimes it's difficult to know which comes first, the chicken or the egg—greater available energy may make suicide possible, or the resolution to end a life which appears hopeless may lighten the depression.

Although anger is more likely to be expressed by those who are not psychomotorally retarded, it is by no means a simple quantitative phenomenon. Classically, depression has been viewed as anger turned inward (anger at parent→anger at introject→anger at self). Suicide then becomes the ultimate expression of anger. Whether such a hypothesis is complete or not, suicidal anger can take many forms.

For example, sometimes it is more or less focused as in Figure 31, drawn by Mike, a young man who had been acutely psychotic and, at this time, was out of work, had no friends, and was returning home to live with his parents. He called the picture *Dragon Breath* and said that he felt this way particularly in the mornings, "lying around in bed with no motivation, feeling stuporous." At such times he would have fantasies of suicide and, in fact, on one such occasion pointed a gun at his head. In the picture the red coming out of his mouth, he said, is his anger, and his hands are indicating that he wants his parents to leave him alone.

Sometimes, the feelings of anger are more diffuse as illustrated by Jane, a young woman who had taken an overdose of sleeping pills following rejection by her lover. She said that she felt better after the art therapy sessions because they enabled her to get things off her chest that she was unable to talk about and that she found picture making easier than talking. Following this statement, she painted *The End* (written in lower right corner, Figure 32) depicting her feelings at the time she attempted suicide. She identified the black dot, lower right, as herself "standing all alone." The rest of the painting is red. She said, "I felt angry and had this feeling nobody loves you and the world is kind of closing in around you." She associated the red with "blood, pain, anger." She drew herself very small and seemingly overwhelmed by a world suffused with the anger she felt. As in Mr. Dunn's view from the window (Figure 29), the style of this painting conveys the angry feelings through the manner of the brush strokes. In this case, however, the content also expresses the anger.

Figure 31. *Dragon Breath*, Mike's anger associated with suicidal feelings.

Figure 32. *The End*, blood, pain and anger represented by the red brush strokes painted by Jane to depict her suicidal feelings.

FEELINGS OF HARMFULNESS TO OTHERS

People who are consumed with impotent rage, as many suicidal individuals are, often experience themselves as harmful to others, for which they feel a great deal of guilt. Such was the case for Joan, a middle-aged woman who drew Figure 17 the day after slashing her throat and wrists. Commenting on this forlorn self-portrait showing the prominent wounds of her self-inflicted injuries, she said she did not want her children to see her as she now appeared and that they would be better off without her. Just prior to the suicide attempt she told her husband that he and the children would not have to be bothered with her anymore. She thought he might have understood her intention and told him,

So he would stop me, but I didn't want him to (note ambivalence) . . . . I'm not worth loving. I don't deserve his love . . . . I've ruined my husband's life and the kids' lives.

She spoke of feeling responsible for her father's heart attack and death a number of years before because,

If I had loved him more then, he wouldn't have had to drive himself when he had a heart condition.

After a few months Joan returned home feeling much better, grateful that her suicide attempt had failed (Figure 18).

SELF-HATE

Associated with anger and feelings of harmfulness to others is self-hatred. An example is the self-portrait drawn by Martha, an attractive, manic-depressive, middle-aged woman who had made suicidal gestures prior to hospitalization. She said that she deliberately chose black in drawing herself, Figure 33, and that she wanted to hurt herself because she doesn't like herself and recognized that she drives people away by her actions. She felt that in her picture she hadn't made the mouth turned down enough. She went on to say,

> I'm going to commit suicide . . . I don't want to live . . . in this Goddamn world . . . I have no place on earth for me . . . I've written out my funeral, every song I want sung.

She had also picked her grave site. Her children were grown and gone from home, and she felt responsible for the failure of her two marriages. On the ward she expressed her anger and destructiveness toward herself by deliberately breaking her false teeth and throwing her jewelry across the room.

The Rat (Figure 34) is also a self-portrait, drawn by Claire, a young woman who had been exceptionally beautiful before she began picking at her face and hands to the point where they were covered with ugly sores. Formerly a member

Figure 33.   Martha's self-portrait of self-hate and suicidal feelings.

of the Peace Corps, she had been sent home after becoming too upset to continue functioning adequately. She felt she had let down people who were important to her. On the ward she was extremely hostile and confided in no one. Describing *The Rat*, she said,

It's hateful, and it's hostile . . . I hate everybody who approaches me because I'm not able to approach people . . . I've had lots of friends and I'm walking out on them all . . . (to me) I don't want you to approach me.

Figure 34. *The Rat*, self-portrait by Claire prior to her suicide.

A couple of weeks after making this picture her behavior became less hostile, and she began to smile for the first time. When I tried to initiate meaningful dialogue, however, she evaded the subject, assuring me that she was dealing with her problems in the sessions with her psychiatrist. The ward staff was so relieved by the change and by the belief that Claire had developed trust in one of us, anyway, that we did not press her further. She begged off further art therapy sessions on the grounds that she was concentrating all her efforts in the sessions with her psychiatrist. As a result of her seeming improvement she was given a weekend pass. She used it to jump from a high building, killing herself. She left a letter indicating that such was her intention all along; the apparent change was only a ruse to gain her freedom. She asked forgiveness from her family and stated that death was the punishment she deserved. For this young woman, feelings of self-hate, failure, and guilt were intermingled.

Another very unfortunate person was Minnie, a frail, child-like woman in her fifties. She had been quite dependent most of her life until she had to care for her husband who was stricken with cancer and ill for many years. Shortly after his death, Minnie was discovered to have breast cancer for which she had a radical mastectomy. At the time of her hospitalization two of her three children had grown up and left home and the third was about to do so. Minnie was hospitalized as a result of an impulsive suicide attempt. Two days later I saw her in art therapy. She was crying and pacing the floor. I suggested she make a picture of her feelings. She smeared flesh colored paint, saying, "I looked at myself and didn't like what I saw." She titled the picture *Mess* and said she had made a mess of the lives of her family. Shortly after this session, she became mute and refused to eat. During her hospitalization a mastectomy of her other breast was necessary. Although Minnie was discharged from the hospital when she became less depressed and held a job for several years afterwards, she eventually killed herself. The misfortunes of her life were more than she could bear. The picture *Mess* and her comments indicated that she held herself responsible.

HOPELESSNESS

Hopelessness is an obvious ingredient of suicide wishes, and empirical studies indicate that in depressed patients, hopelessness is a fundamental precursor to suicidal wishes (Beck, 1967). These studies show that suicidal wishes have a higher correlation with hopelessness than any other symptom of depression. Suicide is seen as an escape from problems, life, or a self the patient finds unbearable.

When Irv, an elderly man, was asked who might be buried in the cemetery he painted, Figure 35, he replied, "Nobody I want to talk about." He went on to

Figure 35. *A Cemetary*, representing Irv's hopelessness and suicidal feelings connected with the death of his mother when he was a child.

say that his mother had died when he was eight, and that he didn't know where she was buried. He said,

I don't know what the hell I'm on this earth for. A man's got a chance to live, and he wants to die. What good is it . . . when your mother dies you might as well go with her, especially if you're a child.

In this case, the feelings of hopelessness were directly related to a profound loss early in life. Irv felt lost and uncared for, just as he had when his mother died almost sixty years earlier. Hopelessness was an early orientation for him. A number of the depressed patients on the ward had suffered the loss of a parent in childhood or adolescence.

Hopelessness is paramount in Figure 36, drawn by David, a middle-aged man, to depict his feelings when he attempted suicide. Though this patient frequently made colorful pictures, he used only charcoal for *Face to the Wall.* He explained that the title is the term used to describe prisoners of war who turned and faced the wall when they had given up all hope and effort to do anything to sustain their lives.

Anger was prominent in the hopeless feelings of Janet, a woman in her thirties. She had experienced recurrent episodes of mania and depression for fifteen years

Figure 36.   David's depiction of a POW who has given up hope, representing his own suidical feelings.

and was convinced that she would never recover. In a picture she entitled *Dreary Day,* she smeared gray paint and described it as follows:

> I kept thinking of a gray, dismal day . . . I don't know whether it's stormy . . . looks angry . . . I decided to make dirty snow . . . I can't express myself anyway so it doesn't matter what I do . . . I never know when I'm going to lash out at somebody . . . I have a lot of anger, and I don't know where to direct it. I should direct it at myself, but that doesn't get me any place either . . . I've put myself in this hospital. I didn't apparently work hard enough to get myself better when I was younger, so now I suffer . . . I'm not going to get well. I'm not even going to get as well as I was five years ago . . . Sooner or later I will do something drastic . . . I'll kill myself . . . medicine has failed me, and whatever I do is out of the control of medicine and psychiatry and everything else.

This patient was preoccupied with death during depression, but ceased to be so when the depression lifted. (She drew Figures 26 and 27, the latter when she was becoming manic.)

COMMUNICATION OR ISOLATION

Hopelessness is often the direct result of feelings of profound isolation. That most of the foregoing patients were able to express their suicidal feelings and know someone was listening, was extremely beneficial in undercutting the hopelessness and isolation. For many of the patients, the pictures and their comments about them were their most complete communication of suicidal feelings. In some instances picture-making probably replaced destructive ways of enacting these feelings and facilitated the patients' own exploration and understanding of their suicidal wishes.

One of the clearest statements of isolation was made by Julia, a sixty-five year-old woman, who drew a minimal representation of herself on the edge of a crowd to illustrate her feelings when she took a lethal dose of medication which resulted in coma and near death. She said:

> I can see the people, but not really see them and not really hear them and not really be able to communicate with them in any way. It's not a very good picture. That's the way it is when I'm really depressed, and I wish I knew how and why I've stopped having contact with other people . . . But it's as if, at some point, I try; I can remember trying to make it clear that something's wrong, and not being able to make it clear, and then, apparently because I can't make people understand I retreat more and more into a kind of shell, thinking nobody understands and there's no use trying.

Connie, an attractive middle-aged woman, seemed to communicate a lot. She was bright and cheery, and usually drew lively, colorful pictures. One day, she appeared quite depressed and tearful and for the first time drew the way she felt when she took an overdose of lethal quantity that came close to killing her. In a picture which was much more stark and pale than her usual drawings, she portrayed her family as they arrived home. She drew herself "removed and apart" from the others and entitled the picture *Removed and Apart*. A chest which divides her from the others resembles a coffin, and is the most developed object in the picture. Through her tears, she said that her family can't possibly understand how she feels, and she's not sure she wants them to. This was one of the few occasions that this woman communicated her painful feelings to anyone. Whereas Julia had been withdrawn, Connie's isolation was disguised by a cheeriness she did not feel, no doubt isolating her even further.

Donald's problem was similar. He was a scientist in his fifties who had achieved high status and prestige, but was convinced that his abilities were obsolete as younger men with more recent training were taking over his field. Hospitalization had been precipitated by his jumping from a high window. He was considered by the staff to be progressing well when he drew a picture he entitled *Rainbow*. He spoke of his lack of confidence in going back to work as he drew, said he should see the beauty in things, and chided himself for seeing only gloom. The bright colors of his rainbow typified his effort to look at the positive and avoid the painful feelings that he probably found overwhelming. The next day, when out on pass, he jumped from a bridge with arches shaped very much like the rainbow he had drawn. He was not killed. At the next art therapy session, he said it was impossible for one person to know another's feelings, indicating his profound sense of isolation. Several years after discharge, he committed suicide by jumping, once again communicating his intention to no one.

On occasion, communication of suicide intent can be very blatant, such as Figure 37, drawn by Shiela, a bitter young woman who had suffered numerous rejections and despaired of ever having a close, fulfilling relationship. In the past she had made several suicide attempts. She drew various means she was considering for self-destruction: on the left a car driving off a cliff, water for drowning below, a gun shooting the circles which represent her head, and her demise symbolized by the black dot in the lower right corner. She said the sun and written messages on the picture indicate that it would be a happy occasion. She covered the picture over with red because she wants "to go down in a blaze of glory" and because she likes "to destroy things."

Although there was an hysterical gallows humor quality to Sheila's preoccupation with death, this seemed in part to cover the seriousness of her feelings. Unlike Donald, she communicated her suicidal feelings sufficiently so that she was hospitalized during periods of high risk.

Figure 37.   Shiela's various means for committing suicide.

SPIRAL SYMBOL

Most surprising was the appearance of the same symbol, a spiral, to convey similar feelings connected with thoughts of suicide. The patients who drew spirals had not seen one another's pictures—in fact they were hospitalized at different times. Nor was any suggestion given to encourage production of the symbol—it appeared spontaneously in every case. Half of the suicidal patients with whom I worked at NIH (twelve out of twenty-four) utilized this symbol to illustrate suicidal feelings. The associations were a whirlpool, turmoil, and anxiety, frequently accompanied by experiencing a narrowing range of possibilities, which led to a feeling of entrapped hopelessness. In each case, the drawing of the spiral began with the broadest circle and became progressively narrower.*

Jeanette was a woman in her thirties who led a rather isolated life. Her depression was so severe that she sat mute and motionless for several months with her face buried in her lap and pressed so hard that her eyes became swollen from the pressure of her knees against them. After becoming mobilized she drew Figure 38 saying that she saw her depression as a downward spiral in which her

---

*These were different from those made by Rachel, described in Chapter 8. Hers were expressions of expansiveness becoming larger as she drew (Figure 25).

relationships with others diminished. She became more and more lethargic until reaching the bottom, at which point she wanted to die because there was nothing to live for.

Some patients expressed their hopelessness with many spirals rather than just one. Virginia's picture, *Life,* Figure 39, is an example. She was a middle-aged woman who had threatened suicide many times. She said she had been going around in circles since she was a child. After drawing these circles, which she said were in her head (the surrounding circle), she said:

> That's exactly what I've been saying since the year one. You're growing up; it will be better. You're going to college; it will be better. When you get married, it will be better. Everything will be better. I know better than that now.

Like the other patients in reference to their spiral pictures, she saw the future as a repetition of the past—no way out of the endless spiral—full of the same pain and disappointment and, therefore, hopeless.

Figure 38.   Jeanette's downward spiral of depression.

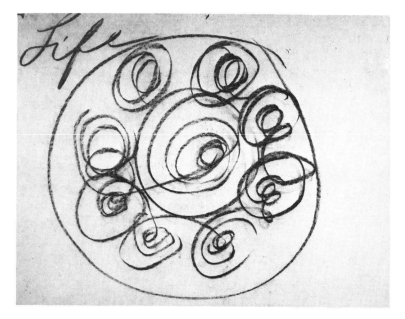

Figure 39.   Virginia's spirals of hopelessness.

Figure 40.   Sheila's suicidal feelings expressed in spirals of "turmoil."

Sheila, the young woman who drew the blatant expression of suicide intent, Figure 37, also drew many spirals to express her suicidal wishes. Associating to Figure 40, she said the spirals represented "conflicts and turmoil"—that the pulls of life are not worth struggling against the current that comes from below. She described the bottom of the whirlpool (spirals) as death. The lines covering the spirals represent "shattering," the result of which is the coffin at right with herself lying in it. The sun is to indicate that it will be a happy day when she dies.

CONCLUSION

Picture-making and the resultant art therapy relationship were important for the suicidal patients with whom I worked for four especially important reasons. The first is what might be called ventilation, release, or catharsis. Particularly where there was pent up anger, often stored over a lifetime of disappointments, the need to release it was a powerful one. Possibly the release achieved in art therapy replaced a more destructive way of enacting violent feelings.

The second reason is communication. Many of the patients were very withdrawn, especially at first. As stated previously, the image expressed graphically was the most complete communication of suicidal ideation for many of the patients. A number of them were much more self-expressive regarding their feelings in pictorial imagery than in other modes of expression. In some instances pictorial communication of active suicidal wishes alerted the staff to take suicide precautions and offer greater support and care at a stressful time.

A third reason is contact. Part of the suicidal ideation was often a feeling of hopeless isolation. The feelings expressed in the pictures were painful and sometimes shameful to the patients. Sharing these feelings through the imagery, seeing them "out there" on paper, and having them accepted and understood by another, went a long way in undercutting the isolation.

Finally, the fourth reason is the patient's own therapeutic work. Looking at their suicidal wishes, conceptualizing them in imagery, trying to understand them and transcend them for many led to a more satisfying life.

Of the four who killed themselves, it seems to me that two could have been helped more. Mr. Dunn (Figures 28 and 29) was not understood, and Claire (*The Rat,* Figure 34) was successful in deliberately fooling the staff. The other two patients, Donald (*Rainbow*) and Minnie (*Mess*) committed suicide several years after discharge, so I do not know what further transpired in their lives. I believe Donald was determined to kill himself and resisted efforts of others to get close to him. He was unamenable to intervention. Minnie's life seemed so overburdened with hardships beyond her control that she was unable and unwilling to cope further. Whether these two could have been helped more, I do not know.

CHAPTER 10

Combining Expressive Therapies in an Effort to Survive on a Depression Ward

As a conclusion to this section on affective disorders, I will describe a creative therapies enterprise I undertook out of sheer desperation.*

Each time I walked into the dayroom of the ward, the gloom and depression hit me like a palpable substance. As I recall the feeling, my imagery is of a gray fog-like nerve gas that infiltrated my pores rendering me inert and helpless.

What was needed were anti-stagnation measures. Despite the variety, intensity, and quantity of the existing therapies, they were not enough. Patients were often mute or at best unresponsive. Some refused to eat, some went through phases of stripping off their clothes and smearing feces. The depressions were occasionally punctuated by manic outbursts of violent proportions. When out of control, manic patients were sometimes secluded, but more often tolerated with fear on the part of both patients and staff. By and large, however, the patients could best be described as unresponsive and individually isolated.

What appeared to me to be needed was a regular group meeting in which activity and communication would be encouraged. Although the patients went to gym daily, had occupational therapy activity and group therapy twice a week at which communication was fostered, these did not suffice. My belief was that activity based on self-expression was needed—that by means of self-expression and communication through more direct modalities than "talking about," the patients would become more activated, energized, less isolated, and maybe (could it be possible?) even discover they could enjoy themselves.

*The following material appeared in Wadeson, Harriet: Combining Expressive Therapies, a Personal Account. *American Journal of Art Therapy,* 15:(1975) 43–46.

STRUCTURE

And so I established "The Experience Group."* Its structure was as follows: the group met once a week in a large activity room on the ward for an hour and a half at a regular time. All patients (there were usually eight to ten) were required to attend, although no one was coerced to participate—it was permissible for a patient to observe. No staff members other than myself were allowed to attend either to participate or to observe. I encouraged the patients to take leadership and responsibility for the activities of the group, although I was willing to take that responsibility when no patient wished to do so. I communicated to the rest of the staff about the group's activities and the behavior of individual patients at weekly staff meetings, as well as in informal contact.

The regulations were devised to enhance patient participation. The underlying reasons were as follows: attendance by the patients was compulsory due to the general lethargy and apathy among the group. In the face of the pervading negativism and passive aggression, it seemed unreasonable to expect that any group activity on the ward would get off the ground without required attendance. Nevertheless, since the very nature of self-expression is based on self-motivation, participation was not made compulsory. Realistically, nowhere more than on a depressed ward is the proverb more self-evident that "You can lead a horse to water, but can't make him drink." I recognized that in addition to required participation being contrary to the spirit of the activity's purpose, it would also be impossible to achieve. My hope was that once there, resistant patients would become interested, motivated, and somehow moved to join in, and that the freedom of expression within the group as well as the lack of demand to participate, would enable usually negativistic patients to join with an ease that would not precipitate a loss of face. And this, in fact, is what frequently happened. Sometimes involvement proceeded very gradually. At other times patients devised unique ways to participate. (See following examples.)

Staff participation was restricted for several reasons. One was the enormous difference between the staff members' participatory skills and those of the patients during severe depression. For example, one evening the staff members on duty initiated a group art activity. When I arrived the next morning, the pictures were hanging on the walls. There were hardly any pictures made by the patients. I believe they must have felt overwhelmed, inadequate, and ashamed.

The feelings of inadequacy and shame characteristic of severe depression constituted another reason for my being the only staff person present. There was

*Although this project was a type of group therapy, I have included its discussion in the section on Affective Disorders because the major emphasis is the effectiveness of expressive therapies with this very difficult population.

an important aspect to my leadership that would not have been found among most of the other staff. I did not mind making a fool of myself. Frequently, I participated in the group's activities in a very uninhibited manner. Because I was willing to risk being a fool for the pleasure I derived from my own spontaneity, others did too.

Finally, a further advantage to my leadership was that as the art therapist, I was identified on the ward as an expressive person working in my particular province which did not usually involve many of the discipline struggles in which patients and staff members were frequently embroiled. As a result, patients did not come to the "Experience Group" meetings angry at me for clashes outside the meeting.

My wish for patients to take leadership in originating and executing activities for the group was based on the obvious recognition that taking leadership is a significant move out of the deadening passivity this group was formed to counter.

In the eighteen months of the group's existence, I cannot recall a session which I entered without fear and trepidation. As the group assembled, usually with several patients arriving late because they were refusing to come and had to be corraled by me and the nursing staff, I would be aware that one patient was mute and refusing to eat; that another had just spent twenty-four hours in the seclusion room because of a violent outburst; another was threatening to sign out of the hospital against medical advice; that another was new to the ward, new to the "Experience Group" and extremely fearful; that one was on close observation because of suicide threats; and that in the preceeding group therapy sessions I had experienced the others as being dead.

Although this represents a composite picture, such conditions in the patient population were typical. Therefore, at the beginning of almost every session, I was convinced that the session would be a total bust—either altogether chaotic or utterly dead. Adding to my anxiety was my belief that it didn't make much sense to plan ahead—that the activities should suit the mood of the group. So I would enter with several ideas in mind and perhaps some appropriate equipment in hand, not knowing what we would do, being ready to scrap plans, invent new ones, or adopt ideas suggested by the patients. Often my feeling on ending each session was proportional to my fear and discouragement at the beginning. Most of the time it was a feeling of exhilaration.

MOVEMENT TO MUSIC

At the beginning of the group's life there was little verbal planning. I wanted to emphasize that we were an activity group and involve the patients in activity immediately. I started out by putting on a record and forming the group in a circle. We did simple non-threatening movements to the music: swaying, clapping, and tapping feet. Gradually we moved into using more of the body and eventually moving around the room. I took a lot of leadership here, often moving more than the patients did. Individuals participated to varying degrees, but all were part of the original circle and moved to the music to some extent.

Patient leadership advanced in this activity in several ways. Initially, patients started selecting the records we would use. Then before too long, I started assigning some leadership. At first when we were in the circle, the patients followed my lead. If I clapped, they did too; when I swayed to the music, the group did also. Then I started designating patients one by one to initiate a movement the group would follow. One of the more surprising moments in the group involved the participation of a fifty-five year-old woman in this activity. For many weeks she had been mute, refusing to eat or cooperate in any activity. At times she smeared her feces. Not only did she follow the lead of others in the movement—when it was her turn, she initiated a movement for the group to follow. This was the clearest communication and only appropriate involvement with others she had had in many weeks.

There were many instances of other negativistic patients becoming involved in this activity as well. An elderly man with an agitated depression who also refused to participate allowed me to dance with him. When the circle had broken up and the group was moving around the room to the music, I took him by the hand and moved with him. Instead of continuing his usual fidgeting, he allowed his body to sway with the music and tried to coordinate his motions to mine. During those moments as we moved together and looked at one another, there was a non-verbal communication breaking into the usual isolation in which this patient existed.

Eventually, some of the more assertive patients involved others in the activity in a similar manner. Obviously, the movement in couples increased communication within the group.

Participation and communication occurred in other ways, too, through movement to music. A woman in her eighties with foot trouble remained seated throughout. Nevertheless, when I took her hand and moved it to the music, she responded by doing sort of a dance with me using only our arms and hands. She seemed to be indicating that she was not too old or too sick to dance, albeit in limited form.

RELAXATION

The physical movement led to its counterpart, relaxation. When the group became more responsible in choosing its own activities, there developed an awareness of choosing to go with the prevailing mood state or to try to counter it. Specifically, the mood of the group was often lethargic at the beginning of the session. At times, a choice was made to do something energizing such as movement to music. But there were many occasions when the group chose relaxation exercises and seemed to derive great pleasure from them. In these instances, passivity reigned supreme. Instead of being a hostile sort of negativism, however, this passivity was a more positive surrendering to directions of an almost hypnotic quality. Although it was difficult for some of the patients to relax, all appeared refreshed by the exercise.

I believe there were several aspects of this activity which made it one which patients requested frequently. One, of course, was the obvious benefit of physical relaxation. In addition, the sort of attention the patients were directed to pay to bodily sensations such as their breathing, temperature, and individual muscles, interrupted the usual painful preoccupations in the minds of most of the depressed patients. Perhaps the most rewarding aspect, however, was the feeling of being given to in a soothing way, almost like a lullaby, while they lay still, listening to my suggestions with closed eyes.

Several deviations from the relaxation were interesting. At one session the group was divided between some who wanted to relax and others who wanted to be active and move to music. We tried both simultaneously, each patient choosing what he or she wanted to do. Some moved from one activity to the other during the session. At the end it was useful to discuss the changes in feeling as one went from movement to relaxation or vice-versa. Surprisingly, neither activity interfered with the other.

Two other examples of a more disruptive nature were significant. One involved a manic man who was just released from several days of seclusion where he was confined for uncontrollable behavior. The group wanted to do the relaxation exercises, but he kept talking, dumping ashes from his pipe on the mats we used to lie on and drawing on them with his pen. I sat next to him and gave him lots of special attention. After a while, he lay down, closed his eyes, and participated with the others in relaxing. Often manic behavior is geared toward winning special attention, particularly in a group setting. Once he recognized he had it, he no longer had to fight for it.

The other disruptive situation was quite different. An extremely hostile and negative young woman refused to participate in any of the activities. She was especially hostile toward me as a result of discomfort at being opened up in an individual art therapy session, as well as some sort of female rivalry she seemed to experience. When the mats were set out for the relaxation procedure, she began doing acrobatics on them. She was extremely adept. I asked her to teach the rest of us some of her skills. She was pleased to have her accomplishments recognized and to take a leadership position in the group. In a sense, she won the battle she had set out to fight before it had even begun, an extremely unusual experience for her.

MURAL MAKING

Another modality of expression was experienced through mural making. The nature of the mural varied from time to time and proved to be an accurate picture of the group at a given moment. For example, at one session the group was sufficiently verbal to plan the mural which was to be ships on a sea. Each patient drew a ship individually. In viewing the mural after completion, the group discussed the different characters of the ships and related them to themselves and each other: One was elaborate and colorful, another simple and drab, another war-like, and so forth. The group noted that each ship was isolated from the others and that only one person had an interest in uniting them by drawing in the sea and sky. In recognizing and discussing their isolation, they appeared to overcome it to some degree.

On another occasion, the mural was very different. The drawing was active and disorganized with individuals spreading over into each other's "territory." The result was more chaotic looking. Of particular interest to the group as a whole was the participation of an elderly woman who had been well-liked because of her sweetness. More recently, however, she had become extremely psychotic, first wildly manic, then totally withdrawn and regressed. In drawing objects on the mural, she communicated with the other patients for the first time in many weeks. There was much interest in what she drew even though she spoke about it very little. On each occasion, the group chose to hang up the mural, apparently taking pride in their joint creation.

DRAMATIC EXPRESSION

Dramatic expression also provided opportunity for patients to express themselves and, therefore, communicate to one another more fully than otherwise. Just as the group was intrigued by the drawing of the elderly lady on the mural, so were they by a middle-aged man's dramatic outburst. He was reserved and withdrawn throughout his entire hospitalization. He always responded appropriately, but never said more than the minimal response necessary. On one occasion during a dramatic activity, he suddenly stood up unbidden, pretended he was carrying a flag, and marched around the room singing *Onward Christian Soldiers* with much vigor. The group was shocked. They later discussed that they had never seen him so exuberant.

Just as the teaching of acrobatics allowed one patient to share her skills with the group, so did drama provide a forum for recognition and involvement within the group for another patient who wrote poetry. He would read it to the group, and the others would act it out. In this way, they joined him in his creativity.

Because spontaneity was a goal, there was not elaborate planning of dramatic events. Therefore, all of the activity was relatively simple. Sometimes we pretended we were animals, crawling, hopping, jumping, and making animal noises. At other sessions, we gestured and spoke gibberish, often with the task of expressing a particular emotion. The purpose of this was two-fold. One was to increase emotional awareness through recognition of voice sounds, gestures, and bodily position. The other was to increase expressiveness. Sometimes one patient would express a particular feeling in this way, and the others would try to guess what it was.

An especially popular activity combining drama and movement was yelling, hitting, throwing, and kicking. We used leather cushions and vented anger on them in as active a way as possible. Some patients really got into it, feeling better afterwards and requesting that we do it again at session after session. They became aware of how much anger was pent up in them. (On one occasion the noise grew so loud that a nurse came in because she thought there might be trouble.) On the other hand, some patients found it difficult and frightening to let go in this way. A middle-aged man recognized that after repeatedly trying to hit a cushion, even with much coaching, each time just as he was about to make contact, he held himself back so that the hits were never full blows. He was a very bright, insight-oriented individual who could make use of this recognition in furthering his self-understanding.

FANTASY

A final activity might not necessarily be categorized as an expressive therapy, but it was very compatible with the spirit of playing that evolved in this group. The activity was to fantasize. Sometimes the group lay on the mats and listened to music, with the instruction to fantasize. Those who wished to verbalize their fantasies did so. Most did, some more elaborately than others. One time I brought familiar objects with pungent smells—coffee grounds, cigarette butts, and so on. The patients closed their eyes and I waved the material under their noses one at a time. Without seeing them, they were to follow where their thoughts led them, triggered by the scents alone. Their associations were interesting to themselves and each other.

RESULTS

As is apparent in the examples, the "Experience Group" experienced a number of modalities of expression, including movement with body awareness, art, drama, poetry, and fantasy experience. Spontaneity and individual leadership were encouraged. My expectation from such activities (were the group composed of a different population) would be a group characterized by fun and enthusiasm. The resistant, isolated nature of the patients on this ward, however, created in me a very low level of expectation and preparation for failure. As a result, the astonishing flowering of some of the patients in this setting was to me, enormously gratifying. Furthermore, each session over a period of eighteen months felt productive. My catastrophic anticipation never materialized.

Two important questions arise from the experience: (1) How was the "Experience Group" received by the rest of the staff? and (2) Did it provide any lasting benefit to the patients?

The first question is easily answered. I would say that the staff's feelings were mixed. They were probably more negative, initially, based on being excluded and envious, and perhaps also being skeptical of such a "far out" enterprise. The staff's resistance was acted out by their failing to get recalcitrant patients to the group meetings, as though the sessions were not important enough to remember. At another time, the idea to form such a group may have been vetoed totally, but the ward was new, and staff people were still feeling their way, so there was relative latitude to allow people to try out their ideas on the part of those responsible for treatment decisions.

The more positive feelings in the staff emerged as interest grew from my discussing with them the experiences of the group. Furthering this process was the development of informal relationships with staff members which served to grease the machinery of working together. Eventually, interest in expressive therapies grew to the point where I became used as a resource person in this regard. I was requested by staff to hold art therapy sessions for the staff and patients together on the ward. We met in the regular meeting room, however, as distinguished from the room used for the "Experience Group," so as not to blur these sessions with the "Experience Group" meetings. In addition, funds were approved for me to engage consultants in dance therapy, psychodrama, gestalt therapy, and family therapy to work with the patient-staff group.

I was treated as the person knowledgeable in these areas and familiar with the appropriate experts. That money was granted for this purpose, indicated the value placed in these modalities of treatment. Finally, the ward chief suggested that I develop a research project to measure the beneficial effect of the "Experience Group." This being a research ward, such a suggestion appeared to be testimony of its worth.

Which leads to the second question. That almost all the patients involved improved, there is no question. Nevertheless, I did not develop a research procedure necessitating a control group and measurable variables. Therefore, it is impossible to determine to what extent the "Experience Group" was influential in the patients' psychiatric course. The only feedback I have is the responsiveness of the patients during the sessions, and their statements that they missed the activity when I was out of town.

It is important to add that although I am an experienced art therapist, I have had no formal training in the other expressive therapies, although I have experienced them in numerous workshops. I was strictly flying by the seat of my pants. I believe the willingness and flexibility to do so is an important attribute of a good therapist. Because creativity is an important element in my life, it is not difficult for me to take the risk of trying to apply it to less familiar modes of expression. I would encourage other therapists to try various expressive therapies. In other words, be creative in helping others to make use of their creativity.

Although much of my efforts at NIMH were funneled into research, my intent in forming the "Experience Group" was my own response to a therapeutic need. As such, I had no wish to modify the group's modus operendi for research purposes. The formation of the group was a personal resolution for me. Therefore, it remained for me a gratifying experiment using the many modalities of expression which to me are personally important in leading a rich and satisfying life.

PART THREE

Schizophrenia

CHAPTER 11

General Characteristics and Clinical Considerations in Schizophrenia

After nine years of depression it was time for a change, so I moved to a new project that was being established for the study of acute schizophrenia at the NIH Clinical Center in the Psychiatric Assessment Section directed by John Straus, M.D., and William Carpenter, M.D. The ward was active and lively, at times chaotic. The patient population was considerably younger than on the depression ward, since most acute schizophrenics have their first episode in late adolescence.

Acute schizophrenia has long held a fascination, not only for mental health practitioners trying to treat what is both the most common of the psychoses and often the most baffling, but also for the larger community in its view of the "split personality." The concept of madness in its common usage refers to acute schizophrenic-like behavior more than to any other diagnostic category. There is often a flamboyance in schizophrenic behavior which is intriguing to others. On the other hand, this same bizarreness tends to alienate family and friends.

Most clinicians and researchers believe schizophrenia is a syndrome comprised of many psychotic conditions rather than one disease. Its diagnosis has posed problems, with criteria having differed over time and place. For example, there have been noticeable discrepancies between European and American psychiatrists in making a diagnosis of schizophrenia. Particularly problematic is a differential diagnosis distinguishing schizophrenic symptoms from organic mental disorders characterized by delusions and hallucinations such as those associated with senile, alcohol, or drug induced conditions. Often there is also difficulty in distinguishing schizophrenia from psychotic forms of affective disorders, especially mania.

Currently schizophrenia is described as a group of disorders characterized by a disorgnization of a previous level of functioning involving delusions, hallucinations, or formal thought disorder. Affect is often either flat or inappropriate. The course may be acute or chronic, the former auguring a more favorable prognosis. The acute and chronic courses correspond to the "reactive" and "process" concepts, respectively. Reactive schizophrenia is associated with a better premorbid state than is process schizophrenia.

Subtypes include the following:

Disorganized (hebephrenic), characterized by formal thought disorder and flat or inappropriate affect.

Catatonic, characterized by stupor, mutism, rigidity, posturing, or catatonic excitement.

Paranoid, characterized by delusions or hallucinations of a persecutory or grandiose nature.

Schizoaffective, characterized by delusions, hallucinations, or formal thought disorder accompanied by a depressive syndrome in the depressive subtype or a manic syndrome in the manic subtype.

Mixed undifferentiated, a category for psychotic symptoms which do not fall into the preceding subtypes.

Residual, characterized by abatement of psychotic symptoms with persistance of some of the signs of the condition.

There is so much variety in schizophrenic manifestations among individuals, often with symptoms of more than one subtype appearing in a single person, that it seems to me that these classifications have limited descriptive usefulness.

Etiology of schizophrenia has posed a perplexing question since Kraepelin first classified "dementia praecox," which was later termed "schizophrenia" by Bleuler in 1911. Both believed the condition to be organic in origin. Since that time many studies have been undertaken and many theories advanced. In the area of genetic transmission there have been numerous twin studies. Comparisons of adoptive and biological parents in families of schizophrenics as well as investigations of pathology in relatives have attacked the nature-nurture question. Biological research has attempted to relate dopamine and monoamine oxidase irregularities to schizophrenia. A prominent psychodynamic theory is advanced by R. D. Laing (1969) who proposed the development of a false self-system in response to parental expectations. Other investigations have covered such areas as information processing, decision processes, attention, eye-tracking, pharmocological effects, communication patterns, obstetric factors, family relationships, and social and cultural influences. Nevertheless, etiology still remains baffling, although current thinking trends point toward a genetic contribution and biochemical correlates (supported by numerous studies) probably in interaction with environmental factors (Wynne, Cromwell, and Matthyse, 1978). On the other hand, Szasz (1970) introduces sociological considerations in describing mental illness diagnosis and institutionalization as our society's method of ostracizing threatening deviancy. Such a brief summary as this, of course, does not do justice to this highly complex and intriguing set of conditions.

Treatment in most settings relies heavily on pharmocologic intervention, particularly chlorpromazine, to combat delusions and hallucinations. Megavitamin therapy, now called orthomolecular psychiatry, is utilized by some clinicians. Psychotherapy, family therapy, mileu treatment, behaviour modification, and rehabilitation are also used, often in combination with pharmocological treatment.

In sum, schizophrenia remains a puzzling array of conditions whose classification has varied across time and place. Its etiology is unknown, and treatment varies according to the condition of the patient, the treatment setting, and the persuasion of the clinician.

THERAPEUTIC RELATIONSHIP AND THE MEANING OF MEANING

Many people in treatment capacities have difficulty in identifying with "craziness," finding it frightening. Some of the staff with whom I worked readily viewed the patients as different from themselves. The issue was often one of management. For example, a young woman who believed a bomb would go off if her feet touched the floor created problems when the staff wanted her to go into the day room, take a bath, and so forth. Her behavior was incomprehensible and unacceptable to them. Instead of trying to appreciate the enormity of the fear these patients experienced, some staff members tried to get them to behave. Sometimes the efforts at management heightened the patients' fears. For example, one patient believed that the male aides who were dragging him to the seclusion room for disruptive behavior were going to throw him out the window. As a result, he increased his resistance by hitting them. (It is important to recognize that the therapist who sees a patient for hour-long sessions has the luxury of a brief encounter without interruption. Nursing staff personnel, on the other hand, are responsible for the management of a whole ward for eight-hour stretches—a very different kettle of fish.)

Although on occasion I did not necessarily understand the reasons for a patient's bizarre behavior, I tried to identify with the feeling expressed. My approach was to convey my genuine interest in the patient's experience *without trying to change it* and to empathize with the patient's feelings—fear, anger, dread, anxiety are not foreign to me. As a result of this acceptance, interest, and empathy, even some very paranoid patients came to trust me. For example, Craig (the young man mentioned in the *Preface*), though diagnosed paranoid, entrusted to me many of the "secrets" of the Mother of the Universe, depicted in Figure 1, overcoming his fear that he was betraying her.

It seems to me that one of the most salient features of schizophrenia is the creation of idiosyncratic meaning. As discussed earlier, the thrust of meaning creation is influenced by many factors, not the least of which is learning from family initially, peers, and the society as a whole. In acute schizophrenia there is a collapse of shared meaning constructs, leaving the individual isolated in a world bearing little resemblance to the views of others. For example, one patient "knew" his psychiatrist didn't like him because the psychiatrist crossed his legs. Leaning on his arm had another specific meaning.

As a result of experiencing little commonality with others, the schizophrenic lives in an envelope of phenomenological isolation. The young woman who thought a bomb would go off in the hospital if her feet touched the floor must have been puzzled, confused, and even more terrified because others were not concerned about the bomb. In my work with schizophrenics, therefore, I encouraged them to inform me of their experience (in both pictures and discussion), and I often responded in terms of how I imagined I might feel if the devil were after me, God had spoken to me, or whatever.

What is being discussed here, of course, are psychotic delusions. Many diagnosticians consider delusions and/or hallucinations the hallmark and indicator of schizophrenia. (These phenomena are discussed in greater detail in the next chapter.) The therapeutic relationship in schizophrenia requires attention to the therapist's attitude toward these experiences. I observed instances of staff members telling patients they were crazy for maintaining such incorrect views and that they should shape up and change to the accepted viewpoint.

The issue of questionable delusions was particularly interesting to me. Many patients believed the NIH Clinical Center to be a concentration camp, prison, or some other politically incarcerating institution. Many staff members had no trouble with this—the patients were delusional. On the other hand, God and the devil were frequent visitors to NIH. Some staff members did not feel on such safe ground in finding a patient's message from God delusional. After all, the patient had some prestigious predecessors. Therefore, although the "delusion" of political incarceration may be closer to reality in terms of society's measures for dealing with its deviants, it was less acceptable than a message from God because the latter is endorsed by the myths of our culture.

In my opinion, the important factor is not how deviant or close one's view is to something we call "reality," which is composed of our shared perceptions, but rather the "reality" of each individual's unique experience. Patients themselves may go through phases of questioning their own perceptions, particularly as delusions begin to fade.

Therapists seem more or less divided on their feelings about working with schizophrenics. Although some are threatened by "madness," there are those who like working with schizophrenics, probably as a vehicle to get into their own craziness or at least to enjoy the imaginative and lively aspects of it. Personally, I believe that other than using one's patients to provide excitement for one's own life (like the psychiatrist in the play, *Equus* [Shaffer, 1974] for example) which can be exploitation, the therapist can benefit immeasurably from the altered views of schizophrenics in their own understanding of themselves and the world. Some who are threatened by schizophrenic thinking probably hold rigidly to the accepted order for fear that their balance could not survive deviation from the straight and narrow and that they too would exist in chaos. It is probably an acceptance of schizophrenic chaos rather than an attempt to control it which helps to foster recovery more readily. (The nature of schizophrenic recovery is discussed in greater detail in Chapter 14.)

In conducting art sessions with these patients, there were many times I did not get full cooperation. One patient found a comfortable place under my desk and refused to come out when it was time to end the session. Another was convinced I was a Nazi impersonating Harriet Wadeson, and since she believed herself to be a Jew at that time, she was understandably suspicious of me. The patient who was convinced a bomb was about to explode refused to come to my office. A young man talked constantly throughout the art session, kicking the easel and throwing pastels. My reaction was to try to understand what the patients were experiencing. I usually felt interested rather than threatened. Many of our patients were combative (they were not medicated), but I was never attacked or threatened. I believe the reason was because I did not try to control them or scare them.

Sometimes communication was not possible. For example, after a number of attempts to reach the young man under my desk, I gave up and read a book until time to end the session. He made a few overtures to me, but it was difficult to understand what he was trying to communicate. Naturally, ''understanding'' did not include accepting abusive behavior. Because I did not try to control or engage in power struggles, but was receptive to what the patients were expressing, patients seldom dealt with me abusively. These patients changed very rapidly (without drugs), so that if it was impossible to hold an art session initially, I was able to gain the patient's cooperation a few days or a week later.

CHAPTER 12

Phenomenology of Schizophrenia Expressed in Art

When I first entered the schizophrenia project, my colleagues urged me to design research for the study of schizophrenia. In considering what sort of questions I would address in research, I realized that I was most interested in what the experience was like for the patient.

For those of us who have not become psychotic ourselves, the subjective experience of psychosis is not readily comprehensible. For the most part, the experience of an acute schizophrenic psychosis is inferred from behavioral observations. Articulate patients have verbalized the experience in some instances, and, even more rarely, understanding has been enriched through such sensitive accounts as *I Never Promised You a Rose Garden* (Hannah Green, 1964) and *The Bell Jar* (Sylvia Plath, 1971). We take verbalization so much for granted as the primary mode of communication, that we are apt to overlook other possibilities. My interest was in finding ways that the art expression might communicate the subjective experience of acute schizophrenic psychosis, in a sense, through the patient's own eyes.

Since acute schizophrenic episodes are treated with chlorpromazine at most facilities, I wanted to take advantage of the research conditions on our ward which provided for drug-free periods at the beginning and end of hospitalization. I was interested in studying the basic condition without drug modification. (Drugs usually have the effect of aborting hallucinations and delusions and often produce some sedation.) In addition, it was possible to see patients in one-year follow-up sessions.

The ward was a twelve-bed clinical research unit at the NIH Clinical Center. Patients were admitted early in a psychotic episode, though usually not their first such episode. Patients considered chronic, non-schizophrenic, or those with organic illness were excluded. While a presumptive diagnosis of schizophrenia was made prior to admission, final classification was based on detailed clinical assessment during the first three weeks of hospitalization, using the categories of

DSM II.* The patients were severely psychotic on admission but generally non-psychotic by discharge. Maximum hospital stay was four-and-a-half months, with most patients being hospitalized at least three months. Patients were also seen twelve months after admission for follow-up evaluation. Admission criteria for this program specified relative adequacy in social and work functioning prior to the present psychotic episode, thus assuring an acute and sub-acute schizophrenic population. Based on Phillips Scale ratings (1953), two-thirds of these patients were classified as reactive and one-third process. The average age was 23.607 ± 7.36 years; the patients came predominantly from social classes II, III and IV (Hollingshead Index); and there were twenty-nine females and twenty-seven males during a three year period.

Treatment goals were increased self-understanding and the restoration and further development of interpersonal skills. Towards this end, patients received psychoanalytically based psychotherapy, group and family psychotherapy, occupational and recreational therapy, and they participated in many ward functions that are part of an of an active therapeutic milieu. Pharmacotherapy was not used during investigative periods, and, in keeping with the unit's treatment philosophy, was used sparingly or not at all during non-investigative periods. Ample nursing and medical staffing enabled even severe management problems to be dealt with by psychosocial rather than pharmacologic means.

SUBJECTIVE EXPERIENCE OF SCHIZOPHRENIA**

During a three-year period, fifty-six acute schizophrenic patients participated in an admission art evaluation session, forty-nine of them in a discharge session, and forty-two in a follow-up session.

Particularly unique in my work with acute schizophrenics was my request that they draw a picture of their psychiatric illness. To my knowledge this procedure had not been attempted before. The visual conceptualization resulting from this task induced the patients to select what to them were the most salient features of the experience and to express them affectually. Obviously the manner in which the task was presented to the patient was important. Sometimes a patient didn't consider him or herself ill, in which case I would phrase the instructions as ''whatever caused you to be hospitalized on a psychiatric unit.'' Following the execution of the picture, the patient was encouraged to discuss it. The patients'

---

*Diagnostic and Statistical Manual of Mental Disorders, Second edition, American Psychiatric Association, Washington, D.C., 1968.

**This material is reprinted with permission from the Schizophrenia Bulletin, 2:302–316, 1976, some of which appeared in Wadeson, H. S. and Carpenter, W. T. The Subjective Experience of Schizophrenia.

verbal explanations and free associations provided abundant data so that interpretations and speculations have been minimal. All sessions were tape-recorded, supplying records of the patients' comments, as well as the art productions themselves.

The context of the psychiatric illness picture production was in the following procedure: All patients participated in individual art therapy sessions during drug-free periods at admission, discharge, and one-year follow-up, and were requested to draw the following pictures in the same sequence at each session:

1. **Free picture**—i.e., no assignment: the patient's spontaneous expression uninfluenced by suggestion
2. **Self-portrait:** patient's view of self
3. **Picture of psychiatric illness:** perception of condition
4. **Hallucination experiences** ⎫
5. **Delusions experienced** ⎭ : expressions of idiosyncratic experience

The first task was selected as both warm-up and to allow the patient to express whatever emerged without suggestion from me. The self-portrait was important in gaining information about the experience of the self, an often distorted perception in acute schizophrenia. The last three tasks were designed to elicit information regarding perception of the illness and its primary manifestations (hallucinations and delusions). It is important to bear in mind in designing specific tasks that the findings will result from the kind of information the researcher tries to elicit. (Further observations gleaned from the picture tasks are discussed in Chapters 13 and 14.)

Examples

The following results reflect meanings the picture of the psychiatric illness held for the patients. They conceptualized in graphic terms their experience of their illness, discussed the intended significance of its various aspects and, in some instances, proceeded to free-associate to the picture, illuminating the ideas represented. I have organized the material into the following categories:

1. Feeling states
2. Depiction of brains
3. Representations of physical illness
4. Locus of illness

Feeling States

Depression. Most prevalent were designations of depressed feelings (fifty-two out of fifty-six patients). Sometimes a person was drawn and described as having a depressed expression. In other instances, patients drew tears, rain, and clouds which they said expressed depression. Often depressed feelings designated by the patient were represented by gray, black, or blue colors. In addition to the picture of the illness, such representations appeared in other pictures as well, particularly self-portraits.

Figure 41 is a picture of the illness, drawn at admission, in which Kevin has depicted himself in the center as "a creature, a blob, everything is gray." His associations were frustration, depression, and "suicidal tendencies." He elaborated the latter further, saying he felt "trapped, closed-in, worthless, and suicidal." The spiral form is very characteristic of depression and is often associated with suicide (see Chapter 9). Although depression has been observed in the behavior of many acute schizophrenics following the psychotic episode, these expressions of depression occurred as frequently during the admission session (acute phase) as well as at other sessions.

Confusion. The experience of confusion was directly expressed graphically by twenty-eight out of fifty-six patients in their pictures of the illness. In a few

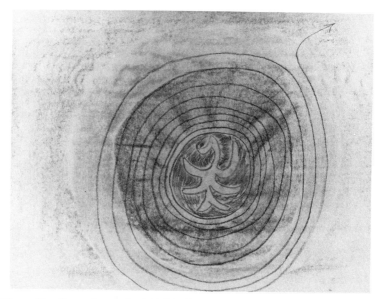

Figure 41.   Depression and suicidal feelings expressed by Kevin, a schizophrenic patient.

instances, the pictures themselves were extremely confused and disorganized. Although the patients were often more confused at the admission session, such representations did not occur in their pictures more often at that time. This finding is not surprising when one considers that in drawing a picture of the illness at discharge and follow-up, the patient was often recollecting a period of confusion experienced earlier.

These representations were often characterized by tangled lines and colors, or people whose facial expressions looked confused to the patient. Figure 42, drawn at admission, is a confused picture of the illness, whereas Figure 43, drawn at follow-up, is a picture of confusion in which the patient represented his brain as being ordered prior to illness (top), confused during the illness (middle), and reordered at discharge (bottom).

Anger. Anger was represented in twenty-three of the pictures of illness. It took the form of associations to the picture more often than direct expression in an

Figure 42.   A confused picture of the psychiatric illness by Donna, a schizophrenic patient.

Figure 43.   An ex-patient's depiction of his brain as ordered prior to his illness (top), confused during the illness (middle), and reordered following recovery from schizophrenia.

image. Often the anger was directed toward staff members, friends, or family for placing the patient in the hospital.

As Richard was drawing Figure 44 at his admission session, he asked if he was making me uncomfortable because he was expressing his anger on paper and could not communicate with his "idiot psychiatrist." This was connected with associations to his father who had abandoned him. He then said that the spirit of the picture was "hate" but amended it to "resentment," saying that one cannot really hate, and "only a crazy person would be glad to see another harmed." The father-psychiatrist transference was obvious. In addition to expressing anger, this picture was also more confused than any of Richard's other pictures.

Positive Experience of the Illness. In the context of the experiences of depression, confusion, and anger, particularly impressive were the positive aspects of the psychosis: eleven patients indicated so specifically. For some, the illness was a rest or respite from life with an appreciation of hospitalization as a means of separation from the turmoil of family life. For others, there was a manic-like euphoria described as feeling happy, high, or being full of energy, enthusiasm, and talent. In her most disorganized picture (Figure 42), Donna expressed the experience of her illness at admission in lots of motion and color. She said she was not ill but had "an acceleration of talent." She used her favorite color combination in the picture which she called "lively and festive." In addition to such direct statements, there were many examples of grandiosity which provided obvious gratifications. In Figure 45, Fred drew himself as a witch doctor who could control others. This picture was drawn at his one-year follow-up, at which time he felt depressed. He said he longed to become crazy again, finding himself more interesting to himself and others when psychotic.

Figure 44.   Anger and confusion in schizophrenia, drawn by Richard.

Figure 45. A follow-up picture in which Fred longed for his previous schizophrenic episode at which time he had felt like a witch doctor.

Depiction of Brains

Since the task of drawing the psychiatric illness is a vague, relatively non-specific assignment, most impressive were the repeated representations of a specific object to symbolize the psychosis. Fifteen of the fifty-six patients drew their brains, indicating pictorially and verbally that something was wrong with them.

When requested to make a picture of his illness at discharge, Richard drew his brain (Figure 46), saying it went "foggy" as indicated by the black. The lightning bolts represent confusion which he said were warnings and cries for help, instead of the normal sending of messages. (Other examples of depictions of brains may be found in Figures 43 and 83.)

Physical Illness

Twelve patients believed they were physically ill or impaired. In some cases, patients thought they were suffering from specific diseases, such as cancer (most frequent) or heart disease. In a number of instances, the concerns were more idiosyncratic, such as the belief by one patient that her corneas had fallen off.

A patient drew her illness at admission in a representation of herself with a sore back she hurt in an automobile accident. At this time, she was delusionally worried about becoming a hunchback.

Locus of Illness

The pictures often provided information about patients' experiences of the locus of their illness. Although there were contradictions, as well as sessions when such information was not forthcoming, in most instances it was possible to determine from the pictures whether the patient believed (a) he or she was not ill;

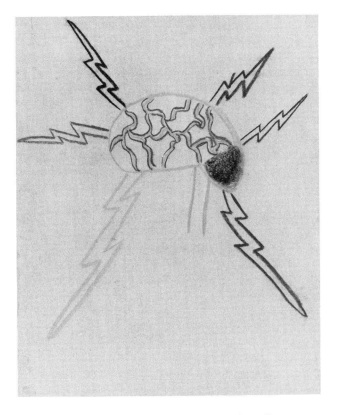

Figure 46.   Richard's brain going "foggy."

(b) the illness was related to external forces; (c) the illness was internal and biological; (d) internal and psychological, or (e) some combination of the above. There were more than twice as many pictures indicating an internal psychological locus than any other. Next in incidence was an external locus. Figures 47, 48, and 49 illustrate a shift in locus.

Diane made similar pictures of her illness at each session, but with a somewhat different view each time. At admission she depicted herself blasted by a drug experience in which she believed she was strangling and being gassed (Figure 47). She is being assaulted by an outside agent, LSD, drawn in purple around her. At discharge a similar configuration appeared with her physical self no longer an element in the picture (Figure 48). She is represented by the "weak blue circle" in the center bombarded by external forces drawn in red, representing drugs, boyfriend and sister. The prominent self of the former picture has disappeared and the focus is exclusively on the external agents.

At one-year follow-up, Diane drew her physical self again looking "helpless, out-of-it, spaced-out" (Figure 49). Once again the bombardment is red. It represents "forces . . . interfering with my being able to perceive reality . . . something that my mind created." Now, the powerful forces she found so frightening are perceived as part of her own mind. Although, initially, the self was drawn prominently (Figure 47), the illness was not integrated as a part of the self. At follow-up, however (Figure 49), an integration has been achieved. This picture appears to be a synthesis of earlier elements: her helpless self and a powerful representation of the devastating forces which she now recognized as part of herself. The biological factor of drug influence had disappeared altogether.

Discussion

The request to make a picture provides a *tabla rasa* on which to project a choice of a view of one's inner experience. It is this selection process which highlights the meaningfulness of the picture's content. Pictorial style adds a further dimension, often less conscious, and more of a reflection of patterned response or present state of feeling. These two factors, selection of content and patterned or affectually determined style, lead to regarding the art material as a particularly significant expression of subjective experience. Therefore, in requesting patients to draw their experience of the psychosis, I believe I maximized an opportunity to view what was most significant and had the greatest impact to the patient. I know of no other instances where patients have been requested to perform this specific task. Not surprisingly, many of the elements expressed in the picture of the illness appeared in other pictures as well, although usually not as pointedly or pervasively.

Figure 47.   Diane's locus of schizophrenic illness perceived as an external agent, LSD, during the acute phase.

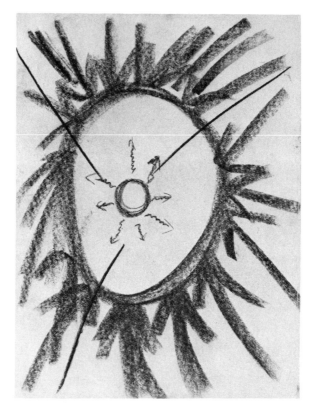

**Figure 48.   Diane's locus of illness as external at discharge, with
the figure of herself no longer present.**

Some of the material conformed to generally held impressions of schizophrenic experience. In regard to feeling states, confusion and anger are expected reactions. Somatization in a delusion of physical illness does not come as a surprise. The frequent representations of disordered brains is congruent with the effort to give meaning to a confused array of experiential phenomena comparable to the more formed delusion of a physical illness. Similarly, shifts in perceived locus of illness represent the patient's developing search for meaning of the experience of the psychosis.

Most intersting, however, are the unexpected elements of schizophrenic experience. When a patient chooses to portray his psychosis as a bleak depression, such as in Figure 50, drawn by Jack, we must recognize the depression as an especially significant component of the experience of the illness. The overwhelming prevalence of depression as the chosen representation of the illness was a surprising finding. Its occurrence during the acute phase, as well as at recovery and follow-up, suggests that it is found not only in the aftermath of the acute episode (so-called post-psychotic depression), but is present earlier, probably only masked by the more florid behavior of the acute phase. A study of the same patient population conducted independent of the art evaluations demonstrated this same phenomenon using more traditional psychiatric assessment techniques (McGlashan and Carpenter, 1975).

Also impressive were the various expressions of positive feelings associated with the psychotic experience. Grandiosity with a euphoric element was, of course, not unexpected. But the quality of stimulation, excitement, and personal enthrallment with psychotic percepts was surprising, expecially where mixed with frightening and confusing ideation. (Further examples of this phenomenon are presented in the next chapter in connection with seclusion room experience.)

Figure 49. Diane's integration at follow-up with the powerful forces now perceived as part of herself.

Figure 50. Schizophrenic psychosis portrayed as a bleak depression by Jack.

Finding the hospital a pleasant refuge from the turmoil of family life was noted by some of the patients.

In conclusion, a general response among the staff members to acute schizophrenics' art expressions was a recognition of the comprehensibility of schizophrenic experience and symptomatology. The pictures often provided illumination of mystifying behavior. Through only three art sessions, it was possible to increase appreciation of the structure and content of the schizophrenic's individual reality and to comprehend it as a reasonable consequence of his or her life experience.

An important benefit of art expression for psychotic patients is the undermining of the isolation experienced by an individual whose view of the world bears little resemblance to views held by others.

HALLUCINATIONS AND DELUSIONS*

Hallucinations and delusions are at the heart of many psychoses, frequently producing disturbed and seemingly inappropriate behavior. In fact, such behavior is often comprehensible to the observer only by knowing the content of underlying delusions and hallucinations. Because delusions and hallucinations are private experiences, they may lead to feelings of isolation in the patient and lack of understanding by family, friends, therapist, and researcher. A patient's behavior may suggest the presence of hallucinations or delusions, but the subjective experience is often imcompletely communicated.

To gain a further understanding of the psychotic experience, I systematically encouraged patients to draw their hallucinations and delusions, as described previously. Both clinicians and researchers on the unit found that pictorial expression of feelings, ideas, impulses, and conflicts served as an important source of data regarding patients' delusional and hallucinatory experiences.

In requesting these drawings from the patients, I asked if they had ever had beliefs that were radically different from those of others or their own previous views or if they had ever heard or seen things radically different from the perceptions of others or their own previous perceptions. Often it was not necessary for me to explain what I meant by hallucinations and delusions, and no one failed to understand what I was talking about. It was clear that I meant not simply individualistic thinking, but a view of experience from a totally different framework than commonly shared meaning.

Other investigators have observed that mental patients seldom portray hallucinations in spontaneous drawings. The same is true of delusions, usually due to excessive preoccupation or disorganization during the acute phase of the psychosis. Once the psychotic episode is over, there has seemed to be little spontaneous impetus to portray these experiences graphically. For these reasons, I structured the art sessions to include a specific request for such pictures. Although there have been numerous individual case studies, I know of no other systematic procedure in which all patients have been requested to draw hallucinations and delusions. Since patients were acutely psychotic on admission, the first session was frequently disruptive. Nevertheless, despite gross disorganization of thoughts, and sometimes behavior, it was usually possible to elicit sufficient cooperation from the patient to produce the requested pictures.

Of almost sixty patients studied, only five did not produce pictures of hallucinations and/or delusions. Of these, three refused to cooperate, and two denied having had hallucinatory or delusory experiences. In a number of

*Some of this material appeared in Wadeson, H. S., and Carpenter, W. T.: Pictorial Presentation of Hallucinations and Delusions. *Japanese Bulleten of Art Therapy,* 5 (1974) 97–103, and in Wadeson, Harriet and Carpenter, William. Hallucinations and Delusions. Publication of exhibit, Annual Meeting, American Psychiatric Association, Honolulu, 1973.

instances in psychiatric interviews patients had not revealed the presence of hallucinations or delusions, but when exploring these phenomena in the art sessions they communicated such experiences. It is impossible to know whether the difference resulted from the enabling quality of the art expression, their relationship with me, or some other factors.

The patients' associations to their pictures as well as the drawings themselves, produced a rich field of information about hallucinations and delusions. From this information, it was possible to delineate various types of hallucinatory and delusional experiences.

At the most obvious level, the request for the drawings elicited the information that at least 95% of the patients experienced hallucinations and/or delusions, underscoring the significance of such experiences in acute schizophrenic psychosis. Delusions were more enduring, whereas hallucinations tended to be fleeting in nature. Often, however, the hallucinations were visual manifestations of the more enduring delusions.

Although almost all of the patients were delusional during part of their hospitalization, some were either too disorganized or fearful at the time to draw their delusions and hallucinations but eventually did so in the form of a recollection at a later session. These latter circumstances applied especially to hallucinations, since patients rarely hallucinated during the art sessions.

Paranoia was prominent in the hallucinations and delusions of most of the patients. Figure 51 is an example of such a hallucination drawn by Beth. She had a "vision" of a "big, black man . . . maybe a killer" walking toward her on a back street. This hallucination occurred repeatedly at her job and was accompanied by dizziness and head pain. She clearly recalled many of its visual details and included them in her picture. She has captured, in the drawing, some of the fearsomeness of experiencing the man steadily advancing toward her.

Paranoia was seen in Eve, a young woman who depicted a delusion shortly after admission which was one of the manifestations of her developing psychosis (Figure 52). She drew herself sitting at her desk "happy, excited, and dumbfounded" about what she was experiencing. The lines around her head represent "electricity" and "buzzing." Her boss had turned away from her while answering the phone, at which point she was convinced it was Jean Dixon (a well-known psychic) calling to tell him something about her. He denied this, whereupon she quit her job and subsequently tried to make him swear that Jean Dixon had called. Other pictures of herself drawn at the same session were neater, prettier, and more organized than this one of her delusion, probably due to the increased anxiety that accompanied this picture.

Figure 53 represents a paranoid delusion experienced by Cynthia earlier, but drawn at follow-up. Objects in the picture are: the TV which broadcasted salacious pictures and information about her; swords, knives and a gun; patients and staff members who would use them to kill her. The black and yellow

Figure 51.   A paranoid hallucination drawn by Beth, a schizophrenic patient.

coloration over the whole picture indicates that she could not distinguish day and night. She thought people wanted to bomb the hospital. Because she felt she had to save it and become a great psychiatrist, they would kill her in order to explode the bomb. During psychosis, she was catatonic, fearing that touching her feet to the floor would cause the bomb to explode.

Paranoid delusions often occurred while patients were in seclusion for combative behavior. These delusions were accompanied by enormous fear.

Figure 54 is an example. While in seclusion, Jill thought she would be "cut open." She has drawn herself as a "clothespin" feeling "trapped and clamped."

Some of the paranoid delusional and hallucinatory experiences involved encounters with the devil. Many patients also "heard" the voice of God and "saw" Christ. The latter type delusions were often grandiose with the patient believing to be chosen by God for a special mission to save humankind. Such religious content, involving the devil or God, appeared in the hallucinations and delusions of over half the patients. This preponderance was surprising in that, for the most part, the patients did not come from backgrounds of strong religious orientations. In our culture, however, God and the devil are significant embodiments of good and evil. Common motifs found in the hallucinations and delusions, such as these, are discussed subsequently.

Other religious personages figured in delusions, also. Figure 55 is a depiction of a delusion which draws its source not only from Christianity, but also from Greek mythology and "hippy" culture. After drawing a "vision" of Christ seen

Figure 52.   A paranoid delusion drawn by Eve, a schizophrenic patient.

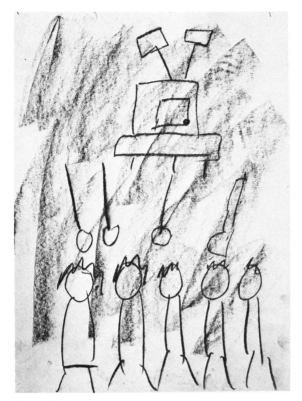

Figure 53. A paranoid delusion drawn by Cynthia, a schizophrenic patient who thought she was being secretly televised
and that others were trying to kill her.

in the shadows, Susan portrayed a delusion of being the Virgin Mary, "the mother of God . . . ethereal and spiritual" but also a "pagan, childlike goddess—Diana" and a "flower child." Susan thought she was pregnant with the child of God.

Figure 55 illustrates another important aspect of hallucinatory and delusional experiences: certainty or doubt about the experience. While believing she was pregnant with the child of God, Susan felt simultaneously "in and out" of this idea. She had doubts about her delusions. Some patients were aware that their hallucinations were unreal in a sort of double awareness. Other patients, however, were totally convinced of the reality of the experience and acted accordingly. An example is Cynthia, who refused to come to art therapy because she was certain that a bomb was about to explode. It was only after she had emerged from this terrifying delusion that she drew pictures of it.

Although many hallucinations were apparitions, such as the appearance of the devil "seen" by many patients or the frightening man depicted in Figure 51, other patients hallucinated transformations of objects actually seen. Live animals appeared dead; strangers were taken as specific acquaintances. Figure 56 represents a stalk of celery which appeared to move and speak. Florence, who drew this hallucination, said that just as she was about to eat the celery, it spoke to her saying, "Don't eat me." It had a soft, male voice like that of her father. She described it as wearing a skirt and moving "the way a penis moves." When this happened, she was so frightened that she dropped the celery and fled. Obviously, the experience was very real to her.

The hallucinations depicted in the art productions were often clear images such as Figures 51 and 56. Other hallucinatory experiences, however, were of a more amorphous nature. Figure 57, for example, represents lights that Donna "saw" when in seclusion. She commented, "I saw lights and felt as though I was dying.

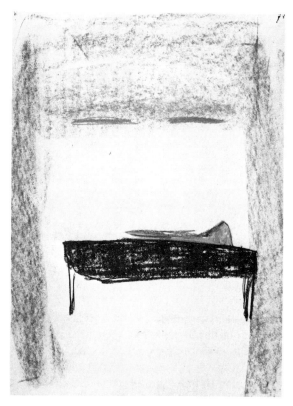

Figure 54.   A paranoid delusion of Jill's belief that she would be cut open while in the seclusion room.

Figure 55.   A religious delusion by Susan, who believed she was the Virgin Mary.

I felt delirious and saw spots of light, like seeing stars when clubbed over the head.'' This fleeting experience was associated with obscure and incomplete ideas connected with Donna's belief that she was dying.

Very different from the fleeting, amorphous experiences, were the highly systematized ideas of some of our patients. Figure 58 by Craig, who drew *The Mother of the Universe* in Figure 1, depicts an extremely intricate delusion about life forces or ''pranic energy'' represented by lightning which changes the molecules on the right. They are vibrating, producing constant cleansing of the body. At left is a double helix series. God, energies, bodily functions, different levels of consciousness, Mother Nature, and the destruction of life were all bound in a complex, internally consistent delusional system. At the time of this drawing, Craig saw himself as ''a little psychotic,'' but his ''delusions'' did not bother him and he felt less ''paranoid'' than previously. His delusional system was less fixed at this time, and he had doubts about its validity. Nevertheless, he

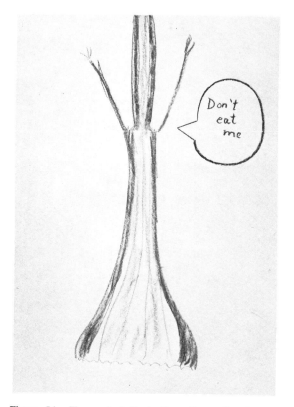

Figure 56. Florence's hallucination of a stalk of celery perceived to talk and move.

still felt he had the "extraordinary ability to change a person's consciousness . . . just by drawing a picture." (Craig is discussed further in the case study concluding this chapter.)

Another highly organized delusional system was revealed in the art work of Fred, who produced Figure 45 at follow-up. Although he was disorganized, excited, and impulsive, he attempted to integrate all percepts into an elaborate mental scheme. He drew himself, true to his experience during his psychosis, as a "witch doctor who had figured everything out and caused people to move." From one "input" stimulation, Fred was flooded with ideas. He drew these ideas as "output." While psychotic, he had taped over one lens of his glasses both to cut down incoming stimulation and to diminish his "power." At the time, he talked incessantly and was unable to screen and process information. Yellow on the sides represents "power and fear force fields" which were "burning me up. I had no internal controls, but would shift back and forth." Frequently, he rearranged furniture in order to gain internal controls. When not feeling omnipotent, he felt totally "at the mercy" of others. His delusional experiences were manifestations of a highly systematized conceptual scheme with which he accounted for his special power. (As mentioned previously, during a post-psychotic depression he longed for the excitement of the feelings expressed in this picture.)

When Sam drew Figure 59 at admission, he was also bizarre and disorganized in his behavior. His thinking, however, was disorganized as well, as opposed to that characterized in Figure 45. Figure 59 began as a representation of air currents which he "saw" outside his childhood home. He mentioned cold and hot air, then became confused and preoccupied with dates, writing over the picture as he spoke so that the initial objects and ideas were almost totally

Figure 57.   Donna's fleeting hallucination of flashing lights in the seclusion room.

Figure 58.   Craig's intricate delusion of life forces.

Figure 59.   Sam's graphic representation of confused thinking as he attempted to draw a hallucination.

obscured. In this way, the development of the picture was a graphic display of the disorganization caused by intrusions of disturbing thoughts. When his psychosis abated, there was a high degree of organization in his drawings.

Comment

The ease with which drawings of hallucinations and delusions could be elicited was remarkable, especially in patients who had failed to reveal these experiences in psychiatric interviews, the ward milieu, or through standardized psychiatric assessment instruments. The examples presented here illustrate the rich variety of hallucinatory and delusional experiences seen in art evaluations. This material demonstrates the ready accessibility of critical symptom information and the opportunity for exploration of its meaning in the art therapy setting. The graphic presentation and clarifying associations to a patient's drawing strongly recommend the art therapy process as a potent investigative tool as well as a therapeutic medium in acute schizophrenia.

PREVALENCE OF RECURRENT MOTIFS IN PSYCHOTIC DELUSIONS*

If sanity is viewed as a fabric carefully woven with threads of various physical and social forces according to a well-organized design, madness might be seen as the cloth's reverse side with its knots, hems, seam edges and pattern colored in reverse. This underside, nevertheless, is woven from the same threads that compose the ordered front that is meant to be seen.

Among the acute schizophrenic patients with whom I have worked, particularly fascinating has been the interweaving of strands from various cultures and eras in the schema of what is labeled their mental illness. Although some delusions were laced with ideation more specific to the individual, there was a prevalence of ideas and concerns shared by a whole culture. Particularly striking was the repeated emergence of specific cultural or historical themes in the psychoses of these patients, despite the variety in their backgrounds.

Most of the patients came from the Washington, D. C. area, a highly sophisticated cosmopolitan locale with a transient population. The parents of some, however, have roots in more rural areas. Socioeconomic class included working class, middle class, and upper-middle class. Most patients had high school educations, some had finished college, and a fairly large number were college students at the time of hospitalization. There was much variety in

*Some of the material appeared in: Wadeson, H. S., and Carpenter, W. T.: Prevalence of Universal Themes and Motifs in Psychotic Delusions. Presentation at International Congress of Social Psychiatry, Athens, 1974.

religious backgrounds. Although age ranged from eighteen to mid-fifties, most were in their twenties.

The material is presented in groupings of manifest content: first religious and demonic influences, then more recent history, and finally, current societal concerns. The varying themes themselves are expressive of repeated motifs which are latent in the underlying conflicts which generated the delusions. They consist of: persecution, conquest of evil, and power.

Religious and Demonic Forces

Perhaps the most dramatic introduction to the recurrent delusional themes manifested in our patients is the presentation of the devil, a frequent visitor at NIH. Although very few of our patients had fundamentalist religious backgrounds where the threat of the devil is ever-present, he became an important influence in the lives of many during acute psychotic episodes. Especially interesting was the pervasiveness of this influence.

When Karl became psychotic, he was living in his parents' house with a friend. He thought that he and his friend were doing bad things in the house, and the house became "eerie, everything was falling down like the devil was eating it up," Figure 60. The manner of pictorial presentation illustrates the totality of the devil's control as he completely surrounds and engulfs the house. The young men were taking drugs there, which they considered indulging in forbidden pleasures. Being controlled by the devil was the psychotic conceptualization of this experience.

Karl said that cats are the devil's workers and the cat is his symbol. Just prior to hospitalization, he had had a kitten who was "wilder than hell," Figure 61. When he picked it up, it bit him and "spirit-wise, what was in the cat got into me and screwed me up for two weeks." As a result, he said, he experienced the feeling of his head and body being polluted and sick. His head felt like a "balloon with water swishing back and forth in it."

At the one-year follow-up session, Karl said that the devil had entered his brain but that now he was happy because he had conquered the devil, thereby preventing him from getting his soul or brain and, as a result, is now a stronger person. In Figure 62, he drew a recent experience in which the devil came to him and his friend, trying to make them "explode."

If I had been a different sort of person, I would have snapped, killed myself or someone else. In one second, we could have lost our minds and become vegetables.

In the picture, Karl is smiling at having conquered the devil, which is "the greatest high leading to total peace." Here the delusion has shifted to conquest of evil forces, a common underlying motif in the delusions of many of the patients.

Figure 60.   Karl's delusion of the devil engulfing his house.

Figure 63 is a self-portrait drawn by Jack while extremely psychotic. He said that he was "King of the Universe." He is smirking because he has just killed Satan after having sex with Satan's wife. Like Karl, Jack had become a savior by destroying the forces of evil. The delusional conquest of evil led to feelings of great power in many of the patients, often to the extreme of grandiosity, as illustrated here.

A female counterpart of the embodiment of evil is the witch, a prevalent preoccupation during the Middle Ages in Europe and prominent in the early history of the United States, as well as in the fairy tales most of us learn as children. One young man drew his experience of seeing a witch fly by his window.

Figure 64 represents the delusion of Sylvia, a young woman who experienced the evil part of herself as a witch who commanded her to burn herself, told her that she was not real, and that she should die. The witch's voice (small figure at top) controlled her sexual feelings which she considered bad. The black crosses which she also painted on her fingernails indicate the witch's evilness. The zigzag lines are the witch's power. When Sylvia was six years old, she was raped by her father. Ever since then, she had hated him and wished for vengeance. This made her feel evil. She became illegitimately pregnant and felt she hurt her father by telling him so. She said it was at this point that she began to hear the witch's voice. The feeling of great evilness here is accompanied by persecution. The tears convey her dispair and the knife and tombstone her suicidal thoughts. Her feelings of entrapment are represented by the box surrounding her.

Equal in number to those visited by the devil were patients who drew pictures of being spoken to by God, or seeing God or Christ. A thirty-five year old woman who drew a large image of the Crucification was very moved by "seeing" it. She felt she was actually present at the event.

Figure 61.   A cat as the devil's worker in Karl's delusion.

Figure 62.   Conquest of the devil by Karl.

Figure 65 is a vision of Jesus seen by Susan, who had believed herself to be the Virgin Mary (Figure 55). It was also common for many of those who had had dealings with Satanic forces to have experiences with heavenly beings as well. For some, the motif was one of redemption from evil. For others, a visit from a diety conferred a special importance to the patient.

Recent History

Perhaps more surprising than these ancient symbols is the prominence of relatively recent historical events in the delusional systems of some of the patients. Although these events are more immediate, they are not as deeply embedded in our cultural heritage. In these instances, however, the connections may be more direct. Nazism exerted a strong influence on several patients

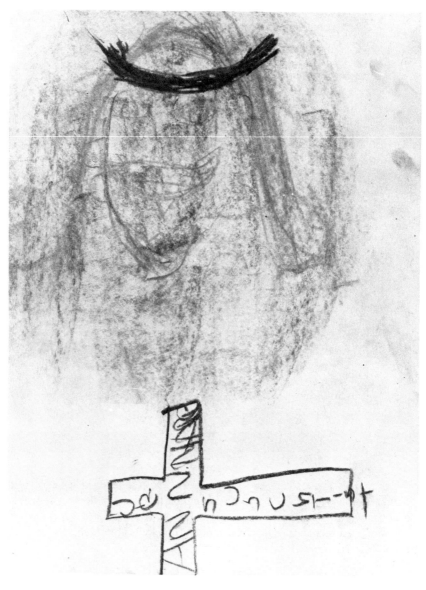

Figure 63. Jack's self-portrait of himself as King of the Universe after killing Satan.

Figure 64. Sylvia's delusion of being controlled by a witch and feeling entrapped in a box.

Figure 65. A vision of Jesus seen by Susan, the patient who believed herself to be the Virgin Mary (Figure 55).

although all had been born since the Nazi era. Several were Jewish, one was having a delusional love affair with a Jewish man, and a few had one Jewish parent.

Several patients experienced the seclusion room as a Nazi-type gas chamber, and depicted it as such. These patients experienced many persecutory delusions which were extremely frightening.

A very disorganized young man was preoccupied with the assassination of John F. Kennedy although he was a child at that time. When extremely disorganized, he drew a picture of his illness, and related a black portion to bullets in the back of Kennedy's head. After recovery he said that during his psychosis he had been sad over Kennedy's death, feeling there will never be another great president. When viewing a TV special on Lyndon Johnson, he hallucinated the ghost of Kennedy.

Current Concerns

Delusions around current concerns in our society more nearly resemble popular thinking than the historical delusions do. At times, their psychotic elements are not immediately apparent. For some of the patients, the delusions were close to reality. For example, a young woman drew a picture of a visitor to the ward whom she believed was an FBI agent coming after her. In fact, her husband had been hunted by the FBI. Eve thought narcotic agents were following her. She had been dealing in drugs. In her picture, Figure 66, she illustrated her confusion over these matters as she pulled into a gas station.

The form of the preoccupations often indicated psychotic processes. For example, preoccupation with war was of great concern to Doris. She believed she was to become ruler of the universe and settle the Mideast conflict. She felt pressured to leave the hospital in order to direct the negotiations. She pictured

Figure 66. Eve's confusion over her delusion of being pursued by narcotic agents.

Figure 67.   A Messianic delusion of being the ruler of the universe who would end war, by Doris.

herself in Figure 67 as the ruler of the universe standing beside her throne. She is dressed in regal garb, carries a scepter and is crowned by a combination crown, halo, and the sun. Once again, we see the motif of extreme grandiosity. Many Messiahs inhabited our ward.

Discussion

The demonic and religious, recent historical, and current cultural themes from which the delusions are woven form the patterns for repeated motifs shared by many schizophrenics:

1. Persecution
2. Evil danger and its subsequent conquest by the patient (for example, those who have conquered the devil)
3. The feeling of power usually in the form of being a savior, or being singled-out to be visited by God

The psychodynamic purposes these motifs appear to serve are as follows: Briefly, delusions of persecution are associated with guilt. Evilness is derived from forbidden wishes particularly in rebellion against parental authority, values, or more subtle commandments. An example of this is the patient who became illegitimately pregnant and heard a witch telling her to burn herself and die. Conquest of evil forces ends guilt and persecution and promotes the individual to a position of power. Finally, being in communication with God or becoming a hero or savior confers a special power and importance as compensation for the helplessness the individual usually experiences. This was exemplified by the patient who drew herself as ruler of the universe (Figure 67). She also considered herself a female black Jew who represents all the oppressed of the world.

Although it is possible to relate the delusional motifs to the individual dynamics of the patients, we still are left with the question of why material from our cultural mythologies, history, and current concerns, in addition to more individualized events from the patient's background, are adapted by so many patients to their psychic purposes in delusional constructs. In other words, what sense can we make of themes shared by a whole culture forming the content of the delusional beliefs of schizophrenic patients?

We see in the visions of madness the eternal battle between the forces of good and evil with which cultures have struggled since the dawn of history. Conflicts within a troubled individual are experienced directly in a larger-than-life drama of events of historical or mythological significance, symbolically representing the conflicts in the narrower realm of an individual's life. Schizophrenic disorganization, in this way, jumbles the levels of significance or meaning, while the essence of the conflict remains the same. It would seem that an individual's conflict between forces perceived as good and evil is experienced as so overwhelming that it takes on the proportions of a battle between God and the devil.

These mythological and historical themes which are part of the fabric of our heritage are learned through acculturation with a low emotional charge (except in fundamentalist religions) but with high symbolic meaning. When organization of thought processes gives way under stress and an acute schizophrenic episode ensues, the epic symbolic frame becomes the more proportionate one to suit the magnitude of the turmoil.

Since mine is not a Jungian frame of reference, it was observation of themes repeated over and over among many patients that prompted my observations, rather than a predisposed belief in universality. On reflection, however, it is not surprising that the sources of turmoil are similar for many. Nor is it surprising that over the ages people have created myths to describe these struggles and have played them out in historical events.

CASE STUDY

The drawings by Craig, who was introduced at the beginning of this book, vividly convey the power of the image in representing the cosmic proportions of his delusions (*Mother of the Universe*, Figure 1). In order to give a fuller picture of how art expression may counter the isolation a delusional individual often experiences, I will present a group of Craig's drawings which helped to form a bridge between his private world and me.

Craig had been working in a factory prior to his admission to NIH, drawing feverishly, probably in an effort to stem the tide of his progressing psychosis. He was dragged into the hospital by seven policemen. Many considered Craig dangerous, particularly his mother and the psychiatric consultant to our ward who interviewed him. He was diagnosed paranoid schizophrenic. At twenty-two he was bearded, sloppy and, in my view, gentle. He never appeared dangerous to me, but rather seemed to experience the world as being out of step with him.

Because of his love of drawing, Craig and I developed an important relationship. He believed he knew the secrets of the universe and through his love of drawing overcame his fear to entrust me with some of them. Eventually he suggested to me that we collaborate. Because he believed that he could "zap" people with a picture, he thought he could cure them also. He said, "I have the extraordinary ability to change a person's consciousness just by drawing a picture," seeing in his art "divine forces which influence the viewer." He devised a plan for making pictures that I would show to patients.

Most of our patients decompensated further shortly after hospitalization. Craig was an exception. His psychiatrist thought that it was his outlet in art that prevented this occurrence. Craig's pictures were always controlled and precise; he said that unless he stayed that way, he would fall apart.

In our sessions, Craig expressed his concerns in the metaphor of a cosmic consciousness, often in a fragmented, confused, or contradictory way. It was up to me to try to fit the pieces together. Nevertheless, at moments Craig recognized some of his personal dilemmas, mainly his difficulties in dealing with his anger and fear of his own power. Themes of world distruction and power were prominent in his pictures. Although sexual themes appeared often, he had difficulty personalizing them.

Craig's delusional system was intricate, complex, and highly systematized. I gleaned various facets of it as he explained his pictures to me. I never gained a full understanding of it. Much of it resembled popular mysticism. Delusional ideas were manifested in Craig's belief that he could control the weather, especially in regard to punishing his enemies: "I make nervous cuts with brain waves through the weather to people." He believed that he was the guardian of Mother Nature's secrets. Threading through the pictures are symbols of sexuality, destruction, and women. They also exhibit Craig's fine sense of design,

Figure 68.   Craig's delusion of being protected from being drawn into the sun-ovum
(upper right) by the astral body in which he is traveling (center) on an astral plane.

imagination, humor, and technical skill. The interest his pictures aroused was
extremely gratifying to him.

Craig believed he was in a "life and death struggle too important to talk
about" because people were trying to steal his secrets. These secrets dealt with
the forces of nature which were usually represented by images of conception or
the figure of a woman. In an early picture, Figure 68, Craig drew himself
traveling in an astral body on an astral plane. He explained that this was an
actual experience, not imaginary. At lower left are sperms emanating from
testicles. At upper right is a sun-ovum which has already been fertilized. The
astral body in which he is traveling (form with eye) protects him from being
drawn into the sun-ovum. Later he labelled this picture "psychotic," and said
that it would make someone who looked at it psychotic.

Figure 69 is also an early drawing, representing "the point of conception"
described as having "a great amount of energy." He recognized that the

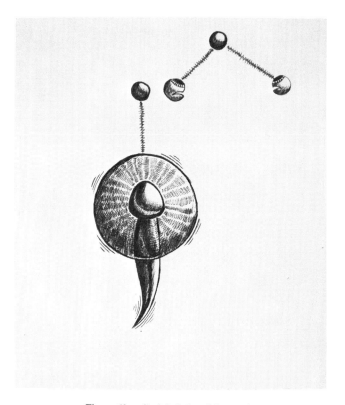

Figure 69.   Craig's *Point of Conception*.

phallic-like sperm cell is larger than normal. In Figure 70, conception looks even more dangerous. From the tip of the phallis-like skull, which he saw as himself, is a faint stream (difficult to see in the reproduced image) leading to the ovum. He said he had made this picture to "zonk" others and that he wanted to paint it on a shirt and wear it. The phallic-skull appears again in Figure 71. This time a female emerges from the fertilized ovum "to prevent a nuclear holocaust." Craig explained that "both countries are married to the same wife."

   This woman appeared in a number of the pictures, sometimes alone and sometimes in combination, as in Figure 72. She was described as representing the marijuana plant. "The head is holy, pure, clean, attractive. To smoke the plant is like drinking mama's milk." The picture was further described as "my way of being in a safe place at the time of judgment." At the top is the "eye of God," depicted similarly in a number of drawings. In the center are symbols of

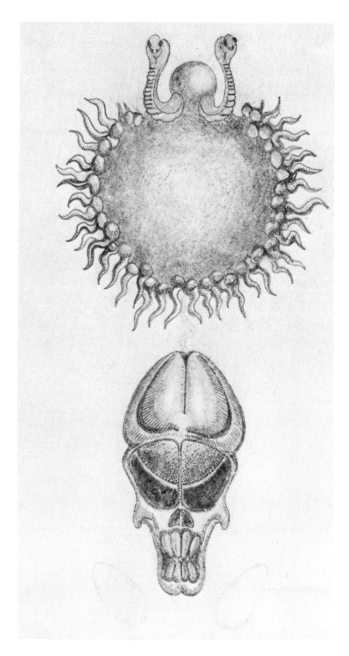

Figure 70.   Craig's picture made to "zonk" others with himself as the
phallic-skull.

Figure 71. Craig's drawing of a female emerging from a fertilized ovum "to prevent a nuclear holocaust," represented by the phallic-skull.

the materialistic world—money, computers, the H-bomb "being retracted from the earth's surface." The face at lower left is his own.

Although Craig was usually convinced of his beliefs, at moments he questioned them. He speculated that when he was no longer "psychotic" he would draw still lifes and landscapes. In fact on one occasion when he seemed less delusional, he did draw a landscape. It was very empty and unimaginative, a striking contrast with his other pictures. Such occurrences raise questions

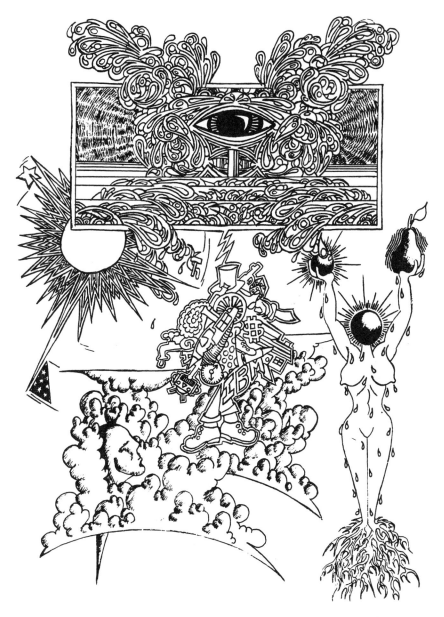

Figure 72. Craig's "judgement day" with the eye of God at the top, the material world in the center, and the female marijuana plant at right.

concerning the loss he would suffer in giving up his delusions. Sometimes serious convictions, such as those described above in connection with Figure 58, gave way to his delightful sense of graphic humor. In a particularly clever cartoon series he made fun of his psychiatrist. Figure 73 is another example of his humor.

In later pictures Craig's female developed a face. In Figure 74, a woman is placed at the interface of the technicological and natural worlds. He noted that his women had become more sensuous and said she was sitting on him. Figure 75 is a mouth with a tongue made of satin quilting. ''It is shiny and slippery like being inside a womb.'' He said the picture of the mouth really scared him because ''it might come out of the paper and swallow me and I would be gummed to death.''

Craig's final picture is a very large drawing of the Mother of the Universe, his guardian angel, on which he worked for many hours, Figure 1. He is seated in her hand under the planet Saturn, which he considered his astrological sign. He said,

I am the only one who knows how Mother Nature works; it's all energy, fluids of different densities, and currents. I know how to harness the energy through electricity which is the cleanest way and easiest to control. People are trying to get my secrets to control Mother Nature, but she can whiplash back, and then we'll all be blown to hell or outer space. The weather patterns have changed which is Nature's way of telling us something is wrong. I'll never tell Mother Nature's secrets, because they could be used to turn her against herself. I'd rather die than cheat on Mother Nature.

I have not heard from Craig for a long time. Following his discharge from NIH, he was subsequently hospitalized elsewhere. The last time I saw him, he had been released, was having trouble holding a job, and was unemployed and living in a tent in the woods. He was planning to do some traveling.

Craig's elaborate representations of man's destruction of the natural world found echoes in my own feelings. From them emerged this poem:

Figure 73. An example of Craig's humor.

159

Figure 74. Craig's depiction of a "sensuous" woman at the interface of the technicological and natural worlds.

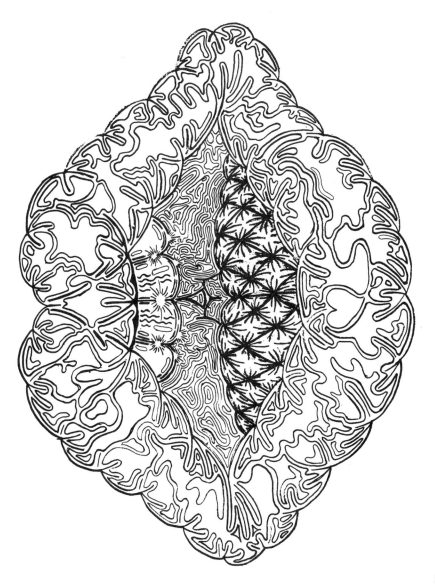

Figure 75. A slippery satin mouth which Craig feared might come out of the paper and gum him to death and swallow him.

My Friend the Paranoid.

My friend, the paranoid,
doesn't inhabit the same void
in which we wander
with only our own ghosts to ponder,
but dwells on an electro-magnetic
astral plane of molecular kinesthetic
pulsations, peopled with ravishing beauties
whose delicious duties
are to give mother's milk and purity,
a pregnant peace and security.
There's a man named Mr. Skin,
smiling and vibrating in
a suit of "pranic" energy.
My friend, as you can see,
is different from the likes of us.
Yet in a time of trust
he opened his world to me
in drawings of exquisite eccentricity.
When enemies label him insane,
he sets about to make it rain
or if they cause severer pain,
he mounts a tropical hurricane.
Here at the hospital, they call him daft
(suddenly I feel a draft).
My many-sighted friend
says the world is coming to its end,
that pollution and avarice
have a risk
to growing things.
On the ward, his musings
are considered crazy.
His parents say he's lazy
because he refuses to work
and that he's plain beserk
when he argues vehemently
against serving a corrupt economy.
My friend, the paranoid,
has learned to avoid
a world that's empty and frenetic
by being labeled schizophrenic.
He dreams and paints the time away
in images of the Judgement Day.

CHAPTER 13

Institutional Impact

From the art evaluation sessions designed to elicit communication of the subjective experience of acute schizophrenic psychosis came some unexpected material. It was only after I had collected a number of pictures that I realized that many patients were drawing similar elements in their environment that had impact on them. Specifically, there were many pictures dealing with seclusion room experiences and television, two prominent influences in the hospitalization. Even after I became aware of some emerging patterns among the ward population over the course of three years, in no way did I try to influence the production of pictures of these experiences. Nor did the picture requests suggest either of these subjects. In other words, in every case, they emerged spontaneously. Thus, their appearance among so many patients indicates the importance these events held for the patients.

IMPACT OF THE SECLUSION ROOM EXPERIENCE*

The seclusion room is a repository of intense feeling and strongly held opinion for members of psychiatric inpatient units. Patients, nurses, and doctors often find themselves in intra-psychic and/or interpersonal conflict over its use and misuse. Perhaps because of general discomfort, relatively little is known about what a patient actually experiences while secluded. Behavioral results (for example, control of violence and reduction of anxiety) are desired and frequently obtained, but accounts of the personal experience of this phenomenon are infrequently encountered. Euphemistically referring to an isolation room as the "quiet room" may represent both the goal of seclusion and the wish that the experience remain private.

Vivid psychotic experiences associated with seclusion as well as nonpsychotic reactions to being placed in seclusion were portrayed spontaneously in art

*Some of this material appeared in: Wadeson, H. S., and Carpenter, W. T.: Impact of the Seclusion Room Experience. *The Journal of Nervous and Mental Disease:* 163 (1976) 318–328.

material collected for other purposes. These materials and the patients' associations to their own work are rich communications about this very personal experience.

The patients admitted to the unit were often difficult management problems. Selection criteria and sources of referrals biased towards behaviorally disruptive patients. Furthermore, the therapeutic philosophy and research protocol made minimal use of pharmacologic restraint with maximum reliance placed on interpersonal techniques. These factors created a setting where the seclusion room was used relatively frequently. At times the door was left open, but more often it was locked. A staff member was always in attendance, usually sitting just outside the doorway, but at times in the room with the patient. While goals of seclusion varied depending on many factors, the general intent was to assure safety of patients and staff and to reduce social stimulation.

At the time these observations were made, sixty-two patients had been evaluated in art sessions during a three-year period. All had admission sessions, forty-nine had discharge sessions, and forty-three had returned for follow-up. Forty-one of the sixty-two patients had been in seclusion sometime during their hospital stay. Twenty of these made forty-three pictures directly reflecting seclusion room experiences. Since most patients participated in only three art sessions, producing three to five pictures at each session, the prevalence of spontaneous depiction of the seclusion room stands out.

These pictures fall into one or more of four categories: hallucinations while in seclusion (seventeen pictures); delusional experiences associated with seclusion (twenty-three pictures); intense affect associated with seclusion (twelve pictures); and drawings focused on a staff member in attendance at seclusion (five pictures).

Hallucinations

Hallucinations in the patient cohort were common with seventy-nine percent reporting such experiences in their initial psychiatric evaluation and ninety-five percent in art evaluation sessions. Visual hallucinations, while not infrequently reported in the clinical assessment, were especially prominent in the art productions. When requested to draw a hallucination, many depicted those experienced in seclusion.

The seventeen pictures reflecting hallucinatory experiences in seclusion were generally rich in their presentational qualities, and usually had a pleasurable aspect. Frightening scenes or intimidating figures were found, but far less than expected considering the patients' disturbed state. More surprising was the prevalence of comforting, reassuring, distracting, or "uplifting" hallucinations. These pleasurable hallucinations conveyed to the patient a sense of special status, or transformed the bleak seclusion room into a beautiful place of color, light, and pattern. For example, one picture depicted the seclusion room bathed in a phosphorescence; another represented a vision of God surrounded by light beheld in the seclusion room. In another instance Mao Tse Tung appeared and gave the patient instructions on how to bring peace to the world. The patient was reassured by this comforting message and enjoyed his special status in this regard.

Hallucinations were usually associated with delusional ideas. A young woman who believed she had travelled backwards in time while secluded, drew herself with Michelangelo in the Sistine Chapel. Colors above them showed the seclusion room ceiling which looked like a "mosaic painting" she and Michelangelo were producing.

Most of the drawings of hallucinations had reassuring qualities, and all provided the patient exciting mental activity with pleasure as one component. Although the patients had undeniable anxiety as part of their mental state at the time of seclusion, as an aspect of the seclusion experience per se, and in realtionship to their hallucinations, the almost ubiquitous experience of pleasure and reassurance associated with hallucinations outweighed those associated with anxiety and fear.

Delusions

In contrast to hallucinatory material, the twenty-three delusions represented in the art were consistently unpleasant, often terrifying. Many were persecutory, entailing a punishing experience in response to some action commited by the patient (for example, taking psychedelic drugs). In other instances seclusion was perceived as a punishment for committing some crime unknown to the patient. Figure 54 was drawn by a young woman, Jill, who believed she was about to die. She said she was tied down (in fact, she was in a wet sheet pack) in order to be cut open and given a heart transplant. She drew herself as a clothes pin, feeling "trapped and clamped." In another example, a college girl drew her belief that everyone in the world had been killed (her mother had recently died) and that she was left to starve to death in the seclusion room. When in seclusion, many patients believed they were in jail, and some thought it was a gas chamber. In Figure 76 Cynthia has drawn herself waiting for the gas to be turned on. (The gas chamber was a common delusion, as noted in the preceding chapter.)

Intense Affect

Patients naturally had considerable feeling about seclusion. When they represented their affect in drawings (twelve instances) it was always negative. This is in contrast to reports in debriefing interviews at discharge and follow-up where various ideas and feelings about seclusion were described, by no means all negative.

Figure 76. Cynthia in the "gas chamber"—seclusion room with a "silent guard" reading a book outside.

The patient who drew Figure 76, Cynthia, said the expression on the face is "gloomy, miserable, frustrated." She drew herself large, she said, because she "was there (the seclusion room) with all my problems and bewilderment." She then redrew the mouth to emphasize her displeasure.

Figure 77, a picture of the psychiatric illness by Donna, was begun with the face in the triangle representing herself in seclusion feeling sad and looking through the window in the door where there is an eye. She spoke of feeling "isolation, confusion, and a lack of understanding." She described "enormous frustration in being confined" and finding that her anger was not "tolerated." The numbers in the picture represent her counting to keep her head clear—sometimes counting the number of times she paced the seclusion room. At lower right is a view of the outside through the heavy screen on the seclusion room window. Although the picture was made at one-year follow-up, allowing Donna distance and perspective, her negative feelings were still intense.

Figure 78, drawn by Nancy, is also a picture of the psychiatric illness drawn at one-year follow-up. Nancy said she sometimes forgets she was hospitalized, but recognized that the seclusion room experience was the most prominent aspect of her illness. She drew herself in wet sheet packs in the seclusion room feeling ''sad and crying.'' She said she remembered the experience only vaguely but found it ''scary.''

Figure 77. Donna's depiction of her psychiatric illness with the central face representing herself in seclusion and a ''compassionate'' eye looking in at her there.

Figure 78.   A follow-up picture of the psychiatric illness showing Nancy in wet sheet packs in the seclusion room.

In a few instances it was difficult to discern the boundary between negative affect and paranoid delusion. For example, Nancy was extremely angry because she believed she had been secluded because the staff did not want to bother with her (which may have been a partly accurate perception).

Attending Staff Members

Five pictures dealt specifically with the accompanying staff person. Themes ranged from hostility at the "silent guard" reading a book (Figure 76) to relief at having a companion as seen in the "compassionate" eye looking into seclusion in Figure 77. Nancy, who drew Figure 78, noted that she was never alone in seclusion even though she depicted herself that way. She said having a nurse present was very important to her.

Discussion

It is part of human nature to divert attention from experiences which are painful and perplexing. The act of secluding a disturbed patient is of no small moment to any of the participants. As an event, it is charged with conflict, fear, sado-masochistic pleasure, fantasy distortion, estrangement, hostility, destructive impulses, retaliation, guilt, confusion, staff splits, and so on. The varied emotional and ideational experiences underline the importance of a more direct appreciation of the seclusion room phenomenon.

The extensive representation of seclusion room experiences in these drawings suggests the impact of the event on the patients. For many it was the seclusion room experience that symbolized the entire psychiatric illness, particularly in recollections at one-year follow-up. Material relating to seclusion was not suggested, requested, or expected. It was only after the material accumulated that I noticed that seclusion was a predominant theme.

The results of reviewing the forty-three pictures from the twenty patients who depicted seclusion suggest certain consistent themes. Delusional material and affective response to seclusion directly represent fear, terror, anger, and resentment. In the art productions, patients presented a universally negative view of the seclusion experience when reacting directly to the event.

The question arises as to whether paranoid tendencies are actually provoked by the seclusion room experience. For example, one of the patients complained of the brutish way he was "manhandled" when dragged to the room with the resultant fear that staff members would throw him out the window. In another instance, a sexually preoccupied college girl responded to the forceful physical contact with a delusion that she was raped in the seclusion room by a male aide. The non-psychotic feeling of bitterness over being placed in seclusion was usually a prevailing attitude, even at one-year follow-up, not simply an immediate reaction. For a few patients, bitterness about being secluded colored their entire perception of their hospitalization.

In sharp contrast to the negative reaction is material seen in the hallucinations. Here we find excitement, pleasure, spirituality, distraction, and a withdrawal to a reassuring inner world. All too often this exciting and comforting aspect of psychosis has gone unnoted while attention is focussed on the obvious anguish of patients. These pleasurable themes reveal at least a powerful attempt to cope with the bleakness of isolation and the tense interpersonal relationships in the clinical environment. The preponderance of hallucinations depicted occurring in seclusion suggests that the seclusion room itself stimulated hallucinatory activity. This observation is consistent with sensory deprivation experimentation in which non-psychotic subjects hallucinated. The depriving nature of the seclusion room (no furniture, bare walls and floor, decreased opportunity for spatial mobility) imposes an environment with diminished sensory as well as human stimulation.

The gratifying nature of the hallucinations experienced there reflects their compensatory attributes similar to the experimental sensory deprivation hallucinations. Such phenomena suggest the adaptive quality postulated in the dynamics of psychiatric symptoms by Arlow and Brenner (1964).

It is clear that the possible increase in hallucinatory experience in seclusion, as well as the production of delusions about seclusion, cannot be attributed solely to its physical and emotional conditions. The obvious factor that seclusion was instituted because of increased disturbance in the patient's behavior presupposes greater severity of psychosis at that time, probably during a period when hallucinations and delusions were more likely to occur.

It is not surprising that several pictures drew attention to the staff person in attendance at seclusion. This human contact can be a supportive and stabilizing influence countering the isolation, confusion, and fear the patient is experiencing. With this in mind, the staff member assigned to care for the patient in seclusion should serve a more important therapeutic function than merely to protect the patient's safety and note behavioral state. In addition to providing emotional support, staff members should be sensitive to the communications involved in the patient's experience in seclusion and apply this information in the therapeutic effort.

Information on the seclusion experience obtained in art productions suggests greater therapeutic attention is warranted in order to increase patients' and staff's awareness of the multiple facets of this event. The patients' pictures and associations to their art reveal the ready availability of material from this conflicted event. In an ideal treatment program, seclusion would be unnecessary. Instead of adequate numbers of personnel with high quality interpersonal therapeutic skills, however, most treatment facilities resort to drugs for management of disruptive behavior.

TV: PROGRAMMING DELUSIONS*

While I had not expected television to be prominent in the patients' art communications, it is not surprising when one considers the enormous exposure to this provocative medium experienced by most Americans throughout their lives. Of the fifty-five acute schizophrenic patients studied, sixteen (twenty-nine percent) drew pictures representing a delusion associated with a program seen on TV. In some instances, patients' delusions were influenced by other electronic media as well, such as the radio and records. Since patients were not expected to

*This is a revised version of a paper first published in the *American Journal of Orthopsychiatry,* copyright 1976, by the American Orthopsychiatric Association, Inc., 46: 434–438, by H. Wadeson and W. Carpenter.

report such an association, I do not know how many of the remaining thirty-nine patients had TV-influenced delusions which were not drawn in the art sessions.

Pictures of TV-related delusions usually emanated from the specific request to draw hallucinations and delusions experienced. Occasionally, TV-influenced delusions appeared in the picture of the psychiatric illness as well. These hallucinations and delusions were most often depicted at the discharge and follow-up sessions, rarely at admission. They were recollections, produced after the acute phase of the psychosis had abated and the patient realized that the TV experience was delusional.

The following examples illustrate several ways television played a part in the psychotic experiences of our patients.

In Figure 79, drawn at one-year follow-up, Kurt depicted a very clear recollection of a delusion stimulated by a specific program. The scene occurred

Figure 79. Kurt's delusion of having committed the crime portrayed on a TV program.

in the unit's day room. Kurt is seated on the sofa watching a program involving a theft on TV. He believed that the three people in the picture, himself, an aide in the chair, and a female patient who is standing had committed the crime. He thought the female patient's pocketbook was filled with money they had stolen, as was the suitcase beside the sofa. He had seen the aide take some bills from his pocket, which he believed were part of the loot. When the aide moved the suitcase to the nursing station, Kurt was convinced that the other two were attempting to cut him out of his share of the stolen money. In this instance, the stimulation of the crime program and details of the immediate scene were incorporated into a delusion. The formation of this delusion appeared related to Kurt's general sense of guilt, the triangular nature of his relationship with this particular patient and aide, and the suggestive content of the TV program.

Figure 80, also drawn at one-year follow-up, is an example of a less precise delusional experience. Nancy drew herself at the top of the picture confronted by armed assassins. She had seen a program about the Arab-Israeli war which

Figure 80.   Nancy being confronted by armed assassins, a delusion stimulated by a TV program of the Arab-Israeli war.

reinforced her belief that everyone was against her. Later, when she saw a protest demonstration on TV, she thought that the people on the screen were her friends. This patient identified with masses of people viewed on TV, feeling either victimized or befriended as she delusionally incorporated emotionally charged content from TV.

The majority of patients experiencing hallucinations and delusions associated with TV, believed that the programs were transmitted in order to send them specific messages. This sort of ideation is different from the preceding two examples where delusional content was stimulated or reinforced by a program's content. In Figure 81, drawn at discharge, Diane depicted an experience just prior to hospitalization in which she thought she received a message from the TV. She believed her boyfriend and sister were involved in a plot to kill her. She became frightened while driving with her sister, and tried to jump out of her Volkswagon (as pictured). Above is the TV set on which she saw a program that

Figure 81.   A delusion of receiving a message from a TV program which Diane thought was about her.

evening about a girl running away. She believed the program was about her, telling her to run away. As a result, she ran out of the house screaming and was "rescued" by her sister and boyfriend, who are drawn coming after her. The TV "message" in this case fitted into a well-developed and detailed paranoid delusional system.

A more complex, pervasive, and grandiose paranoid system is represented in Figure 53, drawn by Cynthia at discharge in a picture of her psychiatric illness. The television set was the first object drawn. The figures depicted below were going to kill Cynthia with the knives and guns drawn above them. Cynthia believed that she was being secretly televised while undressing, and that she had lost her boyfriend because he had seen her naked on TV, and now considered her a "tramp." An important precipitant in this psychotic episode was Cynthia's first sexual experience. Early in her hospital course she manifested catatonic posturing, making it necessary for staff members to dress, undress, and bathe her. At these times she was fearful of being on camera, believing that the entire unit was being video-taped. In this example, the TV itself had become an instrument of fear, rather than a delusional stimulus or transmitter of messages. Cynthia did experience these phenomena as well, believing that everything that happened on TV was specifically related to her personal experience and that the TV commercials displayed prizes for a large numbers racket run by the hospital staff.

A further variation of television's place in psychotic delusion production was illustrated by a patient who believed he could control the TV set with his mind. He claimed the mental power to discontinue any program he did not wish to see. In an elaborate experience of grandiose power he believed he had produced magic to enable a crippled person to walk without crutches. This delusional content sprang from a TV program where a lame person was healed.

Another patient drew an experience where he had heard his unspoken thoughts broadcast over the radio. Still another patient believed he had a computer inside his body, and that he traveled on a rocket ship. He related these and other ideas to the program *Star Trek*. In the preceding chapter a TV hallucination was noted in which a patient hallucinated the ghost of John Kennedy on a program about Lyndon Johnson.

Discussion

While casual clinical observation and common sense suggest that schizophrenic patients incorporate television programs into their psychotic experience, it is surprising that so many patients selected themes involving television for art work when this content was neither requested or expected. The patients appeared to regard the relationship of TV and delusion-formation as significant. These observations raise important questions at the interface of television programming and inpatient psychiatric treatment.

Concern about the television industry's predilection for violence and intrigue has often been voiced but not often heeded. For example, the *Christian Science Monitor* reported the following: "Staff members of this newspaper watched seventy-four and one-half hours of evening programs during the first week of the new season, and during that time recorded two hundred fifty-four incidents of violence including threats, and seventy-one murders, killings, and suicides" (Johnson, 1967). TV violence is readily available for incorporation in personality development, fantasy, interpersonal relationships, and delusions. An official opinion on the character of this influence is supplied in the *Final Report of the National Commission on the Causes and Prevention of Violence:* "Television entertainment based on violence may be effective merchandising, but it is an appalling way to serve a civilization . . ." (Johnson, 1967).

It is not my purpose to discuss the influence of television programming on the public, but rather to address its impact on psychotic patients. It is unwarranted to assert that viewing television has a causative relationship to psychosis, generally, or to delusion-formation, specifically. Evidence related to this question is lacking. One can assert, however, that TV programming provides readily available, evocative material which is frequently reflected in the content of delusions.

If one assumes that TV viewing may enhance delusion-formation—and certainly helps shape delusional systems—then a serious concern emerges regarding the extensiveness of time devoted to TV viewing on many psychiatric inpatient units, and by the social isolate in his or her home environment. Guidelines for the optimal use of time in a psychiatric setting are not well established or agreed upon, but there is abundant reason to question the wisdom of confined patients spending many hours watching television. Hours of passive receptivity to violent entertainment hardly seems beneficial by any stretch of the imagination.

One might point out that such inpatient conditions are no different from those outside the hospital, where in the average home the television set is turned on for some five hours and forty-five minutes a day (Johnson, 1967). Nevertheless, a psychiatric milieu contains the potentiality of developing an enrichment of life, not simply eradicating symptoms and otherwise perpetuating what is deleterious or banal in our society. In any case, it is time for those responsible for the treatment of psychotic patients to pay attention to an important and, perhaps, deleterious attribute of their environment.

CHAPTER 14

Art Expression and Recovery Style
in Acute Schizophrenia

Though etiology of schizophrenia has been widely investigated along with detailed mappings of the roads leading to an acute breakdown, relatively little attention has been given the manner of egress from psychosis. Since both the processes of onset and the processes involved in ''recovery'' have important implications for treatment, it is surprising that the latter phenomena have been subjected to relatively little empirical investigation.

Work of the NIMH Psychiatric Assessment Section has led to a conceptualization of the recovery process in acute schizophrenia according to an integration/ sealing-over continuum. Integration and sealing-over refer to a patient's style of coping with stressful events, conflict-laden ideation, and disturbing affects. These terms may be applied to the way in which a patient adapts to the stress of his or her psychosis upon recovery. Experience with acute schizophrenic patients on a clinical-research unit has led to specific operational definitions of these concepts (McGlashan, et al., 1976).

Briefly, integration describes a process by which a continuity is recognized between thoughts and feelings experienced during psychosis and prepsychotic and postpsychotic mental life. Individuals who make integrative recoveries struggle with the conflicts evident in their psychotic experiences and are gradually able to redefine these conflicts in nonpsychotic ways. They are curious about their psychotic ideas, feel responsible for them, and attempt to use their psychoses as sources of new information about themselves, with the goal of modifying premorbid dispositions and behavior. To a large degree, the use of integration as a descriptive term for a particular individual's recovery reflects aspects of the patient's relatedness to the observer/therapist. There is a degree of interpersonal involvement, therapeutic engagement, and empathic interchange which readily distinguishes these patients from those who seal-over.

Sealing-over describes a process by which psychotic experiences and symptoms are isolated from nonpsychotic mental events and then made unavailable by both conscious suppression and repression. Impenetrance to influence is both its intrapsychic and interpersonal characteristic. Individuals who successfully seal-

176

over are disinclined to discuss the thoughts and feelings they experienced while actively psychotic, often appear to lack awareness of the details of their psychotic episode, and fail to place their psychotic experiences into a personal context. Such individuals see their psychosis as an encapsulated, circumscribed event which is alien to, and distinct from, that part of their mental life they experience as evolving in a continuous, causally related manner. They rarely treat their psychotic experience as a source of new information about themselves, but seek to return to their premorbid styles and behavior—often with remarkable success.

These definitions are distinct for emphasis and operationally represent polar extremes of a continuum. Nevertheless, identification of an individual patient's major style can be made reliably by clinical judgment.

Much of the literature on art expression in mental illness focuses on change in both pictorial content and style over the course of illness with dramatic delineations of graphic reflections of psychotic disintegration and reconstitution. One such example has even reached popular familiarity: the series of cats drawn by the artist Louis Wain (Wilson, 1964) during his course of illness, in which the rendition proceeds from realistic to fanciful to complete abstraction. Little attention has been given, however, to the more enduring modes of pictorial expression which transcend the fluctuations of psychic disturbance and represent the expression of a more basic orientation to self and life and thus reflect a core personality pattern.

In work with acute schizophrenic patients, I have noticed a continuum of pictorial expressiveness along an axis from richly expressive at one pole to impoverished expression at the other. Although there are dramatic changes in the pictures from the acute phase to recovery to one-year follow-up in some patients, for many others there is a remarkable individual consistency of style. Since style of artistic expression was relatively impervious to mental status for these patients, it is here conceptualized as a personality trait manifestation rather than clinical state variable. As such, the differences observed in graphic expression which remained impervious to psychic disruptions of extreme proportions are conceived as indicative of major personality differences. Such differences, I postulated, would predict and reflect adaptational styles, specifically recovery process.

Fundamental to art expression is the processing and communicating of experience. Therefore, it would follow that the richer the individual's awareness of subjective experience, the richer the pictorial communication. Skill, or even fully developed hand-eye coordination, is not essential, as readily affirmed in the art work of young children. Therefore, an impoverished drawing may be viewed as the result of some sort of block to the natural process of self-expression which appears to be spontaneous and effortless in most young children. Because the sealing-over mode of recovery from a psychotic episode implies some sort of denial, encapsulation, or repression, one might speculate that such psychic mechanisms would also interfere with the flow of self-awareness and expression in art production. Therefore, I attempted to study the relationship between expressiveness in art production and recovery style in schizophrenia. I hypothesized that:

1. Integrators are more expressive in their art productions than are those who seal-over; and

2. Those acute schizophrenics who are consistently more expressive in art productions are more likely to integrate their psychoses, and those who are consistently more expressively impoverished are likely to seal-over their psychoses.

The methodology developed to test the first hypothesis is described in more detail in Chapter 21 as an example of art therapy research. In brief, integrators and sealers were designated by independent psychiatrists according to a scale developed for that purpose. All pictures made by twelve pairs of demographically matched integrators and sealers were presented to two independent raters for determination of graphic characteristics associated with expressiveness—color, motion, detail, space filled—and a global rating of expressiveness.* In another procedure designed to test the second hypothesis, an artist scored all the pictures made by all the patients according to expressiveness. Two demographically matched groups of nine each were formed of those patients consistently rich in expression and those whose art expression was consistently impoverished. Determinations were then made as to the number of integrators and sealers-over in each group.

The findings indicated that integrators used more color, drew with greater detail, and were generally more expressive in their art productions than sealers-over. They also tended to have more motion in their pictures but were not different from sealing-over patients in amount of space filled. In the second procedure most of those who were richly expressive were integrators, and most of those whose art expression was impoverished were sealing-over patients. Both hypotheses were supported at a statistically significant level.

EXAMPLES

Expressive and Impoverished Pictures

The following pictures taken from the second procedure illustrate richly expressive and impoverished art expression. Figure 82 is an example of a picture

*Some of this material appeared in: McGlashan, T., Wadeson, H., Carpenter, W., Levy, S.: Art and Recovery Style from Psychosis. *The Journal of Nervous and Mental Disease,* 164 (1977) 182–190.

made by Donna, whose art productions were consistently expressive. This is a graphic conceptualization of her psychiatric illness which she drew during the acute phase of illness. She has drawn internal organs and stated that she has a "rare disease." She deliberately drew the eyes too low to give the figure a "weird" appearance. Donna was delusional at the time, believeing that she was about to die. The prominent heart in the picture is associated with her belief that she was having a heart attack. The metaphoric meaning of her delusion was related to her psychic disintegration at the time, with her heart as her most vulnerable organ. Despite the theme of disease and death, this picture is vividly colored as were all Donna's pictures. At follow-up she drew herself realistically in her current life situation of going to school.

Figure 83 is also a picture of the psychiatric illness drawn at the admission session. Katie's conceptualization is a "confused brain." In this case, the

Figure 82.   A colorful, expressive picture by Donna, who believed she was having a heart attack and was about to die.

Figure 83.   Katie's meager drawing of a confused brain, a picture of the psychiatric illness.

drawing is almost as meager as possible, as were all the drawings of this patient, despite dramatic changes in her mental status.

Figures 84 and 85 are both self-portraits drawn at one-year follow-ups. Note the imaginative and expressive qualities of the superimposed animal faces in Figure 84 in contrast with the non-commital impoverishment of the stick figure in Figure 85. Congruent with these two self-portrait styles were the discussions which accompanied them. Kurt, who drew Figure 84, had much to say about the lion representing his anger and the kitten his meek facade. Jennifer, who drew herself as the stick figure in Figure 85, on the other hand, had little to say about her picture, despite my encouragement to explore it.

Integration and Sealing-Over Evidenced in the Pictures

Particularly interesting are graphic representations which actually illustrate the recovery process. The next pair of drawings was made by Polly, a patient from the first procedure who integrated her illness. In them may be seen the graphic qualities rated to be associated with integration: color, motion, detail, and expressiveness. In this case, the content, as well, reflects integration processes.

Figure 86, drawn at admission during the acute phase, is a self-portrait which she described as a flower and a star. She drew stars for eyes to represent insight and truth. She described the flower-person as feeling much emotion at once. Here, added to her awareness of the strong feelings associated with id impulses, is the element of grandiosity in her belief that she had reached cosmic truth, as elaborated in some of her other pictures.

Figure 87, representing Polly's psychiatric illness, was drawn at one year follow-up. Like Figure 86, it is vividly colored, and otherwise displays the graphic characteristics of pictorial expressiveness found to be associated with the integrating recovery style. Furthermore, the content of this picture illustrates integration as well. Polly believed that her illness was in part the result of feelings which she had kept inside and allowed to build up. These feelings, she

Figure 84. Kurt's expressive self-portrait with the lion representing anger and the kitten his meek facade.

said, came out when she was ill, as described in connection with Figure 86, and illustrated in Figure 87 by red and blue coming out of the head. Other objects in the picture symbolize her delusional ideas, including the planets at the bottom. Polly believed that she had learned from her illness, especially in regard to the degree to which she held her feelings back.

A particularly vivid example of the sealing-over process is furnished by Sylvia, who enjoyed making fanciful drawings which were usually quite constricted in their style. Nevertheless, during psychosis some of her defenses relaxed, and she drew the freer picture of her illness reproduced in Figure 64, described previously. To recapitulate, she said that she had drawn herself in a box like a jail and felt depression, indicated by the tears. She believed she was controlled by the voice of a witch (the figure at the top) telling her she should die, and controlling her sexual feelings which were bad. The black crosses represent the witch's

Figure 85.   Jennifer's impoverished self-portrait.

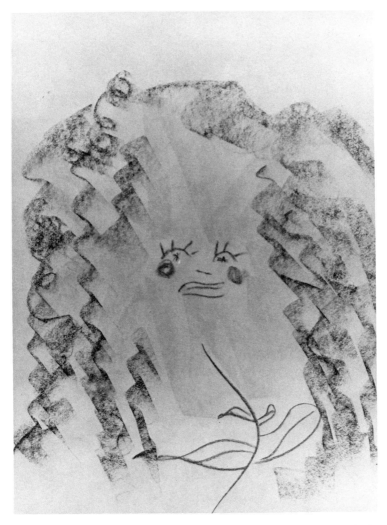

Figure 86.   A colorful self-portrait by Polly, an integrating patient, in which she is a flower and a star. Acute phase.

evilness. The bottom part of the body is a pitchfork "tail." The zigzag lines represent the "power coming in."

Figure 88, Sylvia's picture of the illness drawn at follow-up, well illustrates the sealing-over mode of recovery. There is a lack of color, detail, and motion. Expressiveness is blunted. Sylvia described the picture as a box in which "the sickness is trapped." The richness of the experience available to Sylvia at

Figure 87.　A colorful follow-up picture by Polly, showing bottled up feelings coming out of her head.

Figure 88. A colorless, non-expressive picture by Sylvia, a
sealing-over patient, at follow-up. The illness is trapped in a
box (same patient who drew figure 64).

admission and depicted in Figure 64 became repressed and compartmentalized at
follow-up. In Figure 88, the box has shrunk considerably and its expressive
contents have been replaced with a question mark. The question mark would
seem to indicate that the nature of the illness entrapped in the box was a mystery
to her. The use of the box is a vivid symbol of entrapment in both pictures. In the
former, Sylvia experienced herself as trapped. In the latter, it is the illness which
is trapped, as though the illness is a separate entity from the patient.

DISCUSSION

Although one might conjecture that artistic talent or skill could be a differ-
entiator, this does not seem likely. For example, Figure 76, drawn by Cynthia, a
patient in the study, is expressive but obviously displays little artistic merit.

There is an interesting congruence between personality attributes of creative people, as formulated by Kris (1952), Weissman (1967), Kafka (1967), and Arieti (1976), and psychological mechanisms which would differentiate integrators from sealers in schizophrenic recovery. In the creative individual, the ability to synthesize and integrate primary process material is maximized. Whereas the schizophrenic individual is overwhelmed by id material, the artist is able to use it productively. In recovery, however, the integrating schizophrenic, like the artist, comes to use the new awareness for growth, whereas the sealer still cannot handle the disturbing eruption of id material and recovers by denying it in one manner or another.

In addition to the use made of primary process material discussed by the psychoanalytic writers on creativity, in the area of psychological investigation, Barron (1968b) notes the following personality characteristics of successful artists: (a) a resistance to premature closure, and (b) a view of the complexities of life. These characteristics would be congruent with an integration of the psychosis in which one is fully aware of regressive experiences, remains curious about the psychotic process rather than coming to a premature closure, and likewise has awareness of its many facets, rather than a simplistic explanation. Those who seal-over the event, on the other hand, evidence the antithesis of the creative personality pattern. Through denial or projection they seal off the psychotic experience and come to view it as an encapsulated event unrelated to the ongoing process of their lives. (The patient who drew Figure 83, for example, believed her psychosis was caused by diet pills.)

Levy, McGlashan, and Carpenter (1975) in their discussion of metapsychological concepts of integration and sealing-over recovery styles point up the importance of the relationship to the observer/therapist. In sealing-over patients, they note a "withdrawal from or defense against active drive discharge in interpersonal relationships." They describe integrators by "a degree of interpersonal involvement, therapeutic engagement, and empathic interchange which readily distinguishes these patients from those who seal-over." Viewing the art product as a communication from the patient to the art therapist, these formulations, though not derived from an art setting, readily apply. In this light, it is altogether expectable and comprehensible that integrators would be more expressive (communicative) in their art productions than sealers.

In summation then, where extreme efforts are made to block unconscious flow into awareness, it might be expected that artistic expression would be more constricted. The results in this study support this hypothesis.

There are important clinical implications in the dichotomizing of recovery styles in acute psychosis as discussed by McGlashan, Levy and Carpenter (1975). They note that therapists can be classified by the treatment approaches they employ. A therapist who views psychotic symptoms as mental aberations best treated by pharmacotherapy and the rapid amelioration of symptoms, may well impede the integrative process in patients so inclined, while facilitating successful sealing-over in patients with that predisposition. Therapists invested in the psychotherapy of schizophrenic patients may err by impeding or delaying the sealing-over process in patients who eventually seal-over. Whitehorn and Betz's (1954, 1960) discovery that some psychotherapists (A type) engaged schizophrenics more effectively in treatment than others (B type) certainly relates to concepts of integration and sealing-over, as do the notions that certain patient-therapist matches might be optimal therapeutically. Therefore, the integration/sealing-over determination is a useful one in planning treatment methods and choice of therapist.

The use of pharmocological intervention, particularly chlorpromazine, as it relates to recovery style is questioned by McGlashan, Docherty, and Siris (1976). Although they conclude that information regarding the effects of drugs on integration and sealing-over must await further empirical investigation, they advise a basic guideline of avoiding extremes of disruptive fragmentation on the one hand and asymptomatic, but affectless, sealing-over on the other.

Since integrators may tend to engage more actively and respond better in psychotherapeutic treatment approaches, whereas patients who seal-over may obtain the greatest benefit from a supportive/suppressive treatment regime with or without psychoactive drugs, such determinations would be useful in treatment planning. As demonstrated in this study, expressiveness in art may reflect or predict one or the other style. A patient's art, therefore, can be informative in assessing the suitability of different types of treatment. During the course of treatment as well, art expression may serve as a useful guide for assessing defensive posture at any given period.

CHAPTER 15

Comparison of Art Expression in Schizophrenia, Depression, and Manic-Depressive Psychosis

As stated in my introductory remarks, I had considered writing a chapter entitled "Diagnosis and Misdiagnosis." Many diagnoses rely heavily on subjects' art expression. The House-Tree-Person Test, for example, is widely used, as are more spontaneous productions in art therapy settings. I have seldom felt pressured to apply a diagnostic label. More often, my total understanding of a patient formed a contribution to the dynamic formulations and treatment planning. This understanding developed from my interaction with the patient, the patient's reactions to his or her art expressions, and whatever further information I may have had. In other words, my approach to a picture produced in art therapy would not place undue significance on the observation that the house is in the upper left quadrant or lacks a chimney, for example. I would be more interested in how the house looks to the patient, fantasies about who lives there, and so forth. Because a picture is fragmented, I would not assume the patient to be schizophrenic (although I might surmise that the picture reflects the individual's emotional state at the time). Likewise, a well-organized picture would not necessarily assure me that the patient is not schizophrenic (for example, case study of Craig, previously described).

Nevertheless, since I had had the opportunity to work with a large number of very carefully diagnosed psychotic patients, I felt impelled to try to apply a more systematic approach to diagnostic classifications of patients' art work. The plan was to use independent "blind" raters (See Chapter 21) to test hypothesized distinguishing characteristics. In reviewing the pictures, however, it became clear that there was so much within group variability and between group overlap that such a procedure would be fruitless. Therefore, observations of the hypothesized characteristics were made, instead. In keeping with the original intentions of a systematic study, many significant variables were kept constant, such as art therapy setting and structure, number of sessions, instructions, lack of medication, course in hospitalization. A summary of the study follows.*

Affective psychoses and schizophrenia have traditionally been regarded as distinguishable. Psychiatry textbooks and glossaries of classification describe these illnesses separately, with distinguishing clinical features remaining surprisingly consistent throughout this century. There is, of course, diagnostic debate at the interface of these illnesses, especially regarding differential diagnosis of acute psychoses and the use of schizoaffective schizophrenia as a diagnostic category. Nonetheless, there is substantial evidence suggesting that schizophrenia and affective psychoses are different entities. This evidence is found in genetic, biologic, psychologic and phenomenologic investigations as well as differential pharmacotherapy. Furthermore, the affective psychoses appear to be usefully divided into patients who have both manic and depressive episodes and patients with only depressive episodes.

Observations reported in the literature from clinical settings (without systematic investigation) indicate distinctions in spontaneous art expression among groups with differing psychotic diagnoses. In general, reports describe schizophrenic style as fragmented, bizarre, and deteriorated; manic style is characterized by vivid colors, disorganization, and indications of activity; and depressed style is characterized by dark colors, bareness, and restraint. Content of schizophrenic pictures includes hallucinations, symbols, and body distortions; manic pictures include sexual symbols and euphoric themes; and in depression are seen themes of poverty, death, sin, and grief. These and additional characteristics are summarized in Table I (next page).

Since the observations reported in the literature did not coincide with my own observations, I decided to take a more systematic look. The comparison consisted of art work of sixty-two patients hospitalized on an NIH Clinical Center unit for schizophrenia and 104 patients on units for affective psychoses. Since session design varied among the different populations, I studied the first picture of the first session for each patient, which was always a free choice produced when the patient was in the acute phase of the psychosis and free of medication. I investigated style rather than content because the former can be observed objectively, whereas the latter requires an explanation from the creator. Casual obser-

*Some of this material appeared in: Wadeson, H., and Carpenter, W.: A Comparative Study of Art Expression of Schizophrenic, Unipolar Depressive, and Bipolar Manic-Depressive Patients. *The Journal of Nervous and Mental Disease:* 162(1976) 334–344.

Table 1.   Distinguishing Features of Psychotic Art Reported in the Literature

Schizophrenia	Mania	Depression
Content		
. Hallucinations	Sexual symbols	Poverty of ideas
Symbols	Euphoric themes	Immobile figures
Bizarre or stiff facial expressions		Signs of death
Distorted body parts		Delusions of sin, poverty,
Geometric patterns		hypochondria
"Writing in"		Starless nights
Composite figures		Torture or suicide
		Grief and mourning
		Depressive themes
		Lack of meaningfulness
Style		
Fragmentation	"Wild," vivid or	Somber or dark colors
Bizarreness	"hot" colors	Bareness
Unmixed colors	Lack of color variety	Lack of detail
Unusual coloring	Deterioration in	Indications of restraint
Deterioration of composition	composition	Lack of color
Disturbed spatial organization	Carelessness	Lack of effort or completeness
Disintegration	Disordered lines	Constriction
Detail	Scant detail	Evidence of low energy
Overelaboration	Business	
Precision	Excitement	
Distortion	Indications of activity	
Regression	Motion	
Transparencies	Free style	
Labeling	Paper filled	
Indications of activity		

vation alone revealed no particular patterns of content. Observations were as follows:

UNIPOLAR DEPRESSIVES

Pictures produced by unipolar depressives tended to be characterized by less color and development and greater emptiness and amorphousness than those of the other diagnostic groups. The painting in Figure 89 illustrates this finding. Figure 90 was also drawn by a unipolar depressive and illustrates the variability among patients which was found throughout.

Figure 89. An empty and amorphous picture by a unipolar depressive patient with little color and development.

BIPOLAR MANIC-DEPRESSIVES

Drawings of bipolar patients tended to be more colorful, more full, more formed, and more developed. Those made when manic did not appear to differentiate out as a group. Figure 91 is an example of a bipolar patient's picture. Figure 92 is an exception which looks more like the trend of the unipolar patients' art expression.

SCHIZOPHRENICS

The drawings of schizophrenic patients were highly variable. They tended to be similar to bipolar patients and different from unipolar patients in that most

Figure 90. A vividly colored exception to the characteristics of pictures by unipolar depressed patients.

Figure 91. A colorful, formed, developed, full picture by a bipolar manic-depressive patient.

pictures were colorful, full, formed and developed, such as Figure 93. On the other hand, there were more amorphous pictures among the schizophrenics than the other two groups. A few pictures were impressively colorless, empty, amorphous and minimally developed, Figure 94, for example. This colorless, empty style, previously associated with art productions of psychotically depressed patients (Wadeson, 1971a), was frequently noted in pictures of all three diagnostic groups studied for this report. This finding is surprising in terms of the art therapy literature (Table I).

ORGANIZATION

The disorganization frequently observed in the behavior of psychotic individuals was seldom reflected in the pictures. Particularly impressive in this regard are the

Figure 92. An exception to the characteristics of pictures by bipolar manic-depressive patients; more similar to pictures of unipolar depressed patients.

drawings of the acute schizophrenics, all of whom were free of medication for three weeks prior to the art session. Figure 95, for example, was produced by a schizophrenic woman who was rated* severe in psychosis and was causing much turmoil on the ward at the time. Nevertheless, her picture demonstrates concentrated effort, organization and control. Likewise, Figure 96 was drawn by a bipolar man, rated high in mania, who was provoking frequent fights on the ward. Disorganized, psychotic patients, when motivated, are often capable of

Figure 93.   A colorful, formed, developed, full picture by a schizophrenic patient.

*Independent behavioral ratings by nursing staff.

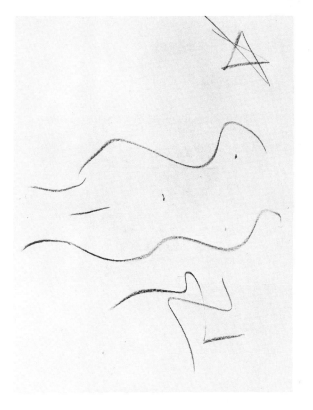

Figure 94.   A colorless, empty, amorphous minimally developed picture by a schizophrenic patient.

purposeful activity. A particularly striking example is provided by the schizophrenic patient who drew Figure 97. His behavior was grossly disorganized, and he seemed unable to focus his direction in the art session. Figure 97, his first drawing, reflects his disorganization. Nevertheless, although the many drawings he produced at this session were similarly disorganized and appeared to reflect bombardment of loosely associated ideas, he was able to organize himself for the final drawing in the same session, and produce a picture not the least bit disorganized.

AGE-MATCHED GROUPS

When the affective psychotic population was pared down to include only those in their teens and twenties (twenty-four patients) in order to be comparable to the young acute schizophrenic sample (fifty-four patients), differences diminished

Figure 95.   Effort, organization, and control demonstrated by a schizophrenic patient during severe psychosis.

Figure 96. Organization and control demonstrated by a patient rated high in mania.

even further. As a group, the younger unipolar and bipolar patients exhibited more color, more fullness and more developed pictures than the older affective psychotic patients.

DISCUSSION

I have often heard and read such terms as "a depressed picture," "schizophrenic art," and the like. My observations indicated that there is so much within group variability and between group overlap that such distinctions are impossible to make. At present, I know of no systematic procedure sufficiently refined to

Figure 97. A disorganized picture reflective of the disorganized behavior and thoughts of a schizophrenia patient.

diagnose a patient simply on the basis of art expression. That is not to say, however, that art productions are of no use in arriving at a differential diagnosis. It is important to consider the art productions in the context of other information: the patient's discussion of the picture, behavior during the session, and historical factors. As indicated throughout the clinical material presented in this book, art expression is extremely useful in understanding the dynamics and current issues of a particular patient at a given time, as well as providing a barometer of change. It is important for therapists to use the art productions for the abundant information they provide and not for the information they don't provide.

PART FOUR

Neurosis and Addiction

CHAPTER 16

Just Plain Folks

Of all the categories in the psychiatric nomenclature, probably neurosis suffers more than any other the burden of the medical model. Since incidence of neurosis has been described as up to seventy-five percent in general medical practice (Redlich and Freedman, 1966), symptomatology is difficult to isolate. Definition is less problematic when distinguishing between neurotics and psychotics—the former exhibiting milder symptoms, not being totally disabled, being in contact with "reality" and aware of their condition. Comparing neurotic distress with "normalcy," on the other hand, raises thorny questions. Although it might be more appropriate to consider people who might otherwise be labeled neurotic as having difficulty in living, the present psychotherapeutic system often requires a diagnostic label. For example, an individual wishing to receive third-party coverage of psychotherapeutic expenses must present the insurance company with a psychiatric diagnostic label supplied by the clinician. Some therapists who believe the medical model is not only inappropriate but harmful in its reliance on a disease concept, have refused to participate in what they consider a medical charade.

In my own private practice, I do not view my clients from a framework of the neurotic categories. I see them, for the most part, as people who have learned some attitudes and behavior, usually in early life, which presently cause them distress. I try to help them sort out the entanglements in which they find themselves and to create for themselves the sort of lives they want. I try not to foist on them my ideas of what constitutes "the good life," but to help them develop and implement their own values. (Such an approach, of course, has its roots in the client-centered therapy model.) For example, a thirty-one-year old woman was totally dependent upon her parents. I pointed out to her that it seemed to me that she paid a heavy price for her parents' support, but if that was her choice with full awareness of the trade-offs involved, that I saw nothing wrong in dependency per se. Obviously, I believe that greater satisfaction in life comes from greater self-reliance, which I told her was my particular bias. In other words, I did not try to impose it on her as a therapeutic goal. Although she made significant changes in her life during the course of our work together and moved from being depressed and suicidal to feeling content and often happy, she never did choose to be independent, substituting the more societally acceptable dependency on a husband to replace support from her parents.

Because what is usually labeled neurotic covers most of the people I have seen in private practice, many of whom have been therapists or therapists-in-training, there are no representative cases. Examples are to be found in other sections of this book, particularly the adults in Chapter 19, and some of the people in Chapter 20.

CASE STUDY

Nevertheless, one example will follow—Laura—mainly because her pictures and words describe her experience quite eloquently. I saw Laura for eigtheen months in one of the adult weekly art therapy groups described in Chapter 18. As did others in her group, Laura responded positively to my request to write comments about some of her pictures for presentational purposes. These remarks were written toward the end of her therapy and supply a more longitudinal perspective than she had at the time some of the pictures were made.

An art therapy student in her mid-twenties when she began therapy, Laura was a practicing art therapist seven months later. She was tall and slender with long blonde hair. Laura was initially quiet, reserved, and often subdued. Her first picture and the comments she wrote about it many months later reflect her awareness of the conflict beneath the outer facade:

Lion Picture—Self-Introduction (Figure 98): This is me, cloaked in my shield of long hair and in my favorite, gentle colors. I am aware that as I smile timidly, there lurks behind me, within me, a fierce, aggressive, hating lion. I am afraid of him in me but want his energy and confidence. Above me flies a beautiful butterfly, delicate and full of life. I want to accept my beauty, inner and outer, and not be ashamed of it. These parts of me were not integrated when I drew this picture but now I am more whole. These parts were in conflict with each other and unacknowledged, although I was well aware of them.

Laura's family had polarized "goodness" and "evilness" within the family, ascribing to Laura's brother the "black sheep" qualities and viewing Laura as "the good one." The suppression of the lion within her caused her great difficulty in expressing her feelings. Because in her position of "good girl" her rage at others was forbidden, it became manifested in self-destructive fantasies.

Scream and Cry (Figure 99): How I felt when my friend killed herself six years ago. Horrified. Shocked to the core. Shaken—my whole philosophy of life assaulted. Tears of sorrow, pain, and anger. I hold my head so it will not explode. I want to scream but I can't. How could anyone think of such a thing? I don't understand. I want to understand. I want to scream, "HELP." It never occurred to me that killing myself was a possibility until my friend killed herself.

The theme of self-destruction was to continue.

Figure 98. *Lion Picture–Self-Introduction*, by Laura.

The scream became prominent in a dream as well. In it Laura was riding in an elevator and was attacked from behind by a man who was trying to strangle her. She tried to scream but the sound whould not come out. Rather than using art therapy at this session, I suggested that Laura "gestalt" her dream. As she "became" first the scream and then the constriction in her throat, she experienced in a very immediate way the conflict within her. The experience was so intense that she became temporarily disoriented and had to hold onto the floor on which she was sitting to be sure it was under her.

Another pivotal experience occurred when I became angry at her for arriving at a session half an hour late. She stifled her feelings, but at the next session was gratified to realize that she had not become demolished and had not run away as was her usual pattern. By this time sufficient trust had developed so that she had the courage not to run away. She made a picture of her feelings of the previous session and wrote the following about it:

Monster (Figure 100): How I felt when I could not speak in previous session. I am trapped inside a monster, and I cannot speak. I sit so sad and silent and fragile when I want to wave my hands for help—I want to scream. I cannot move. I am isolated and alone in darkness—so far from everyone else. They are like flowers in the sunlight, and I cannot reach them or join them. I am not what I appear to be. I am a monster. I am the monster—it is not outside me. I am trapped by it—by myself. I feel crazy. I can hardly feel the floor. I float. I hold myself so I can feel real. Terrified, so sad that I cannot reach out when I need to.

Figure 99.   Laura's *Scream and Cry*.

Figure 100.   Laura's *Monster*.

As she began to free herself, to become more responsive, outgoing, spontaneous, and alive, she made the following pictures of what she was leaving behind. Her comments indicate some of the process of her freeing herself:

In the Dungeon (Figure 101): Many layers between me and the outside world—mountains of ice, Egyptian stone statue, medieval armor, dungeon. So many layers of protection between me and the sun, between me and myself, between what I know and what I will admit to. Slowly I am breaking through the layers—the ways I have felt at times: frozen and immobile, waiting for the thaw. Stone and permanently motionless—the truth about myself—even to myself. Lead and steel—a coat of armor—inside, not a person, but a metal coil tightening. Eyes closed to the world and to myself. Afraid of breaking from the tension. What have I been hiding? My thoughts of self-destruction. God, I can tell someone at last. Fantasies haunt me in my dungeon—bloody daggers. All in the imagination. I hide from them. Perhaps if I share this, I can see the sun again and rejoin life. How can I be so crazy inside—I am so sane. The cool earth supports me, gives me reality despite the fantasies.

Madonna (Figure 102): The attempt to be good and do right has forced me to submerge my mischievous, evil, rebellious self out of acknowledgement. The Madonna, Saint Joan, The Good Citizen, the Smiling Do-Gooder lack luster of life. In being without evil, without death, they lack life and sex. The battleground of the skin showed all was not well. My evil burst through and I sought to eliminate it, to squeeze it out of existence, out of my pimples. The bogey man and murderer, the hater and vile weapon maker is not out there but within.

In this recognition can I now be freed of my investment in pimples—in making them spread and grow? Can I not be my beautiful and ugly self without them complicating and blockading my true self from showing through? The time has come to give them up and express life's human conflict constructively, not self-destructively. Amen—so be it.

In a final mural, Laura pasted together six large pieces of paper to depict the scenerio of a dream:

Fish Dream (Figure 103): On the beach, my husband and I both refuse to take the responsibility and work of cooking a fish (lower left). Both of us say "You cook it." I throw it on the sand after he walks away. Then I'm driving down a black winding road that disappears into the hills and valleys below. I'm mad and won't let him in the car. I'm getting depressed, down, down. Finally I stop the car and let him in. The depression stops when the anger is resolved.

A group of people come along and pick up the fish which has become enormous and snakey—squirming (lower middle). Some people want to throw the fish back into the water, back into the unconscious; others want to take it on shore and cook it. After a struggle the latter win and volunteer to cook it, saying it will only take a couple hours. The group met for two hours.

I help carry the fish to the fire but still protest and resist. The fish is passive. I say other food could be eaten instead of the fish, even though I know it won't do any good. It has to be cooked. To become conscious.

Next, I have consulted a psychiatrist who wants to give me tranquilizers (upper left). I'm afraid someone will look at some pictures I did in a garden and think I am crazy. In the

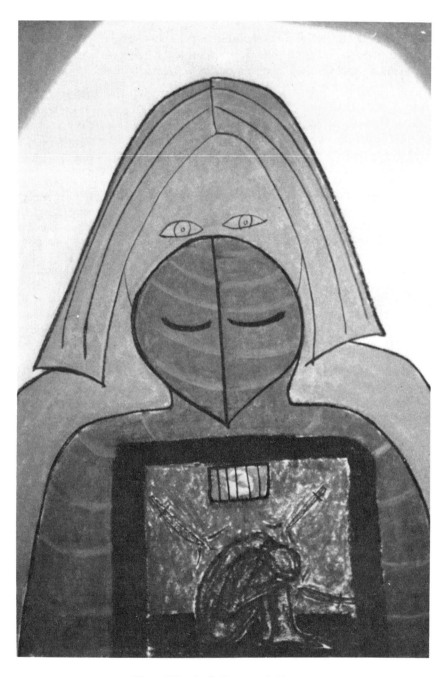

Figure 101. *In the Dungeon*, by Laura.

Figure 102. Laura's *Madonna*.

garden I was psychotic with crazy hair. But it was beautiful in the garden; a fountain flowed full of life, but I was alone (upper left).

In contrast several people are making a large paper fish of beautiful, vivid colors (upper left). They are having fun and never pause and think what they are doing might look crazy. So confident.

The paper fish is beautiful but empty and lifeless. Such might be the tranquilized life. I don't want it despite my tension. Instead I seek to unite with the big fish from the sea. As in real life, I pass up the tranquilizers.

After the dream, I fantasized that the fish exploded in the fire (upper right). At the same time it had a wish to continue to live—''I want to live.'' I faced this scene naked and alone without craziness. I feel the fish is my unconscious which I was afraid to face alone and which the group helped me to face, even when I was resistant. I feel I took a route toward healthiness and resolution and turned away from mere survival and repression and tranquilizers. I took care of my garbage like the garbage collector in the dream (lower right). Now, I want to live.

Like the fish, I was passive, not taking control of my life or myself. At the same time having too much self-control, keeping down the craziness. Now I feel my craziness won't make me crazy—it was my fear of my craziness that was doing me harm—I was stifling myself.

Figure 103. *Fish Dream*, by Laura.

208

I now try to be more active—to be more aware of what it is I want and to speak up. I want to live. My desire to live is greater than my desire to die or to harm myself. I want to make my fantasies of my life come true. I am stronger now.

I believe it took a lot of trust and courage on Laura's part to delve into her frightening and forbidden conflicts. She emerged a more alive, spontaneous, confident human being.

CHAPTER 17

Dreams

Dreams get a chapter all to themselves because they are so special.* Primitive sages recognized them as omens. Joseph became important to the Pharoh for his ability to read them. The western world became Christian as a result of the Roman emperor Constantine's belief in his dream of a cross and the words, "In hoc signo vinces" (In this sign thou shalt conquer). Modern soothsayers agree with Freud that dreams are "the royal road to the unconscious," among them Fritz Perls (1969), who described dreams as the individual's "most spontaneous production."

Perhaps one reason dreams are so captivating is because they speak to us in a strange and mysterious language—a language of haunting images, unexpected creativity, and delightful or frightening surprises. In our dreams we encounter a different reality not subject to the laws which govern our waking life.

Since the purpose of dreaming and the meaning of dreams remain speculative, dreams are best approached in terms of their usefulness to the dreamer. Naturally, people of all diagnostic categories dream, but I have included dreams in the section on neurosis because the greater insight-oriented possibilities with this group make dream work more productive than with some of the other populations.

Current art therapy approaches to dreams were predicted by Freud (1963), who recognized the visual character of dreams:

> We experience it (a dream) predominately in visual images; feelings may be present too, and thoughts interwoven as well; the other senses may also experience something, but nonetheless it is predominately a question of images. Part of the difficulty of giving an account of dreams is due to our having to translate the images into words. "I could draw it," a dreamer often says to us, "but I don't know how to say it."

Jung went further in having his patients draw their dreams. Presently, drawing or painting of dreams may be a major component of a Jungian analysis.

In my own work, I have found Perls' treatment of dream material especially productive. He believed that the different objects in dreams are fragments of the

---

*Some are presented in other chapters as well.

personality, some of which may have been split off or denied. The goal of therapy is to put the parts together so that the individual becomes a unified person. The technique Perls employed was to instruct the individual to relive the dream by ''becoming'' each of the objects in it. The ensuing dialogue between opposing parts often brings about understanding, an appreciation of differences rather than conflict, leading to integration of the separate parts. The results I have obtained from applying his gestalt therapy process have often produced a flooding of emotion accompanied by dramatic insights.

Incorporating gestalt therapy with art therapy, I have asked clients to become the objects and figures they have drawn in depictions of dreams. Sometimes the drawn image may be different from or more complete than the vaguely remembered dream image. It doesn't matter. Both picture and dream are the client's production; both may be understood as expressions of the self.

As in other pictorial subjects, the spatial nature of a dream drawing may add a further dimension of understanding as is illustrated in subsequent examples. There are other advantages to drawing dreams which add to the processing of the material beyond the verbal account. I experienced one of them recently when I recognized that I had difficulty drawing a dream image of myself embracing a grieving friend. In fact, although I have little technical difficulty portraying figures, in this instance, initially I actually drew myself facing away from her. This problem, totally unavailable in a verbal account, put me in touch with deeper and more complex meanings in the image than I had previously suspected. Since dreams are often complex phenomena encompassing many layers of experience, it can be fruitful to relate to them in many ways. Sometimes one modality or approach may augment another, as is illustrated in the following dream exploration where several approaches are combined.

EXAMPLES

Because of the complex subjectivity of dreams, I have chosen two of my own as illustrations. The first dream occurred at a time when I was about to attend a meeting in the city where John lived. John was a former student to whom I had been something of a benefactor. We had been close friends before he moved away, but I felt he had used me. I was undecided as to whether I wanted to visit him or not. The dream: John came to me to say he was leaving. After a while he said it would be tomorrow. I was surprised because I hadn't seen him in some time. (This was similar to his actual leaving.) He wanted something from me—information or a trip ticket—I don't remember what. He was wearing a familiar blue sweater. (Later I discovered he had left this sweater at my house—I didn't know that at the time I had the dream.) His face looked very different. It was smooth like a child's and very white and delicate, as though he hadn't been exposed to the sun. His nose was bulbous on the end like a baby's and his lips were full and sensuous. Two men appeared. One was black, and the other had a missing tooth. I knew they were dangerous and that they were out to get John. I was between him and them. I thought that if I stayed there, he would be safe. Then I realized that I was in danger too, so I moved away toward a door. The man missing a tooth was the boss, and the other was the henchman. As I was leaving I looked back and saw that the latter had gotten John and was putting a black blindfold over his eyes. I was hurrying through the nighttime city to escape, but not running because I didn't want to be conspicuous. I felt a tap on my shoulder and turned to see the missing-tooth-one had caught up with me and was leering at me. I realized that I had stayed with John too long, that by having seen his capture I was a witness and therefore would be captured too.

Analysis: Both Freud (1963) and Faraday (1974) suggest looking to immediate events. It seemed obvious to me that the dream had been precipitated by my conflict around whether to visit John or not. To pursue the meaning further, I associated to the ideas, images, and key words I had used in writing down the dream. (For brevity, I will omit some of the details.) I saw John as child-like. When I "became" John in gestalt therapy fashion, I was aware of his passivity in the dream. Seeing and not seeing are important motifs: John gets blindfolded; I am to be captured because I saw. The two men are alien, dangerous, and evil. They are connected with John. In trying to protect him from evil, I too become trapped by his evil, realizing too late that I must escape and leave him to his own fate. Out of these associations and key words in the written dream description, a

Figure 104.   A drawing of a dream used in conjunction with other approaches to exploring it.

poem emerged quite spontaneously which illuminated my vulnerability to the delicate destructive child in myself and others.

Dark of the Heart
The exotic evil of my dreams
screams from silent soft full lips
of an angel face
still
in the quiet of my heart.

The menace comes
and I
the shield
the mother
guard the delicate child.

Too late I see the child must deal with evil on his own.
Too late I see myself
caught in the glow of that smooth white face—
innocence untouched—
sucking at my life.
Too late I leap.

Leering evil taps my shoulder
for I have seen the selfish child,
the pale white blossom of my dreams,
blinded with black.
I am caught in the exotic dream
of protecting the demon child
from his fate.
Blinded by his whiteness
too late I see the dark
and am tapped to share his fearful fate.

The polarities in the dream are innocence and evil, darkness and light, mother and child, vision and blindness.

The next step was drawing the dream. It was quick and spontaneous (Figure 104). Most significant to me was the placement of the figures. There I am in the middle between the baby-faced John and the evil men, a position fraught with conflict. The picture clarified the polarity in myself: on the left the innocent child, the only passive person in the picture. Although one part of my divided self is reaching out to him and facing him, my eyes are closed. On the right, my eyes and mouth are wide open as I hold up my arm to ward off the evil man who is laughing and touching my shoulder. The other man is reaching also and looking at the child. On the far right, the child is blindfolded. The polarity within myself concerns child-like innocence accompanied by my blindness. With my eyes open, I see the evil and try to protect myself, and only the child is unseeing. Finally, in recognizing the cast of characters as aspects of myself, I see the danger in the non-seeing child-like passivity, the futility and self-destructiveness in the protective mother, and the power in the maliciousness.

Specifically, the message of the dream was that I must not get caught up in John's entanglements, trying to protect him in his "blindness," lest I get caught in his web of difficulties. In actuality, I did visit him (curiosity got the better of me), but I felt quite distant from him. I found him still stuck in his naive fictions of human relationships. He did try to prevail upon me to help him again, but this time I declined. He seemed stuck in his blindfoldedness.

At a more general level, the dream has instructed me toward a greater detachment so that I am less likely to place myself in the middle of the picture trying to control people and circumstances (This time I remained uninvolved when John wanted help). It seems also, that if I can leave off trying to protect what is innocent within myself, I won't feel menaced by what is evil within myself. These aspects of myself will be able to live together more harmoniously.

This example was selected to demonstrate the combining of several modalities in dream exploration: relating the dream to recent events, associating to it, "gestalting" it, writing a poem from it, and drawing the dream. The resultant understanding was then both applied to the immediate situation and used as a basis for instruction in the development of goals in self-growth.

The following is a very different sort of dream experience. Unlike the first where action dominated, the impact of this dream was in a single image. The first part of the dream was only vaguely remembered, but was full of violent activity. I was scared, but also excitedly enjoying it. The scene shifted to an image: my face, a dusky, large, placid moon-face suspended in a dark surrounding. Next to the face was a young cherry blossom tree in full bloom. The image was very beautiful. The contrast between the first and second parts of the dream is striking: the violent activity and the stillness. I have drawn and painted the second image many times. Figure 105 is the first rendition. It appeared to me as though one eye is looking inward, the other outward. It gives me a feeling of tranquility. The message of the dream seemed to be that despite the violence and even my enjoyment of it, that I am whole in myself, that the world that is mine is beautiful and tranquil. The young blossoming tree and the serene face suggested a resolution of mid-life anxieties.

I'd like to add that I believe these "explanations" of the two dreams are far from complete. The images themselves speak more eloquently than their translations into words. For example, John's smooth white dream countenance contrasts strikingly with his actual lined, pock-marked face. Each time I paint the face image of the second dream, it takes on a different aspect, sometimes more solid, sometimes more primitive, but always a lovely peaceful presence. And painting it is a peaceful experience. I think I depict it many times because it is a part of myself I want to develop and know better.

Figure 105.   A haunting dream image.

Another use to which dream pictures can be put is illustrated by a piece of Erica's therapeutic work. A client in private practice, Erica entered therapy at a time when she was recently divorced and working on her Ph.D. Prior to the dream she had expressed her anxiety about undertaking her dissertation, which was in the planning stage. The Dream (Figure 106):

I was alone in my childhood home (upper left) feeling sort of lost and bewildered. I think I was a child. Then the scene shifted and I was getting out of a car to go to a workshop at a house on the Potomac River with rocks in front of it (top center). I walked around inside and found a tiny bedroom which was almost completely filled with a double bed and sun streaming in the window over it (middle left). It was cozy and charming, but I realized I couldn't sleep there because I had to be in the dormitory in the basement (right). The beds there looked small and uncomfortable, and there were no covers. Then a group of people came in (lower right). I realized they were professionals from New York and that the purpose of the workshop was to work on my dissertation. Even though the whole enterprise was for my benefit, I felt terribly intimidated by the professionals, especially the cold looking woman with glasses. Then the man who was in charge came in. His name was Mr. Shepherd (left), and he was very kind looking. He came over to me, and I put my arms around him. I immediately felt reassured.

In processing her dream Erica recognized that although she often felt like the helpless, lonely child she pictured in the bleak house of her childhood, in fact she was a mature, accomplished, and resourceful woman. She saw the workshop

Figure 106.   Erica's dream.

scene as representing her anxiety in entering the realms of professionalism and higher education to which her Ph.D. program was taking her. The rocks she had to cross to get to the house represented for her the difficulties she had experienced in getting into the program. Erica was clear that these New York professionals were her Ph.D. committee, intimidating experts who were strange to her but who were supposed to be helping her with her work. She was mystified by the sunny bedroom and the gloomy dormitory. The identity of Mr. Shepherd was puzzling to her, but she was sure that his appearance and his name indicated that he was someone who would take care of her. She was very pleased with the way she had drawn him, saying that in the picture he looked just as he did in the dream.

Because she was most drawn to the puzzling meaning of Mr. Shepherd and the sunny bedroom, I suggested that she draw another picture about them (Figure 107). Here she has drawn an idyllic scene of herself and Mr. Shepherd asleep in the bed, with the window filled with bright sunlight streaming in on them. Erica became tearful and said that although she knows she is no longer the lonely child in the bleak house as in her dream, she still needs some love and care, and that her life has just been too difficult and too pressured lately—managing her household, her two teen-age children, her part-time job, and her life alone and now feeling overwhelmed by her Ph.D. work. Erica and I agreed that in her generally productive and successful life style, her accomplishments often overshadowed some of her needs and longings. She felt that her dream was a reminder of aspects of herself she overlooked. It was letting her know, she said, that she was not the super-woman that others saw, but rather the needful mortal she is. Combining the elements of her dream picture in a new way enabled Erica to recognize aspects of herself that previously had been only dimly perceived.

Patricia's dream provides an example of a gestalt therapy approach. In a class studying work with dreams through art therapy, she drew a picture of her previous night's dream. In it she showed herself and her two young children in a parked car while her husband and parents were getting out to enter a "girlie joint." In front of the car were people dancing in the street, with a "stripper" drawn the most elaborately of the group. She explained that she had to babysit with the children in the car while the rest of the family joined the revelers. As she "gestalted" the objects in the picture and became each one, several recognitions emerged for her. She was impressed with the delight she felt as her prudish parents in anticipating the forbidden pleasure of the "girlie show." She also recognized the conflict between the responsible, constricted part of herself in the

Figure 107.   Erica's new combination of dream elements.

form of her husband telling her to stay in the car and take care of the children, and a previously unrecognized, more libertine part of herself which loved being the dancing stripper. Most significant to her, however, was her experience of being the road. She felt the pain of having people walk, dance, and drive over her with no concern for her needs and wishes. The content of the dream (herself as babysitter while the others were having fun) reinforced this interpretation. Patricia realized that in returning to school she was only just beginning to do something for herself instead of devoting herself completely to her family, as had been her pattern and the tradition to which she (and so many women) had been raised. Her dream seemed to be a reminder that there was more enjoyment from which she was being held back.

In working with a dream in this fashion, it is important for the therapist to be aware of the emotional balance of the dream in helping the dreamer to identify with one element after another. In this regard the sequence can make a difference, usually with an attempt to build toward the more impactful elements. On the other hand, sometimes unexpected, seemingly innocuous inanimate objects, such as the road in Patricia's dream, may have strong emotional import. There may be occasions, therefore, when the therapist will not be able to predict the emotional balance of the dream objects.

A final example illustrates the use of dream images in work with people who are not insight-oriented. Clark, a six-year-old child, was referred to an NIH study of hyperkinesis because of behavior problems at school and home. He was considered hyperkinetic and diagnosed minimally brain damaged with no hard signs to indicate malfunction. He enjoyed his individual art therapy sessions and did not evidence the disruptive behavior about which his mother and teacher complained. When not on doses of dexedrine, however, he displayed some physical restlessness and flight of ideas. Clark's pictures and the stories he made up about them revealed a strong conflict between his aggressively hostile urges and his wishes to please. Through picture-making and fantasy he was able to ventilate, communicate, and defuse some of these disturbing feelings.

At one session during a period when his dexedrine dose had been reduced, allowing for a greater play of fantasy, he drew the previous night's dream, Figure 108. The trees had turned to monsters, and he and his mother were going to jump into a hole to hide (bottom). Hiding was a recurrent theme in Clark's pictures, probably the result of his felt need for protection in light of the fears connected with his fantasies of monsters, devouring bears, attacking ships, and so forth. In the drawing Clark has depicted his mother as the same size as himself, and in fact she seemed a somewhat ineffectual woman. His relationship with her was a troubled one, partially as a result of the absence of his father the previous year while living with another woman. As the only son, Clark may have experienced himself taking his father's place. Both he and his mother appear tiny in contrast

Figure 108.   Monster dream by six-year-old Clark.

to the towering monsters. It is likely that Clark felt this way too, especially in relationship to his domineering father. Hiding may have been his most adequate defense.

Clark benefited from art therapy through the release of such material as formed his dreams and fantasies, and through the positive relationship he was able to develop with an adult who was interested and accepting of wishes and fears that he and the adults in his world found frightening and/or unacceptable. (A study of Clark's intrapsychic reaction to amphetamine is described in Chapter 21 in connection with research.)

My intention has been to show several ways in which dreams may be approached in art therapy. I certainly do not prescribe any set method, as each dream and each dreamer is unique. Here, certainly, is an opportunity for art therapists to function most creatively in guiding the dreamer to explore the dream.

CHAPTER 18

Alcohol Abuse

In order to gain experience with an addictive population, I worked for a brief period at an outpatient alcohol abuse treatment center and enrolled in several seminars dealing with various aspects of substance abuse. Since this was an area of very limited knowledge and experience for me, I learned a great deal. In addition to what the clients taught me, my studying of alcoholism, in particular, yielded a societal perspective and the recognition that alcohol abuse is a much more pervasive problem than I had realized.

Alcoholism is the third leading cause of death in the United States when alcohol-related traffic deaths are included. Alcohol's effects on functioning in order of occurrence are: impairment of judgement, impairment of voluntary motor actions, confusion, stupor, unconsciousness, impairment of neural centers governing heart beat and breathing, leading to death. It is especially dangerous when mixed with other central nervous system depressants. These drugs multiply each others' effects and may cause death. In addition, long term heavy drinking causes severe physiological damage to many of the organ systems of the body, most noticeably cirrhosis of the liver and irreversible brain damage.

Unfortunately, alcohol consumption is an intrinsic part of the business and socializing patterns of our society, leading to ample opportunity for abuse. As a result, a major effort is necessary in promoting alcoholism prevention. Since denial is one of the salient characteristics of alcohol abuse, the major focus is on identifying problem drinkers and coercing them into treatment and education about alcohol abuse.

Treatment usually consists of management of acute episodes, correction of chronic health problems caused by alcoholism, and promotion of behavior change to eliminate destructive drinking patterns. Psychotherapy has not proven to be particularly effective. Often aversive therapy such as antabuse, is instituted. This drug, taken regularly, causes nausea with the ingestion of alcohol. Alcoholics Anonymous appears to offer the most effective force in combatting alcohol abuse. The strength of this organization is in the support system it provides. In some instances, the alcoholic must give up a familiar social system (such as drinking buddies) when he or she goes on the wagon. AA's describe alcohol as a great solvent—it removes stains, grease, spouses, homes, jobs, and health. AA can supplant some of those losses.

In treating alcoholics it was clear that unless destructive drinking ceased, there was no hope for positive change. In some instances, the client made a decision to stop and stuck by it. In others, the decision was made but not adhered to. These were the most painful efforts. And then there were some who had no intention of stopping. Some who joined AA evidenced the zeal of converts and became "AAaholics," making this organization the center of their lives.

Although some of the treatment center's clients were referred from hospital detoxification units, most had been arrested for drunken driving and were referred for treatment by state Alcohol Safety Action Programs. By entering the center's treatment and educational program, they were able to lighten their sentences. Although all clients technically volunteered for treatment, many felt coerced. Often these people believed that they had been arrested unfairly and that they were not problem drinkers. Naturally, they were resistant to treatment and simply put in time to fulfill their legal obligation. Denial of the problem was a frequent detriment to overcoming it. Others were relieved to be caught in the act. It gave them the impetus finally to do something about the problem they were beginning to recognize.

I saw clients in groups. Most were in their middle years. They came from all social classes with men predominating over women considerably. The groups were scheduled for sixteen sessions, once a week, which was the requirement for reinstatement of a driver's license. There were often twenty group members at once with the population changing weekly as people were admitted and discharged from the program. The purpose of the groups was to enable the members to personalize the learning they had acquired through the center's educational program which they were required to attend. There were two therapists, and at times we divided the groups into smaller subgroups, particularly when I introduced art therapy. There was much greater cohesiveness and revelation of feelings in these sessions. Each person contributed, in contrast to the large sessions where some remained withdrawn. (See Chapter 19 for a discussion of the withdrawn individual in group art therapy.)

The pictures highlighted several prominent themes. One was loss. The broken clock and hour glass in Figure 109 represented, for the middle-aged man who drew them, missed time and opportunities. When he was jailed for drunkenness, he feared he had lost everything.

A sense of passing time was reflected in many of the pictures. Some were representations of a downhill progression with a few peaks during periods of non-drinking. One client drew himself as young and then older saying that it was okay for a young person to act silly, but that an older person looks like a fool when he has had too much to drink, such as the way he had embarrassed himself by saying things repetitiously at business parties.

Figure 109. A representation of lost time and opportunities by an alcoholic.

Figure 110. An alcoholic's good time at a party, left, hangover and possible automobile accident, right.

Ambivalence was common in the pictures. Figure 110 depicts the good time the client was having at a party and the hangover and perhaps a wreck on the way home. The cloud symbolizes the ill feeling when hungover. Many clients drew clouds to represent negative feelings. A middle-aged woman drew a dark cloud engulfing her home and described it as "a cloud of depression."

Some made pictures that expressed the need to drink. In Figure 111, a bachelor who said that all his friends were married, drew himself at a "friendly bar" socializing. This led to a discussion of the difference between drinking alone and with others. Another group member said that when he drinks with others he can blame the situation. He would worry, he said, if he drank alone.

Many drew the scenes of their arrests, conveying some of the shock they experienced. One withdrawn client drew himself smoking in bed when drunk and explained that he had caught the bed on fire. Most bleak was the blackout, Figure 112, drawn by a man who said that he did awful things he can't remember.

Although many of the clients came to a recognition of the gravity of their alcohol problem (a necessary first step), this contact with the treatment center was not of sufficient duration for me to know whether their attempts to deal with it were likely to be long lasting or temporary. As is evident here, my experience in using art therapy with alcoholics is relatively minimal. I have included these few examples, nonetheless, because there is little reporting of such work in the literature. Most of the participants in the personalization groups experienced art therapy in only one session. Nevertheless, and despite the denial of drinking problems or withdrawal that characterized so many of the clients, I believe these

Figure 111.   An alcoholic bachelor's source of social life, his "friendly bar."

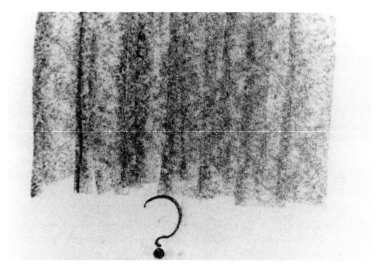

Figure 112.   A blackout drawn by an alcoholic man who said he did awful things he can't remember.

illustrations demonstrate the usefulness of the art expression in helping to focus on feelings connected with problem drinking. For many it was their most complete and/or only expression of feelings about their drinking problem.

EVALUATIONS OF ALCOHOLIC FAMILIES

In addition to clinical work at the alcohol abuse treatment center, I undertook a study of some aspects of alcoholic family patterns. This work was based on investigations indicating that alcoholism flows in family lines, unexplained by genetic evidence of predisposition. This observation has led to the study of psychosocial heritage processes within the family as a basis for understanding intergenerational transmission of alcoholism in families conducted by the Center for Family Research, Department of Psychiatry and Behavioral Sciences, George Washington University Medical Center (Wolin, Bennett, and Noonan, 1979). In conjunction with this research I designed art evaluation sessions to study one of the areas of interest which the larger research was investigating through verbal interviews. In brief, the Center for Family Research approach was to look to the family's psychosocial environment to explain the continuity of alcoholism over generations. The work is grounded in the family systems tradition, in which the family unit is regarded as the locus of pathology in the sense that the pathology becomes so intertwined with ongoing family functioning that the problem cannot be isolated from the rest of family interaction and behavior. The verbal interviews tapped family rituals and myths, which are significant conveyors of the family identity. One area of interest was pattern of family heritage, specifically whether the family studied carried over the rituals and myths of the alcoholic or the nonalcoholic parent.

In contrast with the specificity of questions and resulting data derived from the verbal interviews, I believed family art expressions would tap a more global, nonspecific, less conscious area of experience. I hypothesized that in addition to manifestations of heritage dominance in family myth and ritual, there would be unconscious manifestations of identification processes which could be elicited through art expression. Specifically, I anticipated that symbolic representations of the nuclear family and ancestral families produced by each family member would reveal areas of identification and heritage transmission. Furthermore, I expected that through drawings, feelings about alcoholism in the family might be dramatically displayed, thus providing information about the place of alcoholism in the family. In order to achieve these results, I designed specific procedures which have not been used elsewhere.

Method

All families selected for the research had one alcoholic parent and grown children, most of whom were in the area and available for interviews. Each of five families participated in a conjoint family art expression session lasting approximately one and one half hours.* Materials were simple—pastels and large paper—and participants were asked to make relatively quick drawings. They were told that expertise was not expected. The procedure was as follows: Family members drew concurrently, facing away from one another so that they would not be influenced by each others' drawings. After the completion of each of three tasks, the group faced one another and took turns explaining their pictures. Thus the pictures could be understood in terms of the drawer's intent. The tasks were assigned one by one so that there would be no anticipation of what was to come.

Instruction and rationale for each picture were:

1. "Please depict your family as a whole in a symbolic way. In other words, don't draw people." *Purpose:* To study each member's perception of the family as a whole, tapping significant themes and affect through symbolic content.

2. "Please divide your paper in half and depict on one side the maternal grandparents' family in a symbolic way and on the other side the paternal

*See Chapter 20 for further information on conjoint family art therapy sessions.

grandparents' family in a symbolic way." (After completion) "Please mark with a check which of the two more nearly resembles your first picture." *Purpose:* To discover heritage dominance from grandparental family through pictorial similarity produced unconsciously.

3. "Please depict the consumption of alcohol in your family as it has affected your life." *Purpose:* To understand the nature and pervasiveness of the influence of alcoholism in the family for each individual.

Example

The Tipler family consisted of Mr. Tipler, age sixty, a successful builder and active member of Alcoholics Anonymous for the past ten years after having a severe drinking problem for the preceding ten years; Mrs. Tipler, fifty-eight, nonalcohlic; Paul thirty-two, with a history of alcohol abuse, not present, divorced and living on a boat; Jerry, twenty-nine, in business with his father; and Annette, twenty-seven, married, alcoholic during college, presently a counsellor for alcoholics.

As is usually the case, the family's drawings revealed many aspects of each member and their interrelationships. Only those germane to the study will be discussed here.

Heritage: All members of the family except the father chose their picture of the mother's family as more nearly like their depiction of the nuclear family, based on a strong connection with the maternal grandmother. In terms of graphic style alone, however, Annette's first picture more nearly resembled her picture of the father's family. All family members depicted the paternal grandfather as cold and unavailable (their description). Particularly salient in the nuclear family drawings was the position of the older son Paul, who was not present. Annette drew his representation first in her picture, saying he had had a strong effect on the family. She explained that he has rejected the family and lives as a "loner" on a boat in the Carribean. The others described him as "anti-social," previously engaging in delinquent behavior and abusing alcohol. Annette drew him in black, represented by a boat that is "blocked in" (upper left in Figure 113). She used bright colors for the other family members. Jerry also drew his brother in black and as "outside the family." Similarly, Mr. Tipler depicted him in his boat outside the family circle. He stated that his son's separation from the family was "the greatest hurt the family has had," which he thought might have been caused by his own drinking. Most interesting was the line of identification linking this son to his father and the paternal grandfather. Mr. Tipler said, "I was Paul in my own family," and drew himself as a red frown removed from the others in his childhood family (Figure 114, bottom right). The black square is his father. Similarly, Annette represented the paternal grandfather as a black square (Figure 115, upper right center), saying that he was like Paul. There were many warm

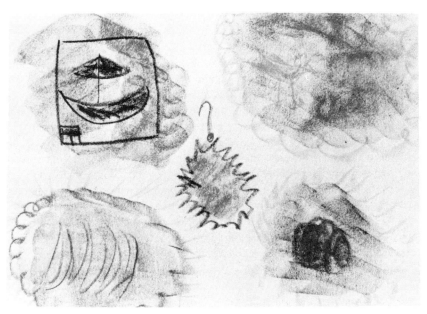

Figure 113.   Annette's symbolic portrait of her alcoholic family.

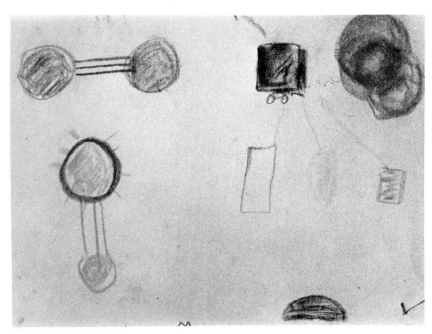

Figure 114.   Symbolic origin families by Mr. Tipler, an alcoholic.

227

associations to the maternal grandmother, especially from Jerry and Annette. These examples and others pointed to an identification with feelings of warmth from the maternal side and of alienation from the paternal side. The strain associated with the latter was less readily admitted.

Further identification was seen between father and daughter, and was acknowledged by both. In describing his representation of her, Mr. Tipler said that they are alike. She drew herself as red like her father (she noted), but with an inner core of green like her mother (Figure 113, lower right). She further identified with her father in the last picture, using the red color again to represent her turbulent early adolescence, when she would sneak out of the house and had become involved in alcohol abuse herself (Figure 116, center). She recalled her father drinking and being angry at that time. She felt that her recovery brought her closer to her parents, a reaction similar to Mr. Tipler's experience that through alcoholism, both the drinking and recovery, he became closer to his family, with the possible exception of the older son, Paul.

In sum, although this family explicitly chose the more desirable identification with the warmth of the maternal family, my assessment was mixed heritage based on the paternal identification described above. The art sessions were especially revealing in this regard. Independent analysis of verbal interview material from many individual and conjoint sessions with this family produced the same results.

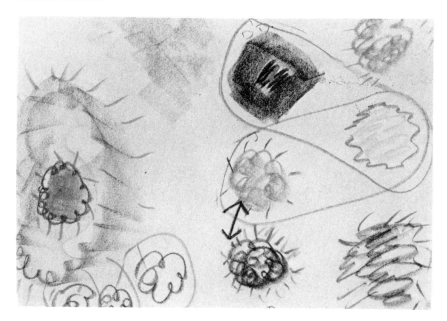

Figure 115.   Annette's ancestral families.

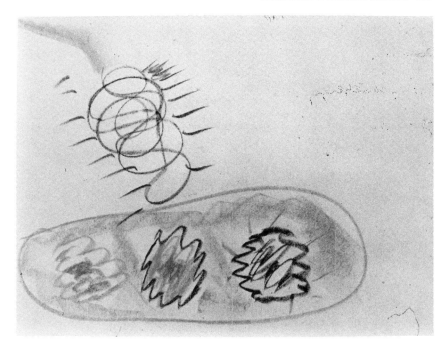

Figure 116.   Annette's depiction of how alcohol consumption in the family affected her life.

Reaction to Alcoholism in the Families

The third picture, "the consumption of alcohol in your family as it has affected your life," provided information about each individual's relation to the drinking behavior. The following patterns emerged: All fathers in the sample were recovered alcoholics who were enthusiastically involved with AA. For the most part, their pictures were positive and optimistic; they felt that recovery had brought them closer to the family, which was symbolized by such images as the sun shining through the clouds. One father described his drawing as follows:

> The most fruit-laden tree I could draw. The fruits are benefits even though the tree's growth is crooked. The sky is glorious. There are deep roots in alcoholism—my father. The fruits are gratitude. Alcohol has enriched my life.

His wife, on the other hand, drew a picture of the sleepless nights she spent waiting for him to come home from his drunken binges. Another wife drew two flowers (Figure 117). She described the larger one as "beautiful or handsome, the way he was when sober." The other, she said, was "wilted with alcohol." The wilted flower may have been related to impotency (a frequent result of

Figure 117.   A wife's representation of her husband sober and drunk.

alcohol abuse), but that was not mentioned. She said she felt "left out." Another wife also felt "left out" until she joined AA with her husband. She represented that period with bright yellow compared to darker colors designating more painful times during his drinking.

The offspring showed greater variety in their reactions. These included anger and withdrawal, confusion, denial, positive feelings, and being little affected. In several of the families the younger children appeared less affected than their older siblings, their father's drinking having stopped relatively early in their lives.

The following are examples of a variety of reactions. In a family where the father's drinking was kept secret, one daughter drew the way she felt when she "heard things at night that weren't discussed." She didn't understand the fights between her parents that she heard at night because their relationship appeared different during the day. She used gray to represent "nebulousness," which she said was like her father's family. The mother was drawn looking at the father, who is "turned away." She drew herself "isolated."

A daughter in another family drew "the taint of alcohol" on the faces of all family members, Figure 118. Although all are colored gray, the gradation varies according to the extent of the "taint." The mother is lightest and the father darkest. On the right are herself, her boyfriend, and other "outlets" which take her out of the family.

On the other hand, the oldest daughter in the same family drew a family scene with lots of people and prominent drinking, saying that alcohol brings about family togetherness. The son drew a similar picture but with himself removed. He said he removes himself from the family because he believes he'll be less likely to become alcoholic if he's less involved with them. He drinks when he's with them, he said, in order "to feel more comforable, like the good old days."

Other Findings

As mentioned above, the art session produced other data in addition to the specific question of heritage dominance it was designed to probe. The overall character of the family emerged in several ways. One was a dimension of liveliness, expressiveness, and engagement. For example, all the pictures made by one family were full and vividly colored, even when dealing with negative feelings. In contrast, a feeling of emptiness pervades all the pictures made by another family. Expressions of anger, withdrawal, and depression were prominent in their pictures.

Figure 118.   The "taint" of alcohol in the family.

Especially striking was the remarkable degree of concordance of symbolization seen in some of the families, similar to Wadeson and Fitzgerald's observation of couples with a manic-depressive member (see Chapter 20). In both studies family members neither saw each other's drawings until completion, nor was there any prior discussion of possible symbols. Three of the four members of one family used trees in their first picture to symbolize the family. In another family, four of the six members symbolized the maternal grandparents' family with a church and the paternal grandparent family with a lake. A family of five displayed the following similarities: two represented the paternal grandfather with a chain and the maternal grandmother with a flower; a brick wall was used by the father to symbolize his own father and by the son to represent his other grandfather; in their first pictures of the nuclear family, two members of the family represented members by trees and two were very similar graphically in the depiction of a road by one and a river by another. Such impressive concordance of symbolization within families is difficult to explain. It has been seen in other families as well (see Chapter 20).

Results

In assessing each family, I made a judgment regarding heritage dominance as paternal, maternal, mixed, or none. (I was unaware at this time of the results of the verbal interviews.) In comparing these assessments with those derived from an independent analysis of the verbal interview material, we found agreement in four of the five families as follows:

Family	Art Evaluation	Verbal Interviews
1	mixed	mixed
2	paternal	paternal
3	mixed (with paternal stronger)	mixed
4	mixed	mixed
5	paternal	maternal

Discussion

Wolin and Bennett's findings regarding the import of heritage dominance has yet to be published. What is interesting here is that the art expression session provided sufficient information for judgments made from many hours of verbal interviews with each family member in addition to a conjoint family verbal interview. Also of interest is that heritage dominance could be studied through art tasks designed to reveal unconscious identifications, as well as through the investigation of family rituals and myths.

Of particular interest to me was the material elicited by the third picture concerning the reactions to alcohol consumption within the family. It was clear that the problem drinker's alcoholic activity affected different family members quite differently: in strongly positive ways for some and in strongly negative ways for others. My experience was that art expression was a particularly sensitive instrument for tapping such feelings. The display of a family's pictures of these feelings gave an especially thorough view of the complexity of the effect of alcohol abuse on family life.

PART FIVE

Group and Family Art Therapy

CHAPTER 19

Group Art Therapy

When one considers the complexities of individual therapy and individual art therapy, the array of considerations becomes exponential in group therapy and group art therapy. The challenge can be exciting. In addition to the many issues brought by each group member, the interrelationships among them and the characteristics of the group itself create a complex and dynamic field. Unless the therapist simply conducts individual therapy in a group setting (as some do), the group dynamics play an important part in the treatment of each individual. Although the focus may be on group interaction, the goal, nevertheless, is still the treatment of each individual.

There are many important considerations in group therapy, such as composition of the group, structure (including rules and contracts), role of the therapist, and so forth. I will not dwell on them here, however, but concentrate instead on the unique aspects of art expression in group therapy. For a comprehensive background in group therapy, I recommend *The Theory and Practice of Group Psychotherapy* by Irvin D. Yalom (1975). I believe his summation of the curative factors in group therapy is especially useful. These factors are:

1. Instillation of hope
2. Universality
3. Imparting of information
4. Altruism
5. The corrective recapitulation of the primary family group
6. Development of socializing techniques
7. Imitative behavior
8. Interpersonal learning
9. Group cohesiveness
10. Catharsis
11. Existential factors (such as inevitability of death)

STRUCTURE

There are many different kinds of art therapy groups. Some may be very informal and loosely structured while others are highly structured. An example of the former might be a hospital art studio where patients may wander in at will, work as long as they like, and discuss their work with the art therapist and/or others in the room or not. Such a group is unlikely to form much cohesiveness, and some therapists would more likely designate it as something more like a gathering rather than a group at all. Groups such as this, and even some that are more structured that meet for the purpose of art production, might more accurately be called art groups which are therapeutic. A more structured group would have a specific membership, meeting time and place, and procedure which would include group discussion. Many art therapy groups fall in between the extremes of loose and tight structure.

Whatever the structure, it is important that ground rules be made explicit from the beginning. (This applies to any form of therapy.) For example, participants in my private practice groups are required to pay for sessions they miss, and this is stated at the outset. I explain that it is important for members to make a commitment to the group. Group cohesiveness and trust are difficult to achieve without it, and members missing sessions frequently produce a disruptive effect.

Certain aspects of structure unique to art therapy differentiate it from conventional group therapy. Space, lighting, and art supplies are obviously important considerations. The art therapist may supply the art materials, or the group participants may furnish them. The sessions will be structured very differently according to the type of media used—material that may be quickly used and requires no elaborate preparation or cleaning up such as magic markers, pastels, ink, crayons, and so on or more time-consuming projects such as clay, stone carving, oil paints, and so on. Materials used and length of the sessions should be determined according to the treatment goals.

Another part of the structure is the use of various techniques. Participants may work spontaneously; they may respond to projects suggested by the art therapist or other group members; and they may work together on shared projects in dyads, small groups, or as a total group.

Obviously, the nature of the population will influence the nature of the group structure. For example, some groups, such as insight-oriented outpatient groups may be eager to share their art expressions with one another; others, such as a group of retarded individuals, may find sharing very difficult. Other aspects of the population will influence structure as well. For example, a group of mothers of institutionalized children no doubt will focus on issues regarding their children, and the art therapist may structure activities for that purpose in accordance with the *raison d'être* of the group.

TIME

A particularly difficult aspect of group art therapy, I have found, is the allocation of time. I always seem to run out of it, even in groups of only four participants meeting for two-hour sessions. Although picture-making may be quick, so much material surfaces that it is usually impossible to deal with it thoroughly in one session. When discussion of a picture is postponed until the next session, often the material is no longer of immediate import, and the picture's author may be in a new place and ready to deal with other issues. When time runs out before adequate picture discussion, my saving hope is that if something needs to be dealt with, it will surface in future pictures. Of course, in groups of populations where verbalization is minimal, insufficient time for adequate discussion is not a problem.

Although in conventional group therapy sessions there may be material that gets postponed due to lack of time, such issues aren't usually recognized in such a way as to incur the frustration that an unexplained, provocative picture does. In conventional group therapy, at any particular session, some members may be relatively passive or simply reactive to others rather than introducing issues of their own. When each member creates an art expression, however, each introduces material, so there is much out on the table, so to speak. In another respect, this phenomenon is advantageous in groups with members who otherwise are withdrawn. Through their art productions, they capture the group's attention, which helps to integrate them into the group.

In considering the structuring of the sessions, the art therapist must make some decisions about time. As already mentioned, the sort of art materials selected will influence the time spent on art work. Naturally, the therapist will not want to interrupt the art work, yet if there is to be sharing and discussion, time must be allowed for it. If the priority in the group is art production, then discussion time may have to be sacrificed, and vice-versa. The art therapist must be very clear about goals for the group in this sense. On the other hand, if an important goal is that the group take responsibility for its own functioning, the art therapist may leave it up to the members to determine the structure around the division of time for art work and discussion.

A further complicating time factor in group art therapy is the problem that not everyone finishes the art work at once. Sometimes one member may cause the group to wait for him or her to finish for an unduly long period of time. In such cases, it is useful to focus the group's attention on this dynamic. In more responsible groups, members will ask for what they want, or enact it, sometimes beginning discussion before a member is finished. The opposite situation is one where a member or members may rush in order not to keep others waiting and thereby truncate some of the value that may be achieved from finishing the art expression. This dynamic, too, can be explored by the group.

In a sense, the time it takes to produce the art work is not time taken away from group interaction, although this is usually a solitary experience spent in getting deeply in touch with oneself. Even when group members don't look at one another's pictures while drawing, much less talk, there is a sort of sharing that differentiates producing art in the presence of others from working in solitude. Certainly, the expectation of later showing the work and discussing it must play a part in this experience. Nevertheless, those expectations do not provide the full explanation. Rather, it might be compared to travelers on different journeys with different destinations feeling the bond of being fellow travelers.

SHARED IMAGES

The most important contribution of group art therapy, I believe, is the sharing of images. As stated earlier, we all think in images to a greater or lesser extent, but seldom share this important aspect of our experience with others. In an art therapy group, members come to know each other and be known by the images they keep. Recurrent symbols, themes, and motifs do not have to be re-explained. There is a feeling of knowing and being known at a very deep and personal level. For example, whenever Lenore used an olive drab sort of color, group members would say, "Lenore is using her ick color." They knew it expressed her unpleasant feeling of disgust. Many aspects of feeling states are noted by group members in this way—change in pictorial style, such as more formed pictures or amorphousness, sensuousness, bleakness, and so forth. At the same time that participants sometimes surprise themselves with the nature of their art expression, they communicate it to others. The reactions of the others are often illuminating for one's own self-exploration.

ROLE OF THE ART THERAPIST IN THE GROUP

The possible roles the art therapist may assume in a group range from being a strong leader to being a facilitator to being a group member. If there are co-therapists they may assume similar or different roles. Sometimes the co-therapist is not an art person but another member of the mental health team, such as a psychiatrist, psychologist, social worker, or nurse. The sort of group leader one chooses to be depends on such factors as type of population, size of group, treatment goals, length of treatment, setting, structure of sessions, and personal style.

I am very aware in my private practice that I serve as a behavior model. The behavior I try to model is that of dedication, acceptance, respect for others, and empathy within a structure of my regulating my own work.

I believe is is very important for therapists to pay attention to power issues. I apply my power to the regulating considerations: length of sessions, admission of members, fees, and so forth. In other areas I make suggestions but don't impose rules: that members take at least a month to terminate, that they arrive on time, and that they be open and honest. I try to model these behaviors. Regarding acceptance and respect, I try not to be judgmental and try to create a climate in the group in which everyone's insights and observations are just as valuable as everyone else's (including mine) and where the client is the ultimate authority regarding his or her own experience. Nevertheless, as a result of transference phenomena, I am usually placed in a position of authority and wisdom, with my reactions carrying more weight than those of others, at least initially.

Related to the sharing of images is the question of whether the art therapist creates art productions in the group or not. At times when I wish to share images with the group, I do so, but more often refrain for the following reasons. My contract with my clients is such that I am being paid to help them with their problems, not to work on my own. Therefore, my sharing with the group, though quite extensive, is limited to what I think will advance the therapeutic process. Often this includes my feelings about the group and individual members and some of my own experience, both past and present. If I am sharing, however, either in pictures or words, only because of *my* need for ventilation, than I am exploiting my clients. Naturally, I do this unaware sometimes, and realize only afterwards that such has been the case. Usually my ventilation is not a gross error, and sometimes may serve the purpose of helping group members to know me better.

Another reason I usually refrain from picture-making in art therapy groups is the time factor discussed previously. An additional picture to explore would reduce the already limited time for the members' pictures. A further reason in some groups is that the art therapist's artistic ability might be intimidating to the members. This might be the case in a children's group, for example. Finally, it's possible that the group might focus on the therapist's picture in order to avoid dealing with their own. This need not be a reason for the therapist's refraining from picture-making if he or she encourages the group to deal with this phenomenon.

Examples of instances when I have participated in picture-making have been when a member wanted to know how others perceived her and requested of the group that each one make a picture of how they saw her; a group was terminating, and I wanted to express my feelings about its ending, along with the others.

An obvious element in the therapeutic relationship in work with groups is the sibling rivalry-like struggle for the therapist's attention, approval, and/or love. Each member may play out this struggle in a recapitulation of the sibling drama of his or her origin family. Hopefully, the group experience will both illuminate these dynamics and provide a "corrective emotional experience." For this to occur, the therapist must try to respond to each member and the group as a whole with honesty and genuineness. Impartiality in the strictest sense is probably impossible as each member stimulates different feelings in the therapist. Nevertheless, if each member feels given to by the therapist, the issue of who-gets-more diminishes. Of significant importance, too, is the creation of a group climate in which members feel they derive much from one another so the therapist is no longer experienced as the only source of nourishment or the hub of the group wheel. This lesson is a milestone for many individuals in their life struggles, helping to supplant the fruitless quest for the all-giving mother or the savior, with the more attainable support they can derive from a constellation of individuals. Certainly no one person, not even a therapist, can live up to the hopes many people have for the perfect relationship. A group, therefore, can demonstrate that a network of people can give more than any one mere mortal.

EXAMPLES FROM ART THERAPY GROUPS

The examples that follow are from two different populations. The first are two groups of adolescents hospitalized at the NIH Clinical Center on a unit studying Family Realtions in Schizophrenia headed by Lyman Wynne, M.D., Ph. D., and A Study in Growth and Adaptation in the Personality Development of the Adolescent headed by Roger Shapiro, M.D. Patients were diagnosed either schizophrenic or adjustment reaction to adolescence. I co-led these groups with art therapist Hanna Yaxa Kwiatkowska early in my art therapy career. The second population came from two groups of women seen in private practice. All were functioning well and many were therapists or therapists-in-training. These groups are more recent therapy experiences without a co-therapist.

HOSPITALIZED ADOLESCENT GROUPS*

Patients on the adolescent unit ranged in age from eighteen to twenty-nine, though most were nineteen. All patients on the unit participated in one of two art therapy groups of four to five patients each. The groups met over a period of six months. We encouraged spontaneous expression in easy media (tempera, pastels, clay) for an hour and a half-hour discussion followed. There was also often significant conversation while the art work was being produced. During the

---

*The following material appeared in Sinrod, Harriet: Communication Through Painting in a Therapy Group. *Bulletin of Art Therapy:* 3 (1964): 133–147.

discussion period, we directed attention to the feelings and reactions of the whole group.

Group art therapy was one of many therapies in which these patients participated. Each met individually with a psychiatrist, took part in group therapy, unit government meetings concerned with ward management problems, family psychotherapy, and family art therapy. Neither the patients nor the therapists, therefore, expected all problems to be explored in group art therapy.

Group art therapy had been conducted on the ward in the past with a different population, and some of the newer patients requested that it be resumed. They wanted more satisfying contact with one another. Although they lived together, they had great difficulty in enjoying anything they did as a group. Several patients also felt that group art therapy would help them to understand themselves. The program was voluntary on a three-week trial basis, after which all who wished to remain were expected to come to each session. No one dropped out after the trial period. We hoped that working together in a non-verbal medium of expression would help the patients develop genuine relationships and learn to understand themselves and each other better.

Communication about Shared Experiences

The common problem most easily handled and discussed by these patients was difficulty in school, which for many had precipitated hospitalization. The subject often appeared in the pictures which led to a great deal of discussion. Henry, at age eighteen, the youngest and noisiest member of the group, wrote several equations that had given him trouble in college but which he no longer found difficult. Then he made a painting (Figure 119) which he described as the two aspects of himself. He said the left side with the square eye and toothy mouth represented his usual self and the messier right side, his disorganized self that couldn't get through school. He continued:

It looks as though there's serenity on one side and distortion on the other . . . a person divided in two, I see myself on the one hand as being a very calm, understanding, liberal-minded person . . . the way I am right now . . . when I am in school . . . a very different sort of person . . . not me . . . very, very anxious. I reached a point where I wasn't able to think. When I saw a car coming toward me, not really caring . . . and after a while this got pretty damn frightening for me.

Many questions could be asked concerning this self-portrait. For example, why did it begin as a house or does the left side really represent a well-organized self? It was the split, however, which caught the group's attention. Others had felt similarly divided. Barbara, for example, to whom academic achievement meant a great deal, spoke of panicking during exams so that she could not produce, although ten minutes later she could recall the material perfectly.

Figure 119.   Henry's picture showing two aspects of himself.

Starting with the shared experience of scholastic difficulties, the group went on to discuss fears of being out of control.

Barbara developed this theme pictorially. At nineteen she was a heavy girl, devoted to academic attainment. She started back to school by taking one college course while at the hospital, and the day after her first class drew pictures expressing the feelings of panic which she had mentioned in response to Henry's picture. Figure 120, in which buses are topsy-turvy, streets one-way, and books scattered around, represents her intense anxiety concerning her return to college, focused on traveling there by bus. "I feel kind of muddled and confused," she said, "as though I don't really know what's going on around me." Others then recalled similar experiences of confusion, especially around the mechanics of entering college, such as registration.

As Barbara worked, she became freer to express the full degreee of her anxiety, and finally produced the entanglement (Figure 121), through which she feels she will have to proceed to get *To Anthropology* as the picture is entitled. Through Barbara's and Henry's pictures the group shared their feeling about the experience of crisis precipitated by college anxieties.

Another college theme was "Paradise Lost." Barbara's picture (Figure 122) of the university she was attending when she "became sick" is much clearer than the disorganized pictures of her current college made at the same session. In the

Figure 120.   Barbara's confusion in returning to college.

Figure 121.   *To Anthropology*, Barbara's anxiety about returning to college.

Figure 122.   The prestigious college Barbara attended prior to her hospitalization.

foreground are ordered hedges and behind them the library where she had her own carrel. With her exaggerated concern about academic achievement, her former college with its greater prestige seemed a "Paradise Lost" as she spoke of it.

At the following session, Barbara continued to make pictures of her local college. George, a less articulate patient, who had been a student there for a short time, was using the same college as his pictorial theme. At age twenty-four, he was the oldest of the group by four years, and was its quietest, most passive member. Next, he made a drawing (Figure 123) representing the college he had attended initially and to which he wished to return. He entitled it *Pipe Dream* and through this picture, without speaking, achieved a very real communication with Barbara.

Another common pictorial subject was war. One of Henry's many war pictures provoked discussion of his preoccupation with war and eventually led the others to delve into their own experiences. Most of their fathers had gone to war during the patients' pre-school years. Peggy said, "We all lost people in the war," but eventually explained with a tone of disgust that her father had used "pull" to stay out of the army. She apparently meant "lost" in an emotional sense. Her family life had been chaotic due to her parents' divorce, their remarriages, and their eventual return to each other.

Henry brought his feeling about conflict closer to home by saying, "It's just like two little boys standing in the street with rocks in their hands. If something

Figure 123.   *Pipe Dream*, George's former college.

should upset the apple cart . . . why do people hate each other?'' Finally Peggy said, "We can all stay at NIH—it has a good bomb shelter," implying that remaining sick and being cared for in an institution is a way to avoid some of life's conflicts.

At a later session, George responded to Henry's many war pictures by making one of his own. He remembered the war years more vividly than the other patients, who were four to six years younger than he. The fighting appears as though on a stage (Figure 124), which is perhaps how he saw the war—as an exciting drama. The picture brought back memories of his jealousy of his father for going to war and his resentfulness at his father's return (when he was about eight or nine).

George seldom contributed to the discussions of other patients' pictures, but often involved himself in the subject with a picture of his own. In this case, he picked up Henry's child-like drawing technique as well. The planes and shower of bullets are typical of stereotyped war pictures made by youngsters. Although this was a regression for George, it is doubtful that Henry had ever progressed beyond the childish level of his drawings (Figures 119 and 126; the latter is typical of his style.)

The Empty Room with Something in It (Figure 125) enabled the patients to share their fears and anger at being considered crazy by others. Barbara painted this picture in great excitement. At the time of these sessions, her behavior was usually giddy. (Earlier she had made several suicide attempts, and later she became severely depressed.)

The solid dark shapes represent furniture, which is covered over with gray and green lines making the figures partially fade into the ground of the painting. Barbara arrived at the art therapy session after having tried to convince one of the building's painters that there was furniture in the locked room she had been using for studying. With much hysterical giggling she recounted the experience:

I said, "I'm not crazy—I know there's something in there. I'm not crazy—please unlock it" (much laughter). This may be the first time he's worked on a mental ward, and he didn't know what to expect. He really looked a bit scared.

To her alarm, when the door was opened she found the room empty. Her confusion and embarrassment are well suggested by her picture and its title. She

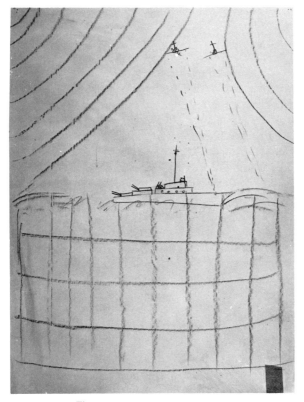

Figure 124. George's war picture.

Figure 125. *The Empty Room with Something In It*, Barbara's doubts about her perceptions and feelings of being considered crazy.

was sure that the painter thought she was "nuts," but her anxiety was due primarily to her own doubts about her perception.

When Barbara first told of the episode, the others responded to the superficial humor of the situation. It was only when they saw her picture, with its ambiguity about what is there and what isn't, that they understood her feelings and were able to voice similar sentiments, especially in regard to being scrutinized by outsiders who looked on them as "crazy people."

Feelings about Each Other

Some of the pictures directly portrayed patients' feelings about each other and others set off a discussion of such feelings. Reactions to Figure 126, for example, taught Henry something about the way he affected people. He often pictured fantasies of omnipotence and aggression; here he shows himself in a soapbox derby which he had wanted to enter as a child. His car is heavily armored and he is smiling while he "annihilates the competition." In the background is a graveyard.

Henry tried to disguise his aggressive and domineering attitudes and apparently saw himself as ingratiating. He tried to win acclaim from the group on the ward by conducting a biology "class" for the others, initiating a charity project in which they would copy him, and suggesting many times that the art therapy group paint to music (his records).

Peggy saw *The Soapbox Derby* (Figure 126) as accurately reflecting Henry's behavior. The group joined her and for the entire half hour discussed their reactions to Henry. Part of the exchange was as follows:

Henry: (referring to his picture) I'm sort of out to get the world. I'm out to win the race.

Peggy: I get that message all the time . . . I feel it's the way you want to control me . . . (angrily) I don't like it one bit.

Henry: One of the motives for the cell class was to do something over which I felt I had some type of control . . . having some kind of respect . . . from other people. But it might turn out that instead of respect . . . I'm sort of alienating them.

Peggy: I feel guilty that I didn't go (to the cell class) and naturally I'm going to feel hostile about it. I don't want these guilt feelings.

Henry: I wasn't really thinking about the reaction I'd get in terms of this.

The group saw his continuous jabbering, whistling, and other efforts to gain center stage as a way of "annihilating the competition." Henry was deeply

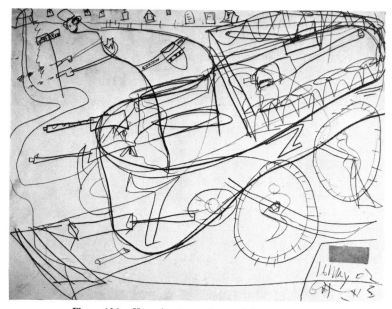

Figure 126.   Henry's attempt "to annihilate the competition" in *The Soap Box Derby* **he had wished to enter as a child.**

impressed when he realized that others saw him as he drew himself, not as he thought of himself.

Stanley, a member of the other group, was the patient who appeared most frequently in the picutures of the others. A slight, nineteen-year-old boy, he was both pompous and quick-tempered, using his red hair as justification for his volatile outbursts. Alan's portrait of him (Figure 127) represents one of his many attempts to needle Stanley.

These two young men were about the same age but otherwise quite different in behavior. Stanley was pedantic and moralistic, maintaining an old-fashioned air of superior virtue. Alan, tall, dark, and good-looking, had discarded his shoes and acquired a shaggy beard. He was bright, often subtly sarcastic, but passive and listless.

While Stanley was afraid of his own violent anger and his poor control over it, Alan took a certain delight in Stanley's tantrums. By provoking Stanley, he could experience vicariously the rage he was incapable of expressing directly. Once when Stanley smashed a Coke bottle in fury, Alan said, "If I got mad, that's how I'd like to do it."

Stanley drank a great many Cokes and had brought one with him to the particular session at which Figure 127 was produced. In the picture the outlandish little fellow seems mesmerized by the overpowering Coke. Alan commented, "Stanley might think that it's him, and I don't want him to be insulted."

On this occasion, however, Alan's teasing missed its mark, and instead of becoming angry, Stanley luxuriated in the attention the picture brought him. He wallowed in his "only vice":

How weak I am—the Coke bottle has complete control . . . you can see I am a slave to the Coke . . . look what it's done to me . . . After all, it's one of the my philosophies of life that life without one vice is no life at all . . . so far Cokes are my only vice.

He happily ascribed his dependency to Coca Cola addiction and dropped his usual officiousness to enter eagerly into the discussion of the other pictures. Alan had portrayed Stanley's oral needs, and the group, through interested comments and questions, had recognized them in a way Stanley could accept and enjoy.

Although Peggy was not in the same art therapy group with Stanley, her feeling about him came out in Figure 128. At age twenty, Peggy was a lively, pretty blonde, often openly hostile. The previous night Stanley had kicked her (notice the big feet in her portrait of him) because she had called him effeminate. She drew him emerging from a dark storm and moving toward a red fire. She said she was glad he was not bigger, but nevertheless found him frightening. She was able to recognize that her fear of his anger touched off concern about her own

Figure 127.   Alan's portrayal of Stanley in an attempt to needle him.

Figure 128.   Stanley emerging from a dark storm toward a fire, drawn by Peggy.

ability to control herself. At another time, she drew a cyclone which she saw as herself out of control, as in her two previous psychotic episodes.

Peggy's picture of Stanley also helped her and Barbara to recognize shared feelings. Barbara often painted fires which were never hot nor big enough to suit her. "Fire," Peggy remarked, "represents conflict." During the discussion of Peggy's drawing of Stanley, the following exchange occurred:

Hanna K.: I wonder how disturbing it is to the group that one member of the group feels . . .

Barbara: . . . like killing another.

Barbara and Peggy thus expressed their understanding of each other's feelings both verbally and pictorially. Fire had the same symbolic meaning for both of them.

The only topic that ever brought Alan and Stanley together was the discussion of plans for the perfect murder. Stanley, the impulsive one, advocated a grandiose and elaborate design for revenge. In his scheme nothing was left to chance. Alan, who was actually unable to act on his feelings, argued for spontaneous violence as a result of sudden anger. Both favored acts foreign to their natures. As Alan spoke, he dripped red paint and linseed oil on his paper and saw the result (Figure 129) as an expression of what he was saying. Referring to the conversation, he said the picture "seems to have been a portent of what was coming." Alan seldom expressed his real feelings this effectively and they never came out in action. Most of his pictures were very empty, and often only intellectual exercises.

Figure 130 is a picture Alan drew when Peggy, who was in the other group, happened to attend a session of his group. The two had been attracted to one another, and their flirtation had made the other patients very uncomfortable. Alan had finally broken off the relationship, probably because it was too frightening. Peggy's presence apparently prompted him to make the picture, which he saw as representing "insidious evil." To his annoyance, Peggy said she found it pleasant. Alan designated the object on the left as claws. He spoke of "little fleshy grasping things" which for him were "terrifying" and said that Peggy should talk to her psychiatrist about "why she thinks evil things look pleasant." She countered: "I don't believe in that sort of evil. I think it's all phony. I don't think people are trying to grab out and claw you."

For the group composed of Barbara, Henry, Peggy, and George, the art therapy experience was relatively successful, although naturally some sessions were more productive than others. The group was continually faced with such problems as Peggy's bossiness, Henry's thinly veiled aggression, Barbara's

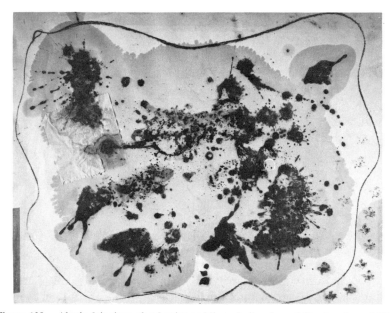

Figure 129.   Alan's drippings of red paint and linseed oil as he and Stanley planned "the perfect murder."

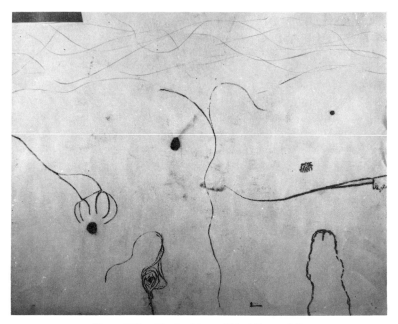

Figure 130.   Alan's picture of "insidious evil."

passive resistance, and George's isolation. Peggy's eventual psychotic breakdown provided an additional difficulty for the others. In general, however, the
pictures tended to become more expressive and communication among the
patients gradually improved. The members of this group came to understand
themselves and each other better.

The other group, however, never really consolidated; each member remained
isolated from the others. The sessions were just beginning to become lively when
one of the members was discharged from the hospital. Stanley had been fond of
her, and on her departure his attacks on Alan became more relentless. Alan
seemed to wither, and withdrew further from the group. The other two members,
who in general isolated themselves, were reluctant to come out of their shells into
the charged atmosphere produced by the constant feuding between Stanley and
Alan.

These inpatient groups were very different from the private practice groups
described below. There are factors more often found in a hospital setting which
influence group functioning. An obvious one is that often patients are not in the
hospital by choice and therefore may be resistant to the activities provided them.
Because adolescents are frequently resistant, as well, we were careful to
compose these groups on a voluntary basis even though we required a
commitment if the patient wished to continue after the three-week trial period. If

there had been no commitment, it would have been even more difficult to achieve cohesiveness. One device we used was to have soft drinks brought in for the discussion period. Although not intended as such, this enabled some of the patients to maintain that they were coming for the drink—a face-saving measure for those who needed to maintain resistance temporarily.

In the hospital setting the tone during art production was often more relaxed than in other therapy situations. Concentration was centered on the activity. In verbal therapy, patients often felt pressured to bring up specific problems. In the art groups, problems frequently come to light naturally and spontaneously as a result of their appearance in the art work.

Paradoxically, art activity in the hospital, which draws some people closer to the group, may also help to isolate certain members. Sometimes patients become so absorbed in their work that they are almost oblivious of others. This is beneficial when they are fully engrossed in creative pictorial expression. On the other hand, solitary absorption in the work may serve as a defense against closeness and exchange with others.

Because each patient produces a tangible object, the experience for the more withdrawn and less verbal patients may take a more favorable course than in conventional group therapy. Patients who remain isolated in verbal therapy groups and on the hospital ward become participants in group art therapy through their art productions. Even when they do not contribute to the discussion, their art work may provide a means of contact with others, as was the case with George. A picture by a withdrawn patient sometimes displays an unexpected aspect of his or her personality which may stimulate interest and eventually serve to draw him or her closer to the group.

As in other group therapies, a common pitfall for the therapist is that of being monopolized by some patients so that effectiveness with the group as a whole is lessened. In some respects, the introduction of art heightens this possibility when the art therapist must make materials available and is occasionally called upon for technical assistance. This problem occurs more often in the hospital with the dependency institutionalization fosters; these demands may be used to manipulate the therapist.

Art production in groups such as these introduces a new element of pride or shame in performance. Added to verbal performance is the production of pictures and sculpture. Some may feel initially inadequate in this activity. Others may derive great satisfaction from it from the start. For some mental patients, art work may be the only area in their lives where they feel some degree of competence. At any rate, it is possible in the art therapy room for people to recognize in themselves and each other expressive abilities they had not seen before.*

*Another hospitalized patient group in which art expression was utilized is described in Chapter 10. The purposes and structure of this group were very different from the adolescent groups.

PRIVATE PRACTICE GROUPS OF WELL-FUNCTIONING ADULTS

I have found results from art therapy groups in private practice to be more substantial than those in the hospital. There are several obvious reasons: higher motivation, longer duration, greater consistency of membership (not influenced by hospital admissions and discharges), and greater intrapsychic and interpersonal resourcefulness of the members.

A group can serve as an incubator for those who wish to molt the constraining shell of painful living patterns during the vulnerable process of developing new patterns. Since my belief is that much of life's problems stem from lack of acceptance of self, usually rooted in childhood family experience, my goal in the group is to foster an accepting, non-judgmental, caring milieu of the sort most people have never experienced. In the supportive group matrix I try to create, there is encouragement in the quest for meaning. The group can be a resource for both nurturance and clarification.

Both private practice groups presented here were composed of all women ranging in age from mid-twenties to mid-fifties. Most were therapists or therapists-in-training, and more than half were art therapists and art-therapists-in-training. There were six people in each group. Meetings were once a week for a two-hour session. Both groups met for approximately eighteen months. There was usually some talking first to determine where people were, to deal with the week-long reactions to the last session, then picture-making, then discussion of pictures. Sometimes a topic grew out of the initial discussion, but most of the time each did her own thing.

The following material illustrates shared experiences and feelings about one another in the group. In some instances, there were feelings and quests for understanding and growth never so fully shared with others before. Experiences of the group as a whole, one another, and me as the therapist revealed present relationships and fostered their growth, including all the transference phenomena and projections one might expect.

These were very verbal groups. It is impossible to reproduce the communication within the group as each person's picture was responded to by the others. A reciprocity ensued whereby each felt understanding of others and understood herself. Often free associations by others to one's own picture were enlightening and much appreciated. Both groups became supportive and cohesive with a high level of trust. Much affection and caring developed as well.

Where possible I have used the creator's own comments about her picture. I requested permission from all group members to use their pictures and invited them to write their own comments about them. Although the comments were prepared months after the pictures were made and, therefore, do not capture the immediacy of the experience or the interchange among group members, nevertheless, the group members' own comments more nearly approximate the meaningfulness of the pictures than what I might say about them.

Shared Experience

Images of experience echoed in that of others in the group, especially around nodal developmental issues, undercut feelings of isolation and differentness, and promoted feelings of connectedness and community. Although much sharing of experience occurred around particular pictures, occasionally there was a central focus which emerged out of the initial discussion. One example was the feeling of being judged. Cindy wrote about her picture (Figure 131):

The first thing that came to my mind was a finger pointed at me. In the actual drawing the figure pointing at me is much larger and I appear as a child. I appear small, weak, helpless—I'm looking at the ground. The feelings that the smaller figure evoke in me are helplessness, worthlessness, rejection and depression. The small figure is also angry but can't express it to the overbearing larger figure. The larger figure represents my mother, (who, by the way, was physically much shorter and smaller than I)—but it also represents the many older authoritarian females in my life that I have feared. The older female figure is chewing me out, demanding that I be perfect and refusing to listen to me. I can hear her yelling "Don't you talk back. You're ugly when you talk back." This thought brought back the memory of three younger boys on the school bus calling me the "ugly old witch" and laughing at me. I was very sensitive to being called "ugly" and they, too, were judges in my life. I pictured them in the upper right hand side watching and laughing at me. As a child and teenager I was convinced I was ugly, and it was hopeless to ever think I might be pretty. It was many years before I felt I was attractive to others—but I still cringe when an older woman has authority over me. I feel that I am reliving a scene with my mother (whose approval I constantly strove for) when she would reprove me or

Figure 131.   Cindy's feelings of being judged.

criticize me. My self worth becomes involved. Disapproval seems to mean worthlessness, but this only occurs with older women.

Many of these reflections had surfaced in Cindy in response to looking at her picture.

Cindy was to explore this theme further when she was interviewed for a promotion by a particularly harsh older woman. She acknowledged an approach/avoidance feeling towards me which was partially based in her early experience of being judged unworthy by her mother. For example, she gave me these written comments almost immediately after I requested them (to please me), and then was certain I wouldn't include them (disapproval).

Marty made a picture related to judgment and spoke of the "dark, angry, dead" face of her mother (Figure 132). Her voice became very quiet and controlled. When I commented on this, she said her mother's voice was like that. This is what she wrote.

The Good and the Bad Mother In Me. I tried to draw that part of me that sits in judgement of myself. I had just become aware of how I criticize myself. How nothing I do is right for myself that sits inside. And that to others I am a good mother—caring about, forgiving, accepting, and I tried to do this each moment for myself. It shows the me now, in the center—the inside hating, yelling at me, and on the left that care-worn, hurting part of me, and above, that good mother, hands holding and caring about all these parts of me. Judgement—I judge myself and began to want to forgive myself.

Linda had felt envious of her husband's career. At the same time she felt judged by him. In Figure 133, she drew him as the large impenetrable solid blob on the right. She is the smaller explosive form on the left. She saw herself as small and angry. She was particularly anxious at this session in relation to getting into graduate school whereby she would achieve professional status comparable to her husband's. She commented as follows:

Feelings about Authority. I don't like how I feel when an "authority" comes on and tells me what to do. If *they* are unruffled and appear to have IT solidly together I feel insecure like I'm all over the place, like I've blown my cover and I'm coming apart. I have lots of anger about feeling in the one-down position—often I don't allow that anger to surface, at least in a productive way. I tend to put a lid on those feelings, the grey stone top on my picture. I don't allow myself to feel, and I function like a robot and do what I should. As a result of the group's input I learned that this picture illustrated how I feel when my husband presents himself as a CRITICAL PARENT. When he's passive-aggressive he cuts through me and I feel shattered and angry.

Several months later she portrayed their relationship quite differently. In Figure 134, they are entwined organic forms without one dominating the other. Linda was particularly pleased with the spaces she had left in their joining. She also took delight in the sensuous quality of the drawing, finding pleasure in rhythmically smearing the colors with her fingers.

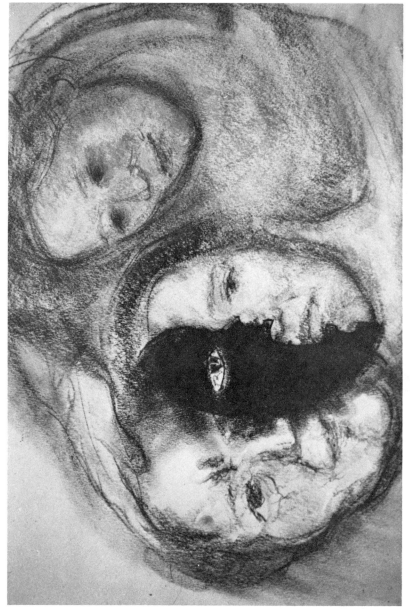

Figure 132. *The Good and Bad Mother in Me*, Marty's judgment of herself.

Figure 133. *Feelings about Authority*, Linda's experience of feeling judged by her husband.

Figure 134.   Linda's subsequent expression of her relationship with her husband in which they are entwined.

At times Sharon took on the role of the free spirit in her group. She was an attractive young woman with a big smile. When she drew a detailed picture of a naked woman with legs spread apart, the group launched on an exploration of sexuality. There was much sharing of childhood prohibitions, fears, and curiosity about penises.

Marty had entered the group in turmoil shortly after the break-up of her twenty-year marriage. She and Sharon, both art therapists and able artists, drew many pictures overtly sexual and sensual. In Figure 135, Marty recognized that she and the man aren't touching. She wrote:

Maybe Someday. Sharon was drawing male organs—her female body. I drew myself—open—soft—felt a softness and sadness in me. Wanting to be with a man but feeling the space that separated me from anyone. A sadness for my sexuality and my loneliness.

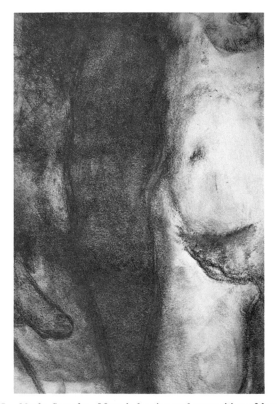

Figure 135. *Maybe Someday*, Marty's longing and recognition of her separation from a man.

The week following, Marty stayed in bed with stomach pains. She drew a picture of it (Figure 136). She began with the stomach, added her body and then the penis. She wrote:

Stomach Tied in Knots. Two weeks previously my separated husband had informed me he was living with someone else. After two weeks of great pain and working through it, a friend invited me to meet a male friend of his. After the evening, I felt in a panic—pushed back against the wall. Those feelings and hating myself for such fears. I actually twisted my stomach in knots—felt old ulcer pains. Talking about it in the group I drew me—wanting—female—a penis about to enter me—and blocked by this horrible painful twisting and knotting of my insides. It felt as tight and wrapped up—walled off as I felt—I wanted to let all those walls open and the tightness out—but I was so afraid to.

Some months later, at a happier time for her, she drew a vividly colored picture of herself and a new man in her life passionately embraced, noting that for the first time there wasn't a space between herself and the man.

Marion began making copious pictures at home which she brought into the group. She depicted bodily parts and her exploding passion in red bursts. She felt guilt and shame over her attraction to men other than her husband. One of the pictures was of me with long "sensuous" hair. Her hair was short. On another occasion she commented that my clothes were too revealing. She seemed to be projecting onto me her conflict about the shamefulness of her sexual wishes.

Ann had had a sexually repressive Catholic upbringing. After raising five children, she moved out of her husband's bedroom, and they had not had regular sexual relations for several years. Ann had difficulty talking about sex and was embarrassed by the others' pictures. This is what she wrote about her picture:

The Anatomical Penis (Figure 137). The issue of the therapy session had been sex. Others had drawn erotic impressions of their experiences, and I said I couldn't *look* at a penis much less draw one. My "homework" was to draw one *from life!* I talked jokingly about it to my husband, but couldn't bring myself to it, though he raised no objections. At the following session, I quickly dashed this one off. I noted that it was quickly drawn, unattached to any body, and becomes part of a hearts and flowers sketch which was derived from motifs of breasts, behinds, and part of a torso. Definitely a discomforting subject, beladen with romantic notions.

(Her "homework" had been to draw a penis; she had assumed it was to be done from life.)

Several weeks later, Sharon seemed to come to a spontaneous resolution involving her sexuality:

Me Swinging From the Tree (Figure 138). This picture was a real high for me. Although I don't have a very good grip on the tree, I feel fresh and free. I felt like telling the group that I feel good about sex, my body and that that gives me a certain amount of freedom. I also wanted to communicate the childlike fun I was feeling. I was amazed to discover that I drew this figure in the branches of the tree. For two years my self portraits

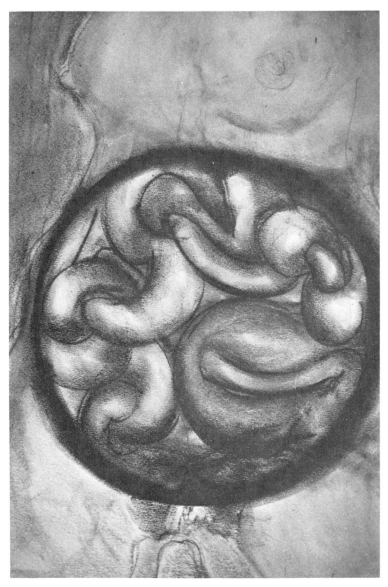

Figure 136. *Stomach Tied in Knots*, Marty's fear of being with a man.

Figure 137. *The Anatomical Penis*, **Ann's discomfort with sex.**

had been intimately linked with the base or roots of trees which I considered grounded, stable, and strong. Yet the role I was playing was also depressing and stifling. This picture gives me the feeling that I've made it through something. I don't have to hide anything and the tree is back together.

Although sex was not dealt with in such a focused manner by the other group, nevertheless, sexual concerns emerged spontaneously from time to time. Hearing others express their warmth and tenderness toward other women and their daughters allowed Sonia to become less fearful of physical intimacy, to become close to other group members, and eventually to hug them. In this supportive environment she dealt with her sexuality in the following pictures and wrote her comments about them. Figure 139:

I tried to draw my thirty-seven-old body and found that at that period in time I couldn't own my adult sexuality; rather I drew myself with pigtails and ribbons about age eight. The eyes are closed—I can't even bare (sic) to ''see'' my own sexuality. The body is that of a slim young female. The realization of this arrested sexual attitude caused me to weep angry tears—the black dot on the shoulder was caused by my tears as I drew the picture. The red and black are anger and rage. Not many months later, I would now be able to draw my present self—accepting, eyes open—I have worked through a great deal.

Figure 138. *Me Swinging from a Tree*, Sharon's good feelings about sex and her body and her resultant feelings of freedom.

265

Figure 139.   Sonia's anger at her "arrested sexuality."

Figure 140:

Variations of this face can be found in several other of my drawings—I see several things in it—a feeling of my own "craziness"—this person—the anima and animus—a kind of temptress with the rose in the mouth, the tropical blossoms at the neck; the red chain that outlines the face is anger. The flowers and smoke at the top grow out of the anger over this whole problem of the struggle to come to terms with my own femaleness. The black patch like the closed eyes is my resistance to look at the issues. The pink background is sensuousness.

Figure 141:

It seems to me I have begun to accept my adult sexuality—the lady is not slim and youthful. It is rather a bit plump and suggests voluptuousness. The blossoms are hibiscus; they are full and lush. Violet means sensuousness for me here; the light blue is a nurturing love; the deep blue is sexuality.

Figure 140.   Sonia's feelings of craziness in trying to come to terms with her femaleness.

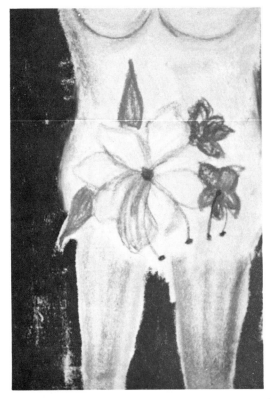

Figure 141.   Sonia's feelings of acceptance of her adult sexuality.

Feelings about the Group and One Another

The aliveness of relatedness found expression in the here and now sharing of feelings about the group, about me, the complex issues of transferential feelings, including anger and idealization, and views of one another. Obviously the communication of these images provided valuable feedback and an opportunity for shared perceptions of the group matrix which was a common experience. Opportunity for the sharing of images around a common experience, especially an emotionally charged one, is rare for most people.

In her picture of the group, Ann remarked that she saw power as masculine and put it central in the picture, giving it a crown (Figure 142). She did not include me among the members, and perhaps identified me with the central power. She wrote as follows:

The Power Thing. It was my feeling that one of the issues we all face is that of power. So I drew the group on a field of growing green, dancing around the elusive crown of power. I show myself as a small circle of blue loosely entwined with green shoots as I relate to each member. The green figure I saw as envious of the therapist's career; the red as aggressively seeking high army rank; the vertical blue as still concrete; the curled-up blue as convoluted with pain; the pink as Pollyanna. I do not admire that I depict myself so small, however, and believe it is connected with not assuming power in my life.

Marion resented Marty's early dominance of the group and felt "unnoticed" by her. In Figure 143, she joined forces with Sharon (at that time one of the group's more outspoken members), in what she conceived as an effort to squelch Marty. She and Sharon are the two large trees, and Marty is the small one between them, deprived of light and space.

At a later time, Marty thought she might have to leave the group for financial reasons. Figure 144 was drawn spontaneously, and Marty saw it as depicting her feelings for the group. She is at left and the group forms a "bridge over troubled waters" for her to cross to the future. She decided to remain in the group and borrow the money if necessary. Despite negative feeling expressed toward her, such as that in Marion's picture, Marty found much support in the group. This is what she wrote:

The Group is the Bridge. I talked about leaving the group—I had gotten so much—I'd changed—it was time to move on. Because that's what I was supposed to do. And on the left I drew me—with the old pain and grief and death behind me now—no longer inside, and the bridge was all the colors of the group—and all the new colors that mean for me new life—and they formed a bridge. Underneath was the deep water I had gone over. Above golden sky and that new turquoise blue—the future color—is the sun. And on the

Figure 142. *The Power Thing*, Ann's picture of the group.

Figure 143.   Marion's resentment of Marty and her effort to pair with Sharon.

Figure 144.   *The Group is the Bridge*, Marty's reflection on her progress.

right all the new colors and new people—arms open for me. And I told the group what I wanted from each of them, at Harriet's invitation, and I did and do want to get something from each one and from the whole group—and so I stay—for me—

Transference Images

In my early work, I was insufficiently aware of the projections and distortions that are the transferential aspects of the therapeutic relationship. In the hospitalized adolescents' group, therefore, there is focus on the patients without discussion of how they related to the therapists. In the more recent adult private practice groups, on the other hand, attention was paid to this all-important phenomenon. What follows illustrates the inflated views, the distortions, idealizations, and exaggerated anger.

At the next session, Marty drew a picture of her relationship with me (Figure 145). She said she enjoyed the picture greatly. She saw it as "a warm intermingling." Marty is a practicing art therapist and at times had taken on the role of therapist in the group. At this point, however, her competition with me seemed to have given way to a mutuality of warm sharing. She wrote:

Harriet and Me: Giving and Getting, the Double Helix, the Chain of Life. There were many feelings about Harriet in the group—some angers. I began to draw—I drew me on the right—lower—but began to draw lines—sharing—back and forth and began to feel warm and happy and sharing. That there were things we gave each other—giving and

Figure 145.   *Harriet and Me: Giving and Getting, the Double Helix, the Chain of Life*, by Marty.

getting—and that interaction was where life and growth exists. This was for me a happy picture.

Laura, an art therapy student in her mid-twenties, described in Chapter 16, was the youngest member of either group. Her image of me was very idealized (Figure 146). She wrote:

I see Harriet as a goddess. I want her to be a goddess, for how else can she help me out of my dungeon. If I am so low down in the ground, she must be high in the sky to pull me up. Then we can both be on earth, human. I know Harriet is not a goddess. She is human and earthy, the earth mother. She too has a shield against the pain radiating inside, like me. But she glows. She carries a goddess behind her—a many-armed Hindu goddess. This is how I relate to her, as a goddess, loved and feared. I cannot get near—I can barely put myself in the picture—so close.

Figure 146.   Laura's depiction of the therapist as a goddess.

The small face at the left is Laura's own.

Lenore's picture of her relationship with me (Figure 147) began as an idealization but she discovered much more in it, leading to important insights about herself:

Woman and Child or Girl and Doll. This picture was drawn to depict my perception of how I saw my therapist. Originally, I had in mind as I began to depict the therapist an all-loving, all-caring figure. As the picture evolved, it developed into something quite different. I saw myself as the doll-like figure arching back ridgidly from this all-too-sweet woman. The blue surrounding me indicated my way of distancing myself and the red in the figure expressed my anger and fear of being possessed and of being deceived by her. The woman's expression appears very sadistic and her grasp almost a squeezing-to-death action. The green around the woman figure was used to denote growth which she wanted and could help foster in the child. As I flipped the drawing and became the woman, I was able to identify with her as the way I keep people at a distance and how I feel the need to be all-controlling and powerful. This is probably one of the most powerful pictures I have done and has a lot more to say to me when I am ready to reap more from my exploration of it.

The other side of the all-giving mother, of course, is the withholding mother. Sonia, an art therapy student, had seen me at a professional meeting the previous evening and felt unbalanced in the brevity and superficiality of our relating there, as compared with the therapy sessions. These feelings gave rise to her picture of her relationship with me (Figure 148). She wrote the following about it:

I picture myself as a hungry little blue bird looking kind of helpless, cut off, pathetic. I have to wait to be fed by Mother bird. The red diagonal is my anger. I am angry about being kept *dependent* (this in relationship to my former psychiatrist who I believe infantilized me with her smother-love). The little bird would like more nurturing without having to ask.

I had seen Ann in individual art therapy sessions for eight months prior to her joining the group. Much of that time was spent on her dealing with her envy and fear of me and the question of making a commitment to therapy. This issue was reflective of her indecision about almost everything in her life. She often became very dissatisfied with herself for not being able to follow through on anything. She reached a turning point in the group, stating that her therapy was the most important thing she was doing in her life at this time. Her behavior changed, too, and she became more assertive and positive. Connected with these changes was a dream she had about me. She drew a picture of it (Figure 149), and wrote the following:

Dream About Therapist. Had had stand-back attitude toward therapist. That is, after having had initial admiration for her—her lyrical voice, good looks, and fine capacity to verbalize information and concepts—a personal booboo of hers toward me had damn near annihilated me. Viewed from my personal angle of low self concept and rejection by

Figure 147. Lenore's *Women and Child or Girl and Doll*, a transference picture.

Figure 148. Sonia's relation to the therapist, anger at waiting to be fed.

Figure 149. Ann's *Dream about Therapist*.

others, it was all I could do for a long time to keep my own feelings from overriding my respect for her ability and integrity as a therapist. Then out of the blue, as I had quit trying to deal with that as I had plenty to think about with others in the therapy group, I had this dream. All very hazy with lots of unremembered figures, but ending with my approaching the therapist with very tender feelings and embracing her, putting my face next to hers. Not a thing I would easily do, even now, but I recognized its importance. She had become trustworthy; and it was good to have someone, for some reliable periods in my life, that I could trust. Other parts of the picture dealt with other troubling issues at that time centering around rejection.

I had seen Sharon also in individual art therapy sessions prior to her joining the group. Figure 150 is her picture of her relationship with me. She wrote:

Harriet and Me. The hot pink and the sun are Harriet, bright and alive yet a bit too flashy. Actually that's a part of myself which I love but gives me a lot of trouble lately. It seems to be too much show. There's an umbilical cord attached to the part of the black tree, representing my conflicts and heavy problems, that I hide behind the flashy colors. Harriet is my link to that. So in a way she's a Mother figure to me or some kind of life-line. Fire is dripping from the sun, destroying a very natural tree that was also me. It's like the process of going through therapy, of attaching myself to disowned parts of me through Harriet, will be painful and self-destructive. I'm a little scared of the power I give Harriet in this drawing.

Sharon was an art therapy student. She made frequent comments about my career, relating it to her own aspirations, identifying with me and using me as a

Figure 150.   *Harriet and Me*, by Sharon.

model in this regard. Her picture of a dream (Figure 151) expresses her anxiety in this area. She described it as follows:

In this dream I'm at an Art Therapy Convention in a large, fancy hotel. I'm attending a seminar (lower left) and feeling very happy because at the end of the hour the professor is going to hand out special invitations to students to attend a fancy tea honoring the greatest art therapists. The reason I am happy is because I am sure I will receive one of these few cards. I followed all the proper procedures and sent in my forms the day I received them in the mail. I am in fact snickering a little because I know I am in and others are out. Alas, the hour is up and I do not receive my card. I ask the professor if there is some mistake. He assures me that there is not. Almost immediately I spring into action with a plan. If I cannot get in with an invitation, then I will be the first one at the door. Either I can sneak in or I can wait tables! Surely no one will object to that. I dash through the lobby. The lobby is transformed into a supermarket (lower right). I don't understand. There doesn't seem to be any way out. I see my daughter. She wants me to push her around on the cart. "No," I say, "I gotta go." I dash out and rush to the room where the reception will be held (upper left). I am delighted because no one is there. I peek in the room and see tables set with fancy china and linen table cloths. I HAVE MADE IT! Just then two of my classmates arrive. They look like high school graduates in their matching white dresses. They explain that they are serving tea at the reception and that this was all arranged in advance. "When?" I shout, "No one told me anything!" They shake their heads. They know and I know that I won't be allowed in without a white dress.

By concretizing the elements of her dream in a picture, Sharon was able to draw together a constellation of concerns—remnants of inadequacy feelings from adolescence, being accepted in her education and career, the intrusion of parental responsibilities, and indirectly, her relationship to me as she tries (and fails in the dream) to make a place for herself in the art therapy profession.

Because people are often stuck in patterns of relating, especially to people in authority (parental roles), the sharing of images around the shared experience of relating to me was very valuable. Seeing both similarities and differences in perspectives as well as relationships to childhood experiences in oneself and one another was important. Also, highly charged feelings, both negative and positive, could be communicated to the group, including me, without untoward consequences. This interaction led to greater trust and confidence, both in the self and in others.

When I told each group that I wanted to present and possibly publish this material, all were interested and eager to participate. They gave me permission to use any pictures I chose with one exception. Cindy asked me not to show the drawing of her husband naked because he's modest. Most took quite a bit of time to write their comments about the pictures I had selected. I had expected some hesitancy due to the personal and confidential nature of the material. I believe the enthusiasm to have their experiences communicated to others is indicative of the value these groups held for their members. They have been growth-producing for me as well—an important and significant part of my life journey, too.

Figure 151.   Sharon's dream about being accepted into art therapy.

Figure 152.   Group termination picture: birth and death of the cat.

I'll close this chapter with a drawing I made at the final session of one of the groups. Shortly before our meeting I discovered that my cat had been hit by a car. I found her dead body in the grass where she must have limped. There were wild strawberries growing beside her. I began my picture (Figure 152) with no idea in mind, but as I smeared the soft colors, my cat emerged covered with the membrane I had seen at her birth. I added the strawberries and was reminded of the story of the Zen monk who reached for the luscious strawberry as he was about to be devoured by a tiger. My association was that my cat was being born into the void of death (the background). A small pale butterfly on the grass was immobile, and I thought it was dead until it flew away. (It is difficult to see at upper left in the reproduction.) The soft colors of the picture expressed my tender feelings toward the group. Unintentionally the picture was a condensation of many feelings: grief for my cat, grief for the death of the group, the beauty and joy of life (grass, strawberries, butterfly) all knitted together with tender feelings toward the group, experiencing in its ending the joy and sorrow of the cycles of life and death.

CHAPTER 20

Family Art Therapy

Family art therapy was developed by Hanna Yaxa Kwiatkowska, working closely with Lyman Wynne, M.D., Ph.D., in the Family Studies Section of the Adult Psychiatry Branch of NIMH at the NIH Clinical Center. Wynne was interested in family studies in schizophrenia to investigate the links between family interaction and the development of schizophrenic offspring. Kwiatkowska, working within the major hypotheses of these studies, introduced modes of art therapy treatment and evaluation of the families studied at NIH. (See Kwiatkowska, 1978.) From her pioneering work in the 1960s, others have branched out to adapt her methods and develop new ones for using art therapy with many kinds of families in various treatment settings.

The rationale for family therapy is rooted in the recognition that an individual's learned responses to life and difficulties in living evolve from and are a part of an ongoing network of family relationships. Before the advent of family therapy there were many instances where a patient showed improvement in the hospital only to return home to a family situation that promoted decompensation. Such occurrences may be reduced by the change in perspective which has been fostered by family therapy, where the individual is viewed as a part of a familial matrix. The resultant pathology, therefore, is viewed as residing in that matrix rather than in the individual alone. As a consequence, it is the family that undergoes treatment rather than only one of its members.

The systems theory approach was applied to families by Don Jackson, M.D., and modified by Murray Bowen, M.D., in the 1950s, and led to the development of family therapy as a discipline of study and treatment. In a systems approach, the family is conceptualized as a homeostatic system in which change in one part affects every other part. There are other approaches as well, but underpinning all family therapy is the concept that individaul development is an outgrowth of relationship experience in one's earliest and most basic social unit, the family.

Family myths have been viewed as both evidence and influence of a pronounced family culture. Sometimes those myths are held so rigidly that no allowance is made for change. For example, there may be no recognition that a mischievous young boy has grown into a responsible adolescent, and the family myth may remain that he is still the rascal within the family, particularly if he has been viewed as taking after another family rascal.

As a result of the recognition of the complex intermeshing of influences within the family, the focus in family therapy is on relationship issues which often involve perceptions and expectations of members. Individual issues are viewed in the context of the family matrix. The range of dimensions of family functioning is broad and complex: boundaries, identifications, bonds, alliances, splits, roles, rules, myths, and modes of communication, to name only a few.

In exploring the family in therapy, "family" may be understood as a very specialized sort of group. Many aspects of group therapy, therefore, apply to family therapy as well. Unique to the family, of course, are generational differences among members, the ongoing (lifetime) nature of relationships, the intensity of involvement over time, and, especially, the breeding ground that the family group provides for its members, fostering primary attitudes toward life, as well as producing extensive needs and expectations among its members.

A common problem in family therapy is the resistance of one member. Frequently it is the member whom the family designates as "the problem," such as a rebellious adolescent. Sometimes the resistant one refuses to come or comes and refuses to participate. If the individual never shows up for a session, there may not be much the therapist can do to reach him or her. If the reluctant member does attend, there is much that can be done. Often he or she feels unheard in the family and finds in the therapy session the opportunity to be "heard" by the therapist and to be taken seriously. Such a person has probably felt picked on and blamed by the family. It then becomes a welcome change to have the focus shifted from his or her misbehavior to the interaction of all family members with all being held accountable.

Art therapy has made some special contributions to family therapy, most especially in its providing a vehicle for the sharing of perceptions within the family and the exposition of fantasy material. Particularly beneficial is the generational leveling aspect of art expression. Although parents are often more articulate verbally than their young children, in art activity the children are usually on an equal footing with the adults. Children often feel quite comfortable with the media and find a way of making themselves "heard" within the family that may not be possible for them in their regular family interactions.

Besides having a generational leveling effect, differences among members in art expressiveness may provide other benefits in reshuffling the usual family hierarchy. The same sort of influence can apply to family members who may be more withdrawn, intimidated, or submissive. Although role relationships are often inflexible or assumed initially, the introduction of this new mode of expression can supply leverage so that a family may provide more space within itself for the movement of its members, both in family roles and position. Through art expression a family member can cause the family to shift its shared perception of him or her quite dramatically.

THERAPEUTIC RELATIONSHIP

The therapeutic relationship in family art therapy poses similar problems to those found in group art therapy with the additional factor of working with several generations in family sessions, a much less likely occurrence in group art therapy. As in group therapy, members may struggle in a sibling rivalry fashion for the therapist's approval. In the family work, however, the therapist is often vulnerable to feeling protective toward the children or to identifying with the parent of the same sex or the person in a family position similar to one's own family position. In such situations, the therapist is particularly vulnerable to counter-transference problems. As a result, it is especially imperative to be aware of these sensitivities. Many family therapists deal with these problems by being "up front" with the family in revealing their own family background and experience.

Another issue peculiar to the family therapeutic relationship concerns controlling the behavior of young children. There may be ambiguity and confusion over what to do when the behavior of a young child is disruptive. Does the therapist run the show and exert controls, or is the child's behavior the parents' responsibility? In most cases it is useful to use the occasion to view the family's interactional patterns around this particular stress. Nevertheless, most therapists would probably choose to step in to prevent chaos. Obviously, there may be any of a number of outcomes: The therapist may be no more successful than the parents; the parents may act helpless since the therapist is "in charge"; they may oppose the therapist's "interference"; they may differ with one another over the matter; and so forth. It is important to consider the feelings engendered which may include embarrassment, anger, resentment, or relief on the part of parents, child, siblings, and/or therapist. Although I don't have specific guidelines to offer, I do believe that a therapist has to feel some degree of comfort and control in order to do effective work. Individuals have different degrees of tolerance for various kinds of disruption. Therefore, I believe that the therapist must know his or her limitations, and structure the work accordingly. In doing so, the therapist must be sensitive to the reactions of the family members and explore them in the sessions. Certainly if children are quite young, it may be unrealistic and unfair to expect them to participate in some forms of family art therapy. For this and other reasons, family therapists may choose to see members in various constellations.

Family work is as complex as families are. There are many problems and many ways of working with families, only a few of which are outlined here. Family art therapy may be used for evaluation and diagnostic purposes as well as for treatment. An example of the former is found in Chapter 18. The following discussions and case vignettes illustrate several ways in which I have utilized art expression in family work.

COUPLE ART THERAPY TECHNIQUES*

One adaptation which has been of particular interest to me has been work with couples. Therapists who have engaged in marital counseling are familiar with its thorny problems: the seductive attempts to inveigle the therapist into taking sides, the unproductive blaming, the rummaging through the past for old grievances, the distorted memories of even recent events with husband and wife each laboring to prove his or her point, to name only a few. The use of art therapy has cleared some paths through this jungle.

Advantages of Picture-Making in Marital Therapy

There are five aspects of both the individual and joint picture-making techniques that I have found particularly beneficial in treating couples:

1. *Immediacy.* Being engaged in the immediate task of making pictures, the couple is able to look at their manner of handling the task, particularly at the way they relate to each other when they are making a picture together. The situation they are exploring is a present one, and their reactions to it are still "hot." The therapist is a witness and may make observations and ask questions concerned with what he or she has seen and heard, not just heard about. Admittedly, this opportunity is not unique to art therapy; marital therapists frequently comment on interaction which they observe at the moment. The art therapy tasks, however, provide a field of *doing together* that is not often seen in conventional verbal therapy.

2. *Genuineness.* Troubled marriages often bog down in a maze of assumptions. Marital therapists are accustomed to hearing a "party line" which may bear little semblance to actuality. Husband and wife may have conflicting party lines or they may agree. At any rate, they are usually adept at dragging out the thoroughly worn assumptions. Because picture-making is a less familiar mode of expression than talking, over-rehearsed assumptions may be undercut by this fresh approach to communication. Unexpected and unplanned material may burst forth in the pictures to challenge the old assumptions.

3. *Spatial expression.* Verbal expression is sequential and, therefore, is not necessarily the clearest way to describe complex relationships. The spatial character of a picture can illuminate many facets at the same time, often more nearly duplicating a situation as it is actually experienced. For example, a picture of a family can simultaneously demonstrate closeness,

*Reprinted by special permission from The William Alanson White Foundation, Inc., from *Psychiatry* (1972) 35:89–98, and Wadeson. Harriet: Art Techniques Used in Conjoint Marital Therapy, *American Journal of Art Therapy* (1973) 12:147–164.

distance, similarities, differences, and feelings among the various family members, thus giving a more complete view of family relationships than does a description of one aspect at a time. In addition, the use of pictorial space in joint picture-making can be very illuminating as a representation of a couple's life space.

4. *Permanence.* Having a tangible record (the picture) can be very important in two ways: First, when something as complex and evanescent as the understanding of a marital relationship is being explored, studying and reacting to a concrete object that represents many facets of the relationship can be immensely clarifying. Perceptions of the self, the other, the family matrix and its various interrelationships can be expressed clearly and vividly in a drawing. Secondly, the pictures form an interesting review over time. Impervious to the distortions of memory, they provide both the couple and the therapist with a permanent record of change. Gaining a perspective on the complex, intermeshing shifts in the individuals and their relationship as they undergo conjoint therapy is often difficult. By reviewing past pictures, both couple and therapist may more readily discern trends of development.

5. *Shared pleasure.* In many troubled marriages there is little shared enjoyment. Even vacations become nightmares. There are times in the art therapy sessions when picture–making seems like play or a game and has the lightness of fun. Particularly in the joint picture–making exercises the shared spontaneity of creating may produce a pleasure in experiencing together that the couple has not had in years.

Where conjoint art therapy is used in evaluations for research or diagnostic objectives, the eloquence of the tangible object and the opportunity for immediate interaction and genuine, spontaneous expression are of primary importance. For example, after a psychiatrist who had been treating a patient individually and conjointly with her husband at the National Institute of Mental Health sat in on their conjoint art evaluation session, he said that he learned more about the couple in the one art evaluation than he had in ten previous conjoint sessions.

The Couples

What follows are illustrations of some techniques I have developed as an outgrowth of art therapy with couples where the sessions were directed toward the study and treatment of marital problems. These illustrations come from conjoint art therapy sessions in private practice, from personal growth workshops for nonpatient couples, and from art therapy evaluation sessions of couples at the National Institute of Mental Health on two wards of manic and depressed patients. The couples seen in private practice were not hospitalized and in all cases were functioning adequately in other spheres of their lives. They participated in art therapy sessions once a week on a long-term basis for an indefinite period. Personal growth groups met either for a weekend experience or once a week for a year. NIMH patients hospitalized at the NIH Clinical Center attended art therapy with their spouses once or twice for the purpose of evaluation for research objectives. Couples in private practice and at NIMH were seen singly, not in a group of couples.

Both members of all NIMH couples and of those seen in private practice were in individual therapy also. A few who were seen in conjoint art evaluation at NIMH participated in conventional conjoint marital therapy as well. Personal growth sessions were not considered treatment, but rather an opportunity for self-exploration with the focus on the marital relationship. None of the members of the year-long personal growth group was in therapy.

In most instances, therefore, the conjoint art therapy sessions were adjunctive to other individual and/or marital therapy. Frequently material from the art sessions carried over into other psychotherapy sessions where it was discussed with the attending psychiatrist. In both private and personal growth group art sessions, the picture-making activity was sometimes interspersed with purely verbal sessions or some other therapeutic techniques.

The Techniques

The picture–making techniques highlight interactional processes in the marital relationship. The focus is not on intrapsychic forces, as is usually the case in individual art therapy, but rather on the complex intermeshing of expectations and interactions arising out of perceptions of self, spouse, and the marital relationship.

The three techniques that I will describe and illustrate are the Joint Picture, the Abstract of the Marital Relationship, and the Self-Portrait Given to Spouse. The materials used in all the exercises were 18″ x 24″ paper and thick pastels in a wide variety of colors. Following execution of an exercise, the pictures were discussed. The couple was urged to reflect upon their feelings while making the pictures and their associations while looking at them. There was usually a great deal of affect expressed at this time, even by couples where one partner was depressed. Occasionally I asked questions and made interpretations, and sometimes produced related pictures from past sessions.

Joint Picture

Instructions. The couple is instructed to develop one well-integrated picture together without verbal communication.

First Example. In a personal growth group of four couples who met weekly for a year, couples took turns at picture–making exercises while the rest of the group observed and contributed to the ensuing discussion. Important dynamics in the relationship of one of the couples, the Kahns, were clearly revealed in their first picture, the Joint Picture exercise. Dr. Kahn was a clinical psychologist, and his wife a social worker at a mental health clinic, so both were psychologically sophisticated. Nevertheless, the action-oriented immediacy of the task undercut the intellectualizations to which they were prone, and they enacted clearly and succinctly a pattern of their interrelating without beclouding it by bringing up many extraneous impinging issues as was their usual custom. In this example can be seen the symbolic significance of the piece of paper, which may serve to represent the life space of a couple.

Dr. Kahn began by taking the pastels out of the box and arranging them in various ways. During this time Mrs. Kahn tried to establish eye contact with him, but he seemed oblivious of her presence. She made a small smear on the paper with pale blue and looked to him for response. He remained busy with his arranging. She added a bit of yellow to the blue and looked to him again. He still didn't notice her. Finally he picked up several vivid pastels which he had lined up together and made a sweeping multicolor streak across the paper, completely disregarding her yellow and blue. He still did not look at her. She added some black to her previous colors, this time bearing down harder on the chalk. It became clear that his streak was meant to be a road as he began to make houses along it.

Figure 153. Joint picture by Dr. and Mrs. Kahn.

At this point, Mrs. Kahn swung into action. As she stated later, it was obvious to her that he had no interest in a cooperative venture but planned to take full control as though she didn't exist. She made her black spot into a torpedo. As he continued to draw without response to her, she became angrier and drew a large black spider with tentacles reaching out and clutching his houses. He finally responded to her by drawing a cannon shooting the spider, but she made another arm with claws grabbing the cannon as well so that it appears quite ineffective against the angry spider (Figure 153).

Dr. Kahn claimed that he was trying to make a street with houses and was surprised that his wife had become so angry. In the ensuing discussion, however, the group called his attention to his total neglect of her despite her nonverbal overtures to him. His need for total control was obvious. Mrs. Kahn recognized her anger and massive retaliation as familiar and realized that her intense reactions when she felt neglected and hurt often compounded difficulties.

Most couples, unlike the Kahns, come to an early agreement on subject matter with a minimum of cues. This sort of communication, or lack of it, is a fruitful avenue for exploration of the marital pattern. The Kahns' picture, however, provided an explicit illustration of how the content of the picture may also be an expression of the marital dynamics.

Second Example. The Kleins were private patients who had been in couple art therapy for many months. They seemed rutted in a pattern where he constantly needled and harassed her, particularly about how to run the household, while she withdrew or castigated him in such a way as to let him know that she loathed him. Up until this exercise, they had spent most of the sessions blaming each other. Their joint picture (Figure 154) is a pleasant, lively, colorful beach scene. The process of its development, however, was very revealing of an aspect of their relationship. In subsequent sessions, Mrs. Klein was to refer to it a number of times.

Mrs. Klein began with the sailboat in a pale color. Mr. Klein went over her lines with a darker pastel. She made small fish in the water and he made a large fish eating them up as well as someone on the boat fishing. She made people on the beach and he put hats on all of them and umbrellas over them and a life guard to look after everyone. Finally, she made the sun in the sky and he responded by constructing a lighthouse with a light far brighter than her sun. The picture very clearly demonstrated Mr. Klein's competitiveness with his wife and the overbearing intrusiveness he used to control her and gain her attention.

Although she had whiningly complained of his harassing behavior, he usually found justification for it by reason of their need to economize, the children's need for discipline, and so on. This picture-making exercise, on the other hand, enabled him to see that his intrusiveness was the result of his own needs and an integral part of their present relationship (the source of these needs is explicated

Figure 154.   Joint picture by Mr. and Mrs. Klein.

in an additonal exercise described below). This example demonstrates not only a particular response pattern (Mr. Klein's intrusiveness) but also the general question of territoriality, a particularly important issue for people living together. The process of development of the joint picture by both the Kleins and Kahns illustrates the importance of observing that process, rather than simply dealing with the finished product.

Third Example. Mr. and Mrs. Barlow had attended private couple art therapy sessions for approximately eight months at her instigation. Treatment was begun after a particularly cataclysmic fight in which Mrs. Barlow was injured and thereupon threatened divorce, insisting on therapy as the only alternative. Mr. Barlow presented himself as a rigid man preoccupied with rationality, while Mrs. Barlow seemed to suffer a mild chronic depression and a feeling of dissatisfaction for which she blamed her husband. This exercise demonstrated the variance between the couple's stated complaints—arguments and fights—and the more significant problems besetting the marriage.

When the Barlows announced that they had celebrated their wedding anniversary the previous evening, it was suggested that they make a joint picture of their thoughts and feelings about their anniversary. In this instance, a topic was suggested for the picture. More often, however, the content is not assigned since the way the subject is chosen can be very revealing, as illustrated by the Kahns' drawing (Figure 153).

Actually, the Barlows' drawing (Figure 155) turned out to be two pictures, each working on one side with Mrs. Barlow taking over more of the paper. They had immediately divided the paper into separate territories, and their activity resembled the parallel play of toddlers rather than more socially creative give and take. (The Kahns and the Kleins demonstrated greater involvement with one another, maladaptive though it may have been.) Although the forms represented specific objects related to their anniversary celebration, the Barlows were asked to respond to the mood of the drawing, forgetting what they had in mind while they drew. They characterized the picture as "bleak, dismal, colorless, sad colors, uninteresting."

They were asked if these descriptive words applied to their marriage as well. This question together with an interpretation of joylessness in the marriage, as evidenced in other pictures as well, elicited feelings of depression in Mrs. Barlow the ensuing week and a strong reaction from Mr. Barlow that will be described in connection with another exercise that follows. This example illustrates a way of focusing on poorly perceived feeling states by examining the mood of the picture rather than the consciously intended content.

In these three examples, the Joint Picture exercise provided insights for each of the couples about ingrained patterns of relating of which they were only dimly aware. In each case, the couples were able to make use of these insights to produce change in their relationships.

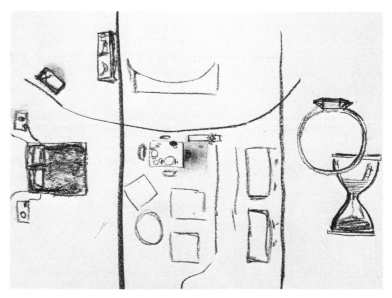

Figure 155.   Joint anniversary picture by Mr. and Mrs. Barlow.

Abstract of Marital Relationship

Instructions. Husband and wife are each requested to draw an abstract picture of their marital relationship simultaneously but separately. (This technique is a modification of one originated by Kwiatkowska, who requested family members to make an abstract portrait of the family.)

The Halls, a young couple, were associated with NIMH as a result of Mrs. Hall's hospitalization following a suicide attempt. Dr. Hall, a research chemist, tended to deny that his wife had any problems prior to her attempt at suicide. They participated in one conjoint art therapy evaluation session as part of a pilot study investigating depression in the marital relationship.

Dr. Hall's abstract marital relationship picture (Figure 156) disclosed perceptions he had not previously acknowledged but that likely had influenced his wife's precipitous action. Mrs. Hall is represented by the form at the right composed of yellow for happiness and black for unhappiness. He is the form at the left composed of more yellow and less black than his wife. The central shape is red and signifies their love for each other. The brown line connecting them he called the "link." The form at the top, colored gold, indicates that he is "connected to other things, such as work, that take me away from her." When I suggested that she might be connected to other things also, he became quite embarrassed, flushed, laughed, and said that he hadn't thought of that. He said that she is lower because she is "dependent" on him. Viewing her as not connected to anything but him, he seems to see her as totally dependent.

She described her suicide attempt as a "cry for help," and indeed it seemed a desperate bid for his attention. The forms in his picture are so placed that she can be seen as a weight holding back his effort to move upward toward his work. In fact, he drew himself closer to his work than to her, placing her at the opposite edge of the paper.

Dr. Hall's subsequent picture strengthened the supposition that he experienced his wife as a weight on him. He drew a test tube and some other objects he uses in his work and spoke of the great satisfaction he was deriving from his current research. He said he had to get back to his lab, and it seemed that he wanted to get away from his wife's dependency and her problems (which he had strenuously overlooked in the past) to his work where he feels more fulfilled. It's unlikely that he had meant to draw his wife as a drag on him. His subtle communication of this feeling about her, however, might have provoked her attempt at suicide.

Figure 156. Abstract of the marital relationship by Dr. Hall.

Self-Portrait Given to Spouse

Instructions. In this exercise each member of the couple is asked to draw a full-length, realistic self-portrait with the paper placed vertically on the easel. They are instructed to make the figure large, using the whole length of the paper. When they have finished, they are told: ''Remove your picture from the easel and give 'yourself' to your spouse.'' When they have thus symbolically given themselves to each other by exchanging pictures, they are told: ''You now have your spouse, and you can do anything you want to him or her.''

First Example. Mr. Long was manic when he and his wife participated in a conjoint art evaluation session at NIMH. Figure 157 is a tracing of his bizarre self-representation, drawn in red. His low self-esteem is apparent. He spoke of his fear that his hand would be cut off (note stump), and the breasts probably indicate a problem in sexual identification.

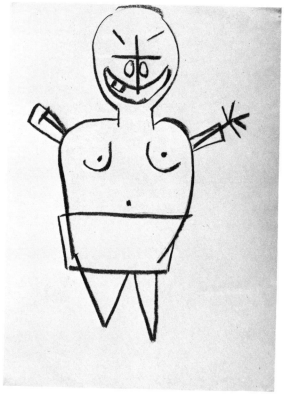

Figure 157.   Bizarre self-portrait by Mr. Long.

When told that she could do whatever she wanted to her husband's picture, Mrs. Long wiped it out with great relish and superimposed a drawing in black of a strong-looking man (Figure 158). She commented, "That's how he should want to look." In many other statements, as well, she indicated that he should try not to act so crazy. His repeated message to her, however, was that he was sick and needed her to care for him.

Figure 158.   Mrs. Long's changes in her husband's self-portrait.

In contrast to her large, bold drawing of her husband, Mrs. Long drew herself as a pale, small image despite instructions to use the full length of the paper (Figure 159). Feeling inadequate, she sought strength in him, probably wishing for the take-charge guy he appeared to be before his illness.

This exercise furnished information about the Longs' mutual dependency, an important item in our study of marital relationship patterns in manic-depressive illness, which is discussed later in this chapter.

Second Example. The Barlows tackled this exercise a week before making their anniversary picture (Figure 155). Mrs. Barlow drew a very heavy, stodgy, immobile-looking woman whom she saw as masculine. Her husband seemed not to dare to change her drawing, and instead drew another image of her peeking out from behind the one she had made (Figure 160). His figure of her is more lithe and feminine, and he said that he did not see her the way she drew herself.

Figure 159.   Mrs. Long's inadequate self-portrait.

Figure 160.   Mrs. Barlow's self-portrait with Mr. Barlow's image of her peeking out from behind.

Mrs. Barlow, on the other hand, readily made changes in her husband's picture of himself (Figure 161). She eliminated the recently grown red mustache he was so proud of, colored his clothes more conservatively because, she said, they were "too loud," and subdued the color of his hair. In both pictures, Mrs. Barlow demonstrated her own constraining and inhibiting nature, showing herself as immobile and toning down her husband. Citing these two pictures as well as Figure 155 and some others, at the next session I pointed out that although the couple said that arguments were the main difficulty in their marriage, the pictures and their associations to them seemed to indicate that a lack of joy with one another was also a major problem.

At the following session Mr. Barlow reported that his wife had been depressed as a result of this interpretation. He had announced that if she wanted to divorce him, so be it; he was tired of trying to change himself in order to prevent divorce,

Figure 161. Mr. Barlow's self-portrait toned down by his wife.

and he was discontinuing treatment. Although his strong stand during the preceding week had initially provoked a fight, when actually confronted Mrs. Barlow had backed off from her earlier threat of divorce, and the couple had sexual relations for the first time in months.

It should be noted that although they discontinued therapy in a somewhat optimistic frame of mind, they were nevertheless running away from the confrontation that grew out of the picture-making exercises. What I want to emphasize here is that the material revealed in the pictures (joylessness) was at variance with the couple's stated complaint (fights). The impact of this newly experienced recognition was evidenced by Mrs. Barlow's feelings of depression and Mr. Barlow's fear of tackling this issue (shown by his decision to discontinue treatment). A more positive result was his realization that he could not take the full responsibility for his wife's depression.

Third Example. For Mr. and Mrs. Klein this exercise proved to be a turning point in their treatment. Both were in psychoanalysis, and Mr. Klein felt that through his analysis he had learned to stop treating his wife as he had his mother, a rather helpless and ineffectual woman. As a boy, he had gained her love through ministering to her by running errands, helping with household tasks, and so on. She died after a long illness when he was thirteen.

When given his wife's self-portrait, his first act was to tear off the bottom because she had "not obeyed the rules" in that she did not draw to the bottom of the paper (the instruction had been to use the full length). He then folded the picture in on itself many times making it small enough to put in his pocket "to keep her close." In reflecting on his own reaction to the exercise, he was able to see that in fact he was still trying to keep her small and dependent so he could serve her and thereby win her love as he did his mother's. In tearing off the bottom of the picture he was doing the same sort of thing he did around the house when he would badger her about budgeting, shopping, and disciplining the children. By constantly correcting her he tried to stress her inadequacy. In folding her up and putting her in his pocket he dramatized his attempts to keep her small and dependent. His intrusiveness and competitiveness in the Joint Picture exercise (Figure 154) served the same purpose.

Mrs. Klein was shy and timid, extremely susceptible to her husband's harassment because of her own low self-esteem. She tended to be quiet and undramatic. She saw his intrusions into her household affairs as effeminate and considered him sexually inadequate. She looked for a long time at his self-portrait. When asked what she was thinking, she said she wanted to give him a penis. She put the picture on the easel and then exploded in an uncharacteristic way. For the first time she vented some of the anger she had been feeling, no doubt stimulated by the opportunity to symbolically *do* something to her husband. She punched the picture in the face, stuck a tack in the nose, angrily added the penis, and said she wanted to strangle him. She was told to do so.

When she took the picture down and proceeded to strangle it (by placing it on a cushion), the eyes smeared, and in Dorian Gray fashion looked as though they were crying. I commented on this, and she said she wouldn't want that to happen so Mr. Klein handed her a pastel and she repaired the eyes.

Her anger was obvious as was the benefit she experienced in actually ventilating it rather than just talking *about* it. Less obvious was their complicity in covering up any suffering he might experience at her hands. Although she had berated him continually for being a "mechanical man" who had no feelings, in the picture she immediately attempted to repair his look of suffering. When she had finished mutilating the portrait of him, Mr. Klein did in fact look sad for the first time in these sessions. I said so, and with an earnestness he had not shown before, he turned to his wife and said, "I'm tired of taking so much shit from you." In subsequent sessions he allowed some of his sadness to show in his pictures and his behavior. Mrs. Klein understood his feelings and began to experience some warmth toward him for the first time in their marriage. The blaming and recriminations decreased, and they began together to try to understand each other's point of view.

These three examples highlight several possibilities of this exercise. Often the most important one is immediate expression of affect. The opportunity to do whatever one wants to one's spouse can have a catalyzing effect as was shown in the relish taken by Mrs. Long in rubbing out her husband's bizarreness and in Mrs. Klein's explosion of anger at her husband.

Further, feelings about oneself become apparent in the self-images, as illustrated by Mrs. Long's portrayal of inadequacy and Mrs. Barlow's of immobile stodginess which was then enacted in her toning down of her husband's portrait. Likewise, the complement of Mrs. Long's feelings of inadequacy and her wish for strength in her husband was enacted in her making over his portrait.

The exercise also dramatizes interactions, for example, Mr. Klein's continued attempt to keep his wife small and dependent despite his belief that he had changed his ways. Perhaps most surprising was the complicity between the Kleins in covering up Mr. Klein's suffering in the face of his wife's complaining that he never showed his feelings. This revelation, as well as most of the others demonstrated in these three examples, had not previously come to light in therapy.

The above examples illustrate only a few of the kinds of pictures couples make in conjoint art therapy. Most frequently, they make free pictures without any instructions—whatever occurs to them at the time. These spontaneous images produce a rich field for exploration and understanding.

Some other art therapy techniques that were originated by Kwiatkowska in work with families have been modified for use with couples and have proved particularly beneficial. Among them are the Family Portrait and Joint Scribble. In the former, the husband and wife are each instructed to draw a family portrait making full figures and including themselves. The results indicate to the subject, spouse, and therapist just who is considered family. There have been many instances where the parental family is included, some pictures in which they are more prominent than the marital family, and some occasions where the spouse has been omitted completely. The arrangement of the figures and similarities and differences in the way they are drawn frequently indicate alliances and identifications within the family. The relative sizes of the figures and the degrees of adequacy of their representation shed light on the relationship between the drawer and the other members of the family. It is usually fruitful for the couple to compare their views of the family as represented in their respective pictures.

The Joint Scribble is begun by the husband and wife each making a scribble with closed eyes. They then look at the scribbles together, discuss what they see in each of them, and decide jointly which one they are going to develop into a finished picture together and what it's going to be. They then work on it together. This technique is similar to the previously discussed Joint Picture, but in this exercise verbalization is encouraged rather than prohibited. I have added a further dimension to the Joint Scribble by asking the couple to tell a story about the picture once it is completed. The information gained from this procedure touches on patterns of leadership, dominance, decision-making, cooperation or sabotage, levels of task involvement, interpersonal involvement, and so forth. The content of the picture and of the subsequent joint fantasy usually helps to identify significant issues in the relationship.

COUPLE ART TECHNIQUES IN MANIC-DEPRESSIVE RESEARCH

In most of the preceding examples the art interactional procedures and shared perceptions were used for therapeutic purposes. These same techniques were also put to use in research with manic-depressives and their spouses. Since the excesses of mania often produce extreme stresses on a marriage (such as uncontrolled spending or extra-marital affairs), the relationship pattern in these marriages was of particular interest. The revelatory aspects of art expression prompted the expectation that some significant interactional patterns in manic marriages might be illuminated through its use.

For the most part, studies of manic depressive patients have focused on the individual's family history of mental illness, psychodynamics, and response to various drug and interpersonal treatment regimens. Insufficient attention has been paid to the ongoing family and marital relationships of these patients. In concentrating on the interactional system of the manic-depressive patient and spouse, the assumption is that whatever the origins of mania for the affected individual, the illness is manifest as part of an interpersonal system.

Description of the Sample

The sample studied comprised all NIMH Clinical Center patients currently hospitalized for mania, who were married, and their spouses.* The rarity of clearcut manic illness resulted in a small sample. (Often the diagnosis is misapplied to agitated patients or those with an underlying schizophrenic disorder.) A combination of careful screening and recruitment throughout the country yielded only seven manic patients on two wards of the Section of Psychiatry, Laboratory of Clinical Science, National Institute of Mental Health, during the year this study was undertaken. Moreover, people with manic illness are often unmarried, probably due to the disruptive nature of the illness. Three of the manic patients had been divorced for many years. Therefore, the sample consisted of four patients, two males and two females, and their spouses. The patients were hospitalized voluntarily for acute manic episodes, as diagnosed by several psychiatrists independently.

All couples were of middle to upper-middle class socio-economic status, though in two of the couples where the husband was the patient, the bulk of the income had been derived from psychiatric disability pensions for several years, and the wives were now working. All marriages were the first and only one for each, were stable in that there had been no separations, except for psychiatric hospitalizations of patients, and there were no plans for divorce. None of the spouses had any significant psychiatric history, and all were living at home, working, and functioning normally. The first episode of psychiatric illness in each couple was a manic one, within the context of the ongoing marriage in every case. Following hospitalization (and this study), all patients were discharged improved, on lithium, to live at home, and continue in some outpatient setting.

One patient, Mr. Long, was on a double-blind medication protocol of alpha-methyl-para-tyrosine. A consensus of the clinical and research staff felt that there were no noticeable effects nor side effects from the drug. Another patient, Mr. Church, was taking L-DOPA and, if anything, the drug was increasing his manic tendencies on the ward. The other patients, Mrs. Rose and Mrs. Young, were not on medication.

Art Evaluation Sessions

Each couple participated in one two-hour video-taped conjoint art evaluation session. They were instructed to spend approximately ten minutes on each of four tasks, each followed by a ten to fifteen minute discussion period:

---

*This material appeared in Wadeson, Harriet and Fitzgerald, Roy; Marital Relationship in Manic-Depressive Illness: Conjoint Psychiatric Art Evaluations, *The Journal of Nervous and Mental Disease*, 153 (1971) 180–196.

1. *Family portrait:* For the first task each person was requested to draw a picture of the family, making full figures of all individuals, including oneself, and no stick figures.

2. *Abstract marital relationship:* In the second task the couple was instructed to draw an abstract picture of the marital relationship, husband and wife simultaneously drawing their own interpretations.

3. *Joint scribble:* The third task was a joint picture. Husbands and wives made an accidental scribble separately with their eyes closed. They were instructed to find associations in the resultant configurations and decide on one to develop into a picture together. When they had finished, they were asked to make up a story together about their picture.

4. *Self-portrait given to spouse:* For the final picture each person was asked to make a complete and realistic drawing of him or herself, filling up the paper. When finished they were told "give yourself to your spouse." After the exchange of pictures, the couple was told, "Now you have your spouse, and you can do anything you want with him or her." Some thereupon made changes in their partner's picture; others took some other form of action directed at the drawing.

Although several investigators have commented on the difficulty involved in completing tasks with manic patients (for example, psychological testing, Bateman *et al* (1954), art productions, Dax (1953)), all these patients were cooperative.

The importance of the marital relationship in mania and the necessity for examining the couple as a dynamically important unit were graphically demonstrated by the art evaluation sessions.

Similarity in Couples

In particular we observed that along certain picture-making parameters couples differentiated out as a unit. Especially striking were the similarities within the couples in the abstract picture of the marital relationship (Task #2). During the procedure each individual was absorbed in making his or her own picture and did not look at that of the spouse until finished (the easels had been deliberately arranged to preclude their viewing one another while drawing); nor did the couples talk with one another as they drew. In addition, the couples had no previous experience with abstract graphic expression, and therefore had no expectations of each other's pictures based on experience in this activity. On the basis of pictorial similarity, patients and spouses were matched with one hundred percent accuracy by independent blind raters. (See Figure 162.) Color, in particular, was a distinguishing variable uniting couples. Raters matching the abstract pictures frequently referred to color as a basis of similarity.

PICTURES BY PATIENTS   PICTURES BY SPOUSES

Mrs. Young   Mr. Young

Mr. Church   Mrs. Church

Mr. Rose   Mrs. Rose

Mr. Long   Mrs. Long

Figure 162. Similarities within couples illustrated by abstract marital relationship pictures matched by blind raters.

There were other stylistic similarities within the couple pair as well. The pictures of Mr. and Mrs. Young are both very vivid with a wide variety of colors. Both fill the paper and give a feeling of movement. The overall impression is a greater liveliness than in the other pairs. Mr. and Mrs. Church both drew closed forms with fewer colors covering less of the paper. Neither Mr. Rose nor Mrs. Rose followed the instruction to make an abstract picture. Both made linear drawings in black producing representational facing profiles. Both pictures of the Longs are monochromatic (his in black and hers in blue). This pair of drawings was matched by the raters through a process of elimination.

Similarities in content were elucidated in the couples' discussion of their pictures. In fact their comments revealed that in three of the four couples the patients and their spouses used the same specific symbols as each other. Mr. and Mrs. Young drew vertical wavy lines that contacted in the center of the paper to represent themselves. Both drew the line representing her in royal blue. Mr. and Mrs. Church each drew the double rainbow that they said appeared on their wedding day. Mr. and Mrs. Rose portrayed in their facing profiles of themselves the issue of closeness and distance in their relationship related to her frequent hospitalizations. Mr. and Mrs. Long, in contrast to the others, did not depict similar material in their drawings. The similarities of content seemed to indicate agreement between partners on important aspects of the relationship which they viewed in similar ways.

In addition to these specific symbols there were other similarities in handling content. The Youngs are further alike and differentiated from the other couples in their plethora of meanings represented specifically by each line and color. The Churches both represented the marriage as a closed form (his a circle, hers a heart) which was, as they said, inviolable by outsiders. The Roses both made a concrete line drawing with only one idea expressed about it. Although the Longs were not similar to each other in their drawings, they, like the Roses, each represented only one idea.

The chronicity of illness in the index patient was found to be an important variable among the couples, as follows:

Color

Use of color for the couples (each partner judged independently by ''blind'' raters) follows the chronicity pattern inversely, from most color used by the couple in which there was least chronicity to least color used by the couple sharing the longest history of manic-depressive illness. Although this result is not unexpected among the patients, what is striking is that the spouses followed the same pattern as their mates.

Chronicity and lack of color paralleled the degree of depression in the patients on the days of the art evaluations as assessed by the independent ratings of the psychiatric nursing staff. (See Chapter 7.) On the other hand there is no relationship with mania ratings. It is not surprising that the more depressed chronically ill patients used less color. What is surprising, however, is that their non-patient spouses did the same. (See Table 2.)

Table 2. Rank Order of Amount of Color Used in Family Portraits, as Judged Independently by Blind Raters, Compared with Rank Order for Chronicity

Rank Order for Color	Couple	Rank Order for Chronicity
Most color		
1	Mr. Young, spouse	
2	Mrs. Young, patient	1 Least chronic
3	Mr. Church, patient	2
4	Mrs. Church, spouse	
5	Mrs. Rose, patient	3
6	Mr. Rose, spouse	
7	Mr. Long, patient	4 Most chronic
Least color	Mrs. Long, spouse	
8		

Expressiveness

Patients and their spouses paired up in amount, type, and manner of affect expressed. In general, we found greater expressiveness in the two couples at the extremes of the chronicity continuum (Youngs and Longs) with greater emptiness, stiffness, or a stereotyped sort of pleasantness among the two couples in the middle of the continuum (Churches and Roses).

For the most part, the pictures of the least chronic patient and her husband, Mrs. and Mr. Young, were the most full, lively, and colorful of the sample. At the same time there was a fair amount of depressive content in the pictures of the patient: people crying in her family portrait, for example (Figure 163). Both the Youngs were quite active in making changes in the other's self-portrait in Task #4, which would seem to indicate a willingness to recognize, tolerate, and express dissatisfaction with the other.

The drawings of the most chronic patient, Mr. Long, were highly expressive but exceedingly bizarre. There were representations of fears of bodily mutilation, extremely low self-esteem, and sexual identity confusion (Figure 157). Most of the spouse's pictures were very empty and pale, and the faces of her figures were practically featureless. She was most expressive in the last task, however, when

Figure 163.   People crying in Mrs. Young's family portrait. She and her husband are at upper left.

she wiped out her husband's image of himself completely and with great relish drew him as she would want him to be (Figure 158). This picture was more forceful than any other she made.

The pictures of the "middle" couples were much less expressive. Mr. Church drew very stiff-looking pictures, both in his figures and the closed geometric forms in his abstract picture. There was little affect conveyed in the images of his people. Mrs. Church's figures were child-like and pleasant. She made no changes in her husband's picture of himself, and he made very few in hers. Few negative affects were expressed by either. This couple preferred romantic stereotyped ways of discussing their family, thereby avoiding examining the material in their picture.

The drawings of the Roses had almost as little color as the most chronic couple. The figures of the patient were mostly child-like, smiling stereotypes, and expressing little affect. Her husband's figures were stiff, and he used no color in any of the tasks. In Tasks #2 and #3 they limited themselves to concrete images and associations. Like the Churches, the wife made no changes in her husband's picture of himself, Task #4, and the husband made hardly noticeable changes in hers. In general, it appears that these two "middle" couples were much more fearful of expressing themselves than the other couples, and conveyed a picture of inhibition and restraint.

Couple Dynamics

A clear-cut marital pattern common to all couples emerged. In order to understand this process it was necessary to consider all aspects of the art session. These included the drawings themselves, the discussion of them, interactional behavior, and background data. (Although the art session produced valuable information for ongoing therapy, the following observations were not utilized for treatment purposes in the evaluation session itself.)

An important factor in the pattern was the strong dependency needs of the patients. For example, in the family portrait Mrs. Young made her large parental family in the foreground with herself and her husband in the upper left-hand corner, drawn after the others and appearing as an after-thought (Figure 163). She drew herself looking in the direction of her parental family, away from her husband. In the discussion of the picture she clarified that her "family" meant the one in which she was a child.

Mr. Long expressed his dependency directly. In his abstract picture of the marital relationship he said he was going to draw his wife as a heaven and drew several suns which resemble breasts as well (Figure 162, lower left). He said of his wife, "she is my whole life, my oxygen; I need her to live." He recognized that he hadn't even included himself in the picture. His association turned to sons (of whom they have eight), and he spoke of his wife as a mother. Much of his behavior revealed his wish to have her take care of him. To her he said, "Just tell me what to do and I'll do it." When she asked why he couldn't do that himself, he responded, "Because I'm sick; I have a God-given affliction."

Complementing the patients' dependency needs were wishes for strength in the mate. For example, after making a very inadequate self-representation in Task #4, Mrs. Young changed the image of her husband "to look more strong."

The spouses' position in this regard is dramatized by the Task #4 pictures of the Longs. The self-image of Mr. Long was extremely bizarre (Figure 157). With great relish his wife wiped it out and superimposed a drawing of a strong-looking man (Figure 158).

Despite the feelings of inadequacy and dependency, three of the four patients had been in complete control of family matters prior to the illness. In the fourth, the Youngs, the patient managed the relationship prior to the marriage with the husband reacting by exerting over-control of both traditionally male and female roles subsequently.

The spouses, as well as the patients, made quite inadequate self-representations, which would indicate their needfulness as well. (See Figure 159, Mrs. Long's pale, small self-portrait, despite instruction to use the full paper.) As a result of these inadequacy feelings plus their passivity, the spouses probably welcomed the patient's control of family affairs prior to illness and continued to acquiesce to the patient's dominance. (Compare Mrs. Long's self-representation,

Figure 159, with the large, bold image of the way she would like her husband to be, Figure 158.)

In general, the marital pattern is one of inadequacy feelings in each member, mutual dependency, and a wish for strength in the other. Patients and spouses differ, however, in that patients were, and had been prior to illness, more dominant and controlling, and spouses more passive and compliant.

Another aspect of the marital pattern is the perception of closeness. In the family portraits, all patients, with the exception of the most chronic, Mr. Long, drew the figures of the couple closer together than did their respective spouses. In the one exception, Mr. Long did not include himself at all because as he said, "I don't count." In the spouses' pictures, the couple was either separated by other people or by space, and others were closer together than husband and wife.

The implication of this difference in perception of closeness is possibly that the problems imposed by the illness had alienated the spouses to some extent or that, in actuality, the patients were more dependent on their spouses than vice-versa.

Discussion

In each case, the data derived from only a single two-hour art evaluation session with each couple was corroborated by many hours of conventional couple therapy. There were a number of aspects of the couples' relationships which first became apparent in the art evaluation, despite much previous psychotherapeutic work.

The emergent pattern in the couples evaluated can be summed up as mutual dependence and inadequate sense of coping expressed complementarily: verbally and psychopathologically by the patients, and in the bahavior and words, but indirectly, by the reluctantly but heroically coping spouses. It may be this sort of mutual dependency that keeps these couples together despite the tremendous strains placed on married life by manic behavior. The spouses may have been attracted initially to the take-charge manner of the patients-to-be in the hope of realizing fulfillment of their own dependency needs. A relevant issue for future study in mania is the extent to which mutual dependency might differentiate those marriages which endure from those ending in divorce.

The explicit demonstration of leadership by all the patients in our couples tallies with the implication of the viewpoint expressed by Goffman (1969) and Janowsky, et al (1970) that the manic acts and the spouse and others react. Our observations of patients in manic and non-manic states, as well as consideration of the marital histories, indicate that the patients were in charge of family matters prior to illness. Humiston (1969), on the other hand, has emphasized the provocative nature of the spouse's role. He noted the manic disorder to be a two-person process, where the manic feels in a "plastic wrapper" of depressing rules, being smothered by the utterly "reasonable" spouse. As the patient systematically rebels, the spouse tries harder to control, and the patient becomes totally unreasonable, that is, manic. During the art sessions the spouse's behavior evidenced passivity rather than "reasonable overcontrol," and we hypothesize that this lack of responsiveness tended to produce the escalation of abusiveness toward the spouse that we observed in the patients.

Cohen *et al* (1954) noted the pseudo-closeness displayed by manics in interpersonal relationships as a result of their failure to take into account the individual characteristics of the other, producing a stereotyped sort of response. Our findings suggest that the spouses also responded according to a familiar script. That our patients drew themselves and their mates closer together than did the spouses may indicate the latters' more accurate perception of the lack of genuine intimacy in the relationship.

Most striking of our observations was the similarity of pictures within the couples and the lack of differentiation between patients and spouses. The similarities included color, style, content, and affect. Even along the continuum of chronicity where less color paralleled greater chronicity in the patient, spouses followed the same pattern as their manic mates.

The implication of similarity in pictorial expression within the couples is difficult to explicate. It may be reflective of assortative mating. Another possibility is that the stereotype observed by Cohen *et al* (1954) in their patients makes for a family myth and style of presentation shared by the spouses that is restricted to a very narrow range of expression. Other data from the sessions supports this notion. For example, the Churches talked about their relationship in a manner characterized by extremely rigid role definitions and quite idealistic values. It seemed from verbal family therapy material, as well, that they had agreed upon a family myth that was unshakable, and contradictory evidence was denied.

The above ideas, however, still do not provide a satisfactory explanation for the similarity in pictorial expression observed within these couples. Nevertheless, the similarities in the pictures and associations point toward a remarkable concordance within the marital system. This finding of similarities was quite unexpected and certainly merits further investigation.

Since this study is based on only four couples, the findings can be only tentative ones. Also, the marital dynamics range far beyond the factors which can be objectively verified in the art sessions.

MULTI-FAMILY ART THERAPY

In more recent times I have been impressed with the changing character of families and some of their needs. Particularly interesting to me has been the changeable constituencies of families and the problems faced by what I have come to call "fluid families."*

Fallout from today's not-so-nuclear family often takes the form of confusion and hurt over just who is family. In family therapy, when we previously thought of family we were usually referring to a mother, a father, and their children. In our contemporary culture, however, this nuclear family is often blasted apart and family boundaries have become fuzzy and fluid. Families consist of people living together in various ways. For example, a man and a woman may be living together with the woman's children and having regular visits from the man's children who are living with their mother. The man and woman may or may not be married. Children may be living with only their mother and seeing their father infrequently or not at all. He may or may not be remarried. Children may be living with only their father, or some with one parent and their siblings with the other, and so forth. Such living arrangements are likely to be subject to frequent change.

Multiple family art therapy has been useful in addressing the problems families of this kind encounter. In addition to doubts about what people make up the family, these special living conditions raise questions about the durability of the familial relationships. Often the pictures reveal that members of the same household have very different perceptions of who belongs in the cast of characters considered "family" as well as differing experiences of the strength of the bonds between particular people.

Having several families participate together in family art therapy offers some particular advantages. An individual often learns from the attitudes of a member of a different family who has encountered similar problems but developed a different perspective and a different mode of coping. Some families feel isolated and benefit from contact with others who are facing the same kind of difficulties. This is especially true of the children, who may feel confused, frightened, angry, hurt, even victimized by experiences that they perceive as unique to their own situation.

Illustrative Case Material

Some responses to one procedure used in multi-family art therapy exemplify the effectiveness of this method. The adults in the three participating families in the following example were all psychotherapists and were self-referred. They were interested in working on some of their family problems

*Some of this material appeared in Wadeson, H.: The Fluid Family in Multi-Family Art Therapy, *American Journal of Art Therapy* 15 (1976) 115–113.

and recognized that picture-making would provide an intriguing activity for the children which, they hoped, would induce them to participate.

Structure of the session

During the six-hour session, several drawing tasks were assigned. After each, the entire group had a chance to discuss all the pictures. Because there were fourteen participants, discussion would have become an unwieldy free-for-all without some structure. First one family discussed their pictures, sitting in a circle on the floor with each one's pictures placed in front of him or her. The other families sat in a larger circle around the central family. First one person talked about his or her own picture and then heard responses from others within the family. Only after all the central family's pictures had been discussed in this way were members of the other families allowed to comment. Thus, feeling within the family was not dissipated nor was the focus shifted away from the family. Furthermore, those in the inner circle were looking at each other and at their family's pictures. Those on the outside were silent observers until the family in focus had finished. Then they joined in, bringing themes which had surfaced in the central family into relationship with their own concerns. When this process was completed, the families shifted, and another family moved into the center to discuss their pictures.

With so many people present, discussion of the pictures was time-consuming. It seemed unreasonable to ask children to sit still for such a long time, so they were permitted to go outside and play when it was not their family's turn to show and discuss its own pictures. Nevertheless, all the children chose to stay until close to the very end of the session, appearing to be totally absorbed in the other families' work. The lunch break, at the end of the first three hours, was a picnic, also allowing for physical activity.

One family's pictures

The material that evolves from this procedure is so rich that it seems best to limit detailed consideration to the pictorial responses of a single family to just one assignment. The first task was a family portrait to be drawn by each participant with large pastels on 18″ x 24″ paper.

The cast of characters in the family whose work will be illustrated included Leonard and Crystal, both divorced, who had been living together for a year. Living with them were Crystal's son Jonathan, twelve, and her daughter Nanette, ten. Leonard's children, Allison, nine, and George, seven, lived with their mother. They visited Leonard on weekends, and they took part in the art session. Leonard and Crystal were living in a house they had obtained for their new family, rather than either moving in with the other.

In presenting the pictures, the focus will be on the intrafamilial relationships, as it was in the session, rather than on individual dynamics. In Figure 164, Leonard demonstrated that he experienced the family in pairs, himself paired with Crystal and each child with its sibling. Nanette, Crystal's daughter, spoke about her picture (Figure 165), next. For her, the family consisted only of her brother, her mother, and herself. It is noteworthy that not only her father but also Leonard and his children were excluded. Leonard said that he felt hurt at being left out, whereupon Nanette began to cry. Apparently she felt humiliated, and her tears seemed to convey a sense of guilt over having done something wrong. Leonard tried to comfort her and offered forgiveness, but Nanette was still upset. It was as though she recognized that the truth was in her picture, and words would not undo it.

Leonard's daughter, Allison, a year younger than Nanette, was very proud of herself when she talked about her picture (Figure 166). It was obvious that she was trying to show up Nanette. She included everyone, but she

Figure 164.   Leonard's family portrait showing dyads.

Figure 165.   Nanette's family portrait with many left out.

Figure 166.   Allison's family portrait including everyone.

placed herself as far as possible from her mother, aligning herself with Leonard's new family.

Crystal said that her picture (Figure 167) was closely related to her daughter's. She drew Leonard meditating and her son Jonathan withdrawn into his art work, stating that her strongest bond was with her daughter. She questioned the permanence of her relationship with Leonard and brought up Jonathan's tentative plan to move out and live with his father. Jonathan said nothing, and Crystal went on to say that she and Nanette are in this life together, whereas the males of the family may be here today, gone tomorrow.

Jonathan's manner was subdued and unexpressive, a dramatic contrast with the activity and turmoil expressed in his picture (Figure 168). On the right is his mother yelling at the dog. Leonard is yelling at his crying children, and Jonathan and his sister, on the left, look forlornly at one another. Jonathan had previously wished to attend an art therapy workshop I had conducted, perhaps realizing that he can say in pictures what he cannot put into words. The picture eloquently expresses why he wants to leave his home.

George, Leonard's seven-year-old son, was the most upset of all. His family portrait (Figure 169) reveals that he was living in the past or, more

Figure 167.   Crystal's family portrait showing her bond with her daughter.

Figure 168.   Turmoil in the family by Jonathan.

likely, in a world of fantasy. He drew his divorced parents, his sister, and himself taking a vacation together. He talked about his picture in a very confused way, saying something about a hurt bird. He would not explain why he is lying down in the picture, but it seemed as if he was the hurt bird. Crystal and her children were not included, and in fact George's behavior when he visited their house almost denied Crystal's existence. George further confirmed his pictorial statement by refusing to join in the next task, a family mural. It was as though he was demonstrating his refusal to be a part of Leonard's and Crystal's family.

Within the limits of what can be expected from one task in a single therapy session, we see that much had been accomplished. Sources of difficulty were effectively delineated. In particular, the pictures vividly reveal that almost everyone of the six family members had a different perception of just who constituted the family, with only Leonard and Jonathan in agreement. The pictures revealed various ways that alliances were perceived, led to the airing of questions about the permanence of bonds between people, and clearly conveyed the emotional tone of the family members who made them. Furthermore, the children in all the families had a positive reaction to this family therapy experience. Despite the surfacing of family tensions, the children all asked when they could have another art therapy session. When Jonathan moved in with his father and began experiencing further difficulties, it was decided that individual art therapy would be useful for him. He had resisted conventional individual and family psychotherapy but as a result of this session was very positively inclined toward art therapy.

Another family's responses to the same assignment

To make clear the gains that can be had from observing the work of other families, a second family's work in the same session will be discussed briefly without pictorial illustration.

This family was composed of Tom and Betty, each married for the second time, and Betty's two children by her former marriage. Each drew this foursome as the cast of characters in the family. Through observing the other families, however, they became aware of the "ghosts" left out by all of them: the children's father, who was figuratively, as well as literally out of the picture, and Tom's daughter by his first marriage. She lived with her mother in another city, but spent summers with her father's present family.

Figure 169.   George's disturbed and unrealistic view of the family.

The family felt that exclusion of the children's father, with whom there was no contact, was appropriate, but they seemed somewhat consternated over the missing child. Finally Tom said that his commitment was to the present family, not the one that included his daughter. The family's discussion of this topic led them to become aware of the premium they had placed on cohesion and conformity. Deviation and individuality were discouraged. Betty, the central figure through whom the others were related, became most alive to this issue and was determined to make some changes.

In summation, having several families work together is especially useful in dealing with the difficulties peculiar to the hybrid family groups so common today. Just as group therapy helps the individual recognize that his or her special problems are not unique, so in multi-family therapy the family recognizes that other families share similar struggles. This is especially worthwhile for the children, with their frequently more limited scope of experience and observation. In addition to its already well-known expressive and communicative values, the art activity helps to provide a structure wherein each member of a large group of people can be seen and heard.

PART SIX

Research

CHAPTER 21

Problems in Art Therapy Research

Those concerned with the growth and development of the art therapy field recognize the need for art therapy research. By producing solid and credible research, art therapists will gain increased recognition and respect in the arena of the behavioral sciences through the systematic demonstration of the vehicle of art expression, a most potent instrument in furthering understanding of the human condition.*

Since the thrust of art therapy training is directed toward the development of clinicians rather than scholars, there has been little research of substance in the field of art therapy. Some of the work that has been produced has been guided by behavioral scientists from other disciplines who are not necessarily sensitive to the special attributes of communication through art expression.

The research problems posed in the study of art therapy data are extremely complex. Although art therapy researchers may borrow heavily from the methodologies traditionally employed in the behavioral sciences, art therapists may have to refine, modify, and adapt them to the peculiar problems posed by this field. Art therapists may even have to develop new methods.

Since 1962, I have wrestled with the problems and embraced the gratifications of conducting research through art therapy. I say ''through art therapy,'' not ''in art therapy,'' because it has not been the art therapy itself that I have researched, but rather conditions of emotional disturbance that I studied utilizing data derived from art therapy sessions. The gratifications have been many, because the richness of the subjective expression in art provides fertile ground for comprehension of intrapsychic and interpersonal phenomena. This point cannot be overemphasized. It is an exciting challenge unique to this profession, with high potential for significant contribution to wider realms of human understanding.

My own research work has changed over the years as I have been exposed to various influences in the settings where I have worked and as I have come to

*An expanded version of the material presented in this chapter was awarded the American Art Therapy Association First Prize for Research, 1978, and a modified version appeared in Wadeson, H. Some Uses of Art Therapy Data in Research, *American Journal of Art Therapy,* 18 (1979): 1.

evolve my own ideas of what is most useful and interesting in art therapy studies. I worked for fourteen years at a research institution (NIH) where there was heavy pressure to use a strict scientific methodology utilizing statistical analysis of quantifiable data. Such procedures often require a reductionistic approach to the material; for example, characteristics of pictorial style might be broken down into compoents such as use of color, space, and so forth. Obviously, in pictorial style and content the whole is often more than the sum of the parts and cannot be adequately described by such a reductionistic process. The result of frustration in this regard has led me, in recent work, to prefer a more holistic approach, albeit with some sacrifice in precision.

Because the understanding of an art expression often requires explanation from its creator, the treatment of patients' comments about their art work poses another methodological problem in terms of a strictly scientific procedure that would require quantification and a statistical analysis. In my more recent studies patients' comments were necessary and included, though not submitted to statistical analysis. Although not so exact, often a more holistic method, such as this, preserves the richness and meaningfulness of the art therapy material.

A particulary fruitful possibility in art therapy research is the structuring of the art evaluation sessions to elicit specific data. This method is a very efficient one, supplying an abundance of relevant material, often with less expenditure of time than would be required in more traditional procedures (such as psychiatric interviews or less structured art therapy sessions).

The research projects I have enjoyed the most have been findings resulting from the discovery of unsuspected patterns among a number of patients. In such cases I was not seeking information—it came as a surprise. Typically, I would begin to notice a similar theme emerging in the art productions of many patients. The investigation, therefore, would be stimulated by the art work itself. Although the other forms of investigation (applying statistical analysis or structuring sessions to elicit specific data) might not be feasible for many art therapists, the discovery of emerging data is.

OVERVIEW OF TYPES OF RESEARCH

Because my intention is to present an overview of a variety of art therapy research, it is not feasible to discuss all the details of background material, methods, or results for each investigation. These are available in the original sources for which reference information for each study is supplied.

In reviewing the art therapy research projects I have designed and conducted, I find that the studies are of four different types, with some overlap. The differences include the nature of the data, the manner in which it is obtained, and the way in which it is processed. Proceeding from the least structured to the most structured research approaches, they are as follows:

1. Observations of emerging data. Such material is not specifically elicited or searched for, but becomes apparent only after art productions have been collected from numerous patients.
2. Art tasks designed to elicit specific data.
3. Judgments I have made concerning the art productions when blind to the variable being studied (for example, drug dosage).
4. Predictive hypotheses tested by pictorial ratings made by judges blind to information about the patients and the hypotheses being tested.

All the studies described in the following examples were conducted at the NIH Clinical Center on wards of NIMH. Of the four investigations illustrating the four kinds of research methods I employed, three were a part of schizophrenia investigations conducted in conjunction with the Psychiatric Assessment Section, directed by William Carpenter, M.D., in the Adult Psychiatry Branch. All sessions were tape-recorded.

In the schizophrenia studies, my objective was to use art expression to gain an understanding of the subjective phenomenology of the acute schizophrenic episode—a nebulous subject, to be sure. My NIH research colleagues urged me to rush into a design, but I was able to convince them that I needed time to get the feel of schizophrenia so that I would know what was important to look for. At first the sessions were unstructured, but gradually I evolved the following structure:

Patients participated in individual art sessions during drug-free periods shortly after admission, just prior to discharge, and at one-year follow-up. Materials were simple—pastels and 18″ x 24″ paper on an easel. Sessions were scheduled as a part of the research evaluations in which the patients participated. They were held in my office on the ward. At each session patients were asked to make the following pictures:

1. "Free" picture (patient's choice)
2. Self-portrait
3. Picture of the psychiatric illness
4. Hallucinations experienced
5. Delusions experienced

The sequence of pictures remained constant throughout all three sessions.

From this simple design of only three sessions per patient have come five papers and an exhibit (Wadeson and Carpenter, 1973, 1974, 1976b, c, d; McGlashan, Wadeson, Carpenter, and Levy, 1977).

EXAMPLES

Three of the following examples are summaries of studies presented in Part Three *Schizophrenia,* where their clinical import is emphasized. They are repeated here, in brief, to compare various strategies and kinds of results that may be obtained through art therapy research. As noted previously, for a complete description of each study, please see its original source, listed in the References and footnotes for each study.

Observations of Emerging Data

Observations of emerging data constitute the least structured of the procedures described. The studies resulted from the preceding tasks, designed to elicit data about the patients' subjective experience of schizophrenia. I began to notice the emergence of some unexpected themes in the art work of a number of patients. This unexpected material has been the most exciting of all because it has come as a surprise, an unsought treasure. It is this sort of data which art expression is most generous in furnishing. The following report (Wadeson and Carpenter, 1976b) describes the surprising emergence of pictures about the seclusion room from the assigned tasks described previously. At no time was there a suggestion that a patient portray this subject.*

Forty-one of the project's sixty-two patients had been in seclusion sometime during their hospital stay. Twenty of these made forty-three pictures directly reflecting seclusion room experiences. I neither suggested nor expected this subject to appear in the pictures. Its prominence in the pictures suggests its importance to the patients.

These pictures fall into one or more of four categories: hallucinations while in seclusion (seventeen pictures); delusional experiences associated with seclusion (twenty-three pictures); pictures portraying intense affect associated with seclusion (twelve pictures); and drawings focused on a staff member in attendance at seclusion (five pictures).

Hallucinations in our acute schizophrenic patient cohort were common with seventy-nine percent reporting such experiences in their initial psychiatric evaluation.

The seventeen pictures reflecting hallucinatory experiences in seclusion usually had a pleasurable aspect. Delusions associated with seclusion, on the other hand, were usually persecutory. When in seclusion, many patients believed they were in jail, and some thought it was a gas chamber. In Figure 76, one

*What follows is a summary of some of the material found in Chapter 13 from Wadeson, H., and Carpenter, W. Impact of the Seclusion Room Experience, *The Journal of Nervous and Mental Disease,* 163:381–328.

patient drew herself waiting for the gas to be turned on. (Note the staff member in attendance outside.)

Five pictures dealt specifically with the accompanying staff person. Themes ranged from hostility at the "silent guard" reading a book (Figure 76) to relief at having a companion.

Figure 78, a picture of the psychiatric illness drawn at one-year follow-up, is an example of negative affect. The patient said she sometimes forgets she was hospitalized, but recognized that the seclusion room experience was the most prominent aspect of her illness. She drew herself in wet sheet packs in the seclusion room feeling "sad" and "crying." She said she remembers the experience only vaguely but found it "scary."

The results of reviewing the forty-three pictures from the twenty patients who depicted seclusion suggest certain consistent themes. Delusional material and affective response to seclusion directly represent fear, terror, anger, and resentment. In sharp contrast is material seen in the hallucinations. Here we find excitement, pleasure, spirituality, distraction, and a withdrawal to a reassuring inner world. The preponderance of hallucinations depicted occurring in seclusion suggests that the seclusion room itself stimulated hallucinatroy activity. This observation is consistent with sensory deprivation experimentation in which non-psychotic subjects hallucinated.

Information on the seclusion experience obtained in art productions suggests that greater therapeutic attention is warranted in order to increase patients' and staff's awareness of the meaning of the experience to the patient. It was observation of the emergence of the seclusion room theme expressed in the art productions which made manifest its significant impact on the patients. Attention to the pictorial emergence of information such as this provides art therapists an opportunity to make important research contributions.

Tasks Designed to Elicit Specific Data

A particularly fruitful possibility in art therapy research is the structuring of the art evaluation sessions to elicit specific data. This method is an efficient one, supplying an abundance of relevant material, often with less expenditure of time than would be required in either psychiatric interviews or less structured art therapy sessions.

The systematic collection of results from the specific request to draw a picture of the psychiatric illness in the previously described procedure is unique to the following study by Wadeson and Carpenter (1976c).* The results of this exercise

*What follows is a summary of material found in Chapter 12 from Wadeson, H., and Carpenter, W. Subjective Experience of Acute Schizophrenia, *Schizophrenia Bulletin,* 2 (1976): 302–316.

revealed some interesting facets of subjective experience in the acute schizophrenic episode.

During a three-year period fifty-six acute schizophrenic patients were evaluated. The resultant material was then organized into categories of subjects most commonly represented:

1. Feeling states
2. Depiction of brains
3. Representations of physical illness
4. Locus of illness

A few representative examples follow.

Feeling States: Depression

Most prevalent were designations of depressed feelings (fifty-two out of fifty-six patients). Figure 41 is a picture of the illness in which a young man drew himself in the center as a "a creature, a blob, everything is gray." His associations were frustration, depression, and "suicidal tendencies." He elaborated, saying he felt "trapped, closed in, worthless, and suicidal." The spiral form is very characteristic of depression and suicide. (See Chapter 9.)

Positive Experience of Illness

Eleven patients expressed what was in their view a positive experience of psychosis. In Figure 45, a young man drew himself as a witch doctor who could control others. This picture was drawn at one-year follow-up, at which time the patient felt depressed. He said he longed to become crazy again, finding himself more interesting to himself and others when psychotic. Apparently the powerful witch doctor was a more desirable and positive experience than his nonpsychotic state.

Depiction of Brains

Particularly impressive were the repeated representations of specific objects to symbolize the psychosis. Fifteen of the fifty-six patients drew their brains, indicating pictorially and verbally that something was wrong with them.

At discharge, a young man drew his brain (Figure 46), saying it went "foggy" as indicated by the black. The patient said that the lightning bolts represent confusion which he said were warnings and cries for help, instead of the normal sending of messages.

Discussion

Most interesting were the unexpected elements of schizophrenic experience. The overwhelming prevalence of depression as the chosen representation of the illness was a surprising finding. Its occurrence during the acute phase as well as at recovery and follow-up suggests that it is found not only in the aftermath of the acute episode (so-called post-psychotic depression), but is present earlier, probably only masked by the more florid behavior of the acute phase. Pleasurable experience of the psychosis was another interesting finding.

As is evident, the research design elicited some unexpected phenomenology of acute schizophrenia, in addition to the more predictable subjective experiences of an acute schizophrenic episode. As such, the art evaluation structured to focus on specific data can provide a valuable research tool for the enrichment of understanding of subjective states.

Blind Methodology

An example of my being blind to the variable being tested is a study of the intra-psychic effect of amphetamine in a hyperactive six-year-old child, Clark (Wadeson and Epstein, 1976).* Although there have been numerous studies demonstrating behavior change in hyperkinetic children from amphetamines, there has been little investigation of its intra-psychic effect. Art productions were used to gain a view of the child's inner experience.

In order to make assessments of the child's psychic state, unbiased by expectation of drug effect, I remained blind to drug dosages and placebo used during the course of the sessions and subsequent evaluations. This was a double-blind study in that the child and his family were blind to drug dosages and placebo as well.

I saw Clark in five sessions over a period of several months when he was on and off varying doses of amphetamines. The sessions were semi-structured to include runny and more controllable media at both table and easel and a self-portrait along with a number of other pictures of his choice at each session.

The study provides an analysis of the behavior and pictures from each session, which I made while blind to drug dosage. The most significant changes in the pictures were related to the handling of aggression and self-concept.

On a low dose of dexedrine (10 mg.) or placebo, there was much expressiveness and play of fantasy, particularly around conflicts between hostile feelings and the need to please, accompanied by positive relatedness, physical restlessness, flight of ideas and perseveration. On a high dose (30 mg.), there was

*Wadeson, H., and Epstein, R., Intrapsychic Effect of Amphetamine in Hyperkinesis, *Mental Health in Children, III,* Sankar, S., ed., PJD Publications (1976): 35–60. Clark is discussed briefly in Chapter 17, as well.

self-contempt and self-punitiveness, depression, less play of fantasy, and much frustration and lack of warm relatedness. On 20 mg., there was self-satisfaction, less expressiveness and play of fantasy, remote interpersonal relatedness, greater concentration, and a less troubled condition.

A self-portrait made when on a high dose compared with one made when on a moderate dose illustrates the change in intrapsychic state. Whereas on placebo and low dose there were monsters, killer bears, attacking navy ships, and so forth, on 30 mg., aggression took the form of self-punitiveness. In Figure 170, the child made the facial features three times, at first smiling, then sad looking, then jack-o-lantern type features, each time smearing them over. Finally, he smeared the background and extended the smearing to cover the whole figure.

On 20 mg, his self portrait (Figure 171) was more complete and mature than any other. He thought it looked "nice" and saw himself "standing here

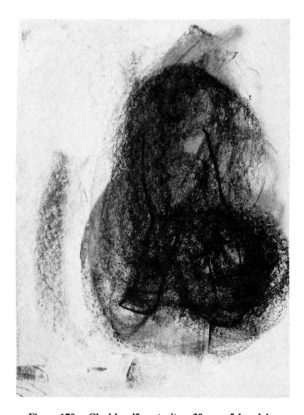

Figure 170.   Clark's self-portrait on 30 mg. of dexedrine.

Figure 171.   Clark's self-portrait on 20 mg. of dexedrine.

drawing'' and ''happy.'' He expended much effort in writing his name in large letters of various colors (covered over in reproduction here), indicating a positive identification with this self-portrait.

In this sort of blind methodology it was possible to make a number of observations about drug influence on subjective state, free of expectation of drug effect.

Predictive Hypotheses

The most substantial research entails the ability to predict because in that manner it is possible to come closest to supporting the assertion being made. Validated predictions are at the opposite end of an investigative continuum from speculations.

In the following study my colleagues and I predicted that expressiveness, or lack of it, in art productions would distinguish modes of recovery style in acute schizophrenia (McGlashan, Wadeson, Carpenter, and Levy, 1977).*

Briefly, integration describes a process by which continuity is recognized between thoughts and feelings experienced during psychosis and prepsychotic and postpsychotic mental life. Sealing-over describes a process by which psychotic experiences and symptoms are isolated from non-psychotic mental events and then made unavailable by both conscious suppression and repression.

It was hypothesized that integrators would pictorially represent themselves and their illness with greater expression, ideational fullness, and affective force than patients who sealed-over. Twenty-four patients were divided equally into integrator and sealing-over groups (based upon independent ratings at follow-up) and matched for age, sex, race, and socio-economic status.

Independent judgments were made of the patients' art productions in the following way: Color slides of the pictures were projected one by one in random order for ratings by two psychiatrists unfamiliar with the patients and the hypotheses being tested. The sample of pictures was composed of nine pictures drawn by each of the twenty-four patients: the "free" picture, self-portrait, and picture of the psychiatric illness produced for the first time at the admission session, again at the discharge session, and for the third time at the one-year follow-up. Raters were requested to score graphic characteristics which I believed would measure pictorial expressiveness: amount of color, motion, detail, and space filled. A global rating of expressiveness was also made. Each variable was scored on a 6-point scale (with 1 being the least and 6 the most for any variable).

The raters exhibited a satisfactory inter-rater reliability coefficient (.63). Statistical analysis utilizing paired t-tests (two-tailed) yielded the following results: The integrators used more color ($p < .05$), drew with greater detail ($p < .01$), and were globally more expressive ($p < .05$). Integrators also tended to depict more motion ($p < .10$), but were not different from the sealing-over patients in amount of space filled.

These results support the validity of integration and sealing-over as defined and demonstrate the use of art as a medium through which differences in individual styles of coping with the psychosis can be discriminated.

The following are examples of each mode of recovery. Figure 83, a picture of the illness drawn at follow-up, well illustrates the sealing-over mode of recovery. There is lack of color, detail, and motion. Expressiveness is blunted. The patient described the picture as a box in which "the sickness is trapped." Its contents appear unknown.

*The study summarized here is reported in Chapter 14, from McGlashan, T., Wadeson, H., Carpenter, W. and Levy, S. Art and Recovery Style from Psychosis, *The Journal of Nervous and Mental Disease*, 164: 182–190.

Figure 87 is a picture of the psychiatric illness, also drawn at one-year follow-up. It is vividly colored, and otherwise displays the graphic characteristics found to be associated with the integrating recovery style. Furthermore, the content of this picture illustrated integration as well. (This information was not available to raters, who scored on style alone.) This patient believed that her illness was in part the result of feelings which she had kept inside and allowed to build up. These feelings, she said, came out when she was ill as illustrated by red and blue coming out of the head. Other objects in the picture symbolize delusional ideas. The patient believed that she had learned from her illness, particularly in regard to the degree to which she held her feelings back.

Our hypothesis centered around our belief that art seemed likely to be revealing since image-making readily taps unconscious phenomena. Therefore, where extreme efforts are made to block unconscious flow into awareness (sealing-over), it might be expected that artistic expression would be more constricted. The results of this study support this hypothesis.

Findings such as this may have important treatment implications. Through art evaluation, a patient's coping style may be assessed and treatment planned accordingly—an insight-oriented approach for those who are likely to integrate their psychotic experience and a more suppressive approach for those who are likely to seal-over the experience anyway.

PROBLEMS INTRINSIC TO ART THERAPY RESEARCH

One of the most apparent problems in researching art therapy products is that a piece of art doesn't tell it all, although some would lead us to believe that a diagnosis can be made on the basis of a picture.* At present our assessment techniques are not sufficiently refined to perform that sort of magic. We still need a great deal more data, such as the patient's behavior during the session, his or her comments about the art product, and in some instances a history. How, then, is this additional data subjected to research in a manner which is as objective as possible?

Another pressing question in considering art therapy research is the method of assessing a piece of art work. Examining pictorial characteristics such as color, use of space, detail, and so forth, usually requires a reductionistic approach. Since the whole is more than the sum of the parts in art expression, such an approach may be meaningless. Focus on pictorial content, too, presents problems in that an understanding of content usually depends on the creator's explanation of its meaning. For example, I worked with a manic woman who repeatedly drew

---

*I attempted to deal with this problem in Chapter 15.

the Star of David. Since her Jewishness was very important to her, I assumed that the symbol's meaning was related to this significant aspect of her identity. Eventually she told me that the symbol represented her husband whose name was David.

The most flagrant travesty in art therapy studies, especially some of the early work, in my opinion has been the resort to speculation without substantiation. In some instances it may be appropriate to advance speculation, but it should always be labeled as such. There are many passages in the art therapy literature where statements are made about art expression characteristics of a diagnostic group or the meaning of an individual's picture without adequate supporting evidence. This medium is particularly vulnerable to speculation due to the provocative nature of art expression, which can be both the beauty and the beast of art therapy research.

In my own art therapy research, I have tackled these problems in a variety of ways. In the study of schizophrenia recovery style (described previously), I did not think the individual pictorial characteristics would necessarily give the complete picture so I added a global rating of "expressiveness," even though this category is far less precise than such characteristics as amount of color or space filled, for example.

In studying content as I did in the seclusion room material (described previously), I relied completely on the patients' descriptions of their pictures rather than hazarding interpretations or speculations.

APPLYING METHODOLOGIC RIGOR

In utilizing the more traditional research methodologies of the behavioral and physical sciences, there are several strictures that are important to note. The first is the necessity of isolating the variable being studied. For example, an attempt is made to isolate the variable of artistic expressiveness in the recovery style from schizophrenia study (described previously) by matching patient groups for age, sex, race, and socio-economic status. These factors, which might otherwise cause a differentiation, become cancelled out. In other words, the researcher must be careful not to be comparing apples and oranges (and perhaps calling them all peaches).

Another important aspect of these "scientific" studies has been the use of independent "blind" raters. They were independent in that they were not involved in the study and therefore uninfluenced by the concepts and the hypotheses of the investigation, which might otherwise bias the rater. They were "blind" in that they knew nothing about the patients whose art productions they rated. By using raters in this way there is greater assurance that the judgements made about the art products achieve greater objectivity than the involved investigator has.

Many "blind" methodologies employ a "double-blind" procedure. What is meant here is that both the investigator and subject are "blind." This design is used frequently where reactions to drug dosage are being studied, as in the amphetamine study, described here. Amount of drug and placebo are manipulated during the course of the investigation. The purpose of the "double-blind" procedure is to insure that the patient's reaction and the investigator's assessment are not influenced by expectation of drug effect.

COMMENT

From my experience, I have come to see value in each of the four kinds of methodologies described. Obviously certain research questions lend themselves more readily to one form than another. Where particular variables can be isolated, a "blind" methodology with a statistical analysis provides greater objectivity and rigor of investigation. The problem here, of course, is that much of the richness in communication through art expression may be lost when the integrated results of complex processes are reduced to a collection of quantifiable elements.*

Predictive studies usually offer the greatest possibility of substantial statements which advance the field of knowledge. The problems here are in obtaining a large enough sample from which to generalize and to have replication studies to insure reliability.**

Designing tasks to elicit specific data is a fruitful procedure which has yet to be explored to its full potential by art therapists. The possibilities in this area for a medium as rich in communication as art expression are almost limitless. There is much knowledge that can be amassed in this way by most art therapists without the necessity of scientific rigor of the previous methods. The advantage of applying a systematic approach to this process is in focus and efficiency. It is important to know what to look for and how to find it. I have found this sort of focus very exciting. One problem is that in applying a specific structure, one may preclude spontaneous expression. In order to avoid this in the structured sessions

---

*In addition to the example presented, I employed this method in a study of the marital relationship in manic-depressive psychosis (Wadeson and Fitzgerald, 1971).

**Predictive methods were used, in addition to the example presented, in studies of characteristics of art expression in depression (Wadeson, 1971a) and in manic-depressive art (Wadeson and Bunney, 1969, 1970.)

I conducted with acute schizophrenics, the first picture they made at each session was always a spontaneous one. The subsequent ones were "assignments."*

Finally, most exciting of all have been the observations of emerging data. In some ways, this process seems to me the most natural sort of research. Rather than some sort of system being imposed on the data by the researcher or the situation being manipulated to produce results in a certain area, the material emerges spontaneously. In this sense, it has greater credibility. The problem here is that once the researcher becomes aware of a particular pattern, he or she must be careful not to interfere with its spontaneous emergence in order to confirm its existence. Any art therapist may take advantage of this possibility simply by being a sensitive observor. A setting providing the supports for a rigorous methodology is not necessary. For those wishing to employ methodologic rigor, however, the emerging data patterns may point out directions for more structured study.**

I do not, by any means, believe that the types of research presented here exhaust the possibilities for art therapy research. In fact, I think art therapy research has only just begun. It is my hope that the creativity which is the essence of the profession will be applied to new means of exploration of the human condition through the fertile expressiveness art therapists are trained to perceive.

---

*Besides the example presented, reports on hallucinations and delusions (Wadeson and Carpenter, 1973, 1974) resulted from the tasks described.

**Reports of emerging data, in addition to the example presented, may be found in studies of suicide (Wadeson, 1971b, 1975c) and delusions influenced by TV (Wadeson and Carpenter, 1976d).

Concluding Remarks

Attempting to distill eighteen years of experience and the ideas that have germinated from that experience has not been easy. So much of the work felt consequential that it was difficult to omit many colorful case vignettes. (Fortunately, perhaps, forgetfulness pared away at some of them.) It has been my hope in writing this book that those engaged in the art of psychotherapy may find my journey in the development of a relatively new mode of therapy illuminating to their own.

My own reason for continuing to choose art psychotherapy as a preferred way to work resides in the power of the image. Through it, I come to know others in new and more intimate and imaginative ways. They come to know themselves as they create and communicate a symbolic language. Particularly those who live behind walls of fear or dwell in a land no one else has seen can begin to build bridges of contact by sharing their images of their reality.

Figure 172.   An image of life and death.

As I opened this book with an image, so I would like to close with one. This time one of my own. Figure 172 was drawn at a time when a routine physical exam revealed that I might have cancer. I was driving out in the country early in the morning to drop off this manuscript at the home of a typist. A split-second view seen at sixty miles-an-hour lingered in my memory. I drew the image and my own face full of longing, superimposed upon it. The beauty of life and my own sadness at the thought of its loss spoke to me in an image.

Several weeks later, after tests had revealed that there was no malignancy, the memory remained and surfaced in a poem. The picture illustrates the "art" of art psychotherapy. These words express the other side of the equation—the contact with another.

Termination

Exit you and exit me
and whatever twining has been ours.
A word
a smile
a touch—
the luminous gosimer
ot a dragon fly's wing—
flickering.
Gone.

Exit you and exit me,
soon from all we know.
For each other, we linger a little,
more or less,
in whatever lights and shadows
memory casts,
and echo in the hidden harmonics
each has created in the other.

Exit you and exit me,
each our separate way,
trailing memories like flowing robes
that soften footfalls
in the night.

Appendix

TECHNIQUES

The following are techniques I have found useful. They can be executed with any drawing medium. Since I prefer to work with relatively quick, spontaneous productions, these techniques are all simple. Many are evocative, non-specific subjects. Most can be used in individual or group sessions. Those designed specifically for groups or families are so indicated. Please bear in mind, however, that most often my clients and patients produce "free" pictures, that is with no suggestions from me.

Loosening Up Techniques When the Client is Stuck

Draw with Your Eyes Closed. Especially good for those fearful of being unable to control their drawing or who are too product-oriented. Control and perfection are recognized as impossible to achieve with this technique.

Draw with Your "Wrong" Hand. Same as above, but usually a little more control is possible.

Meditation. "Close your eyes and relax. When ready, open your eyes and look at your colors, letting a color pick you. Allow your drawing to flow without planning." This procedure often evokes different material from more planned efforts.

Scribble. "Close your eyes and draw one continuous line that loops back on itself. Look at the scribble and develop into a picture whatever you see in your accidental forms." Like the previous techniques, this one is good when the client is having trouble deciding what to draw (or what not to).

Generalized Subjects for Pictures

Present Feelings.

Specific Feelings. Such as anger, joy, sadness, contentment, love, hate, envy, excitement, anxiety, fear, etc.

A Wish. This may lead to recognition of sadness and disappointment that the wish is not attained.

A Specific Fear.

A Secret.

A Hallucination. (See Chapters 12 and 13).

A Delusion. (See Chapters 12 and 13).

One's Psychiatric Illness. (See Chapters 12 and 13).

A Fantasy. This may be a recurrent one, what would happen as a consequence of a fear, the outcome of a plan, a spontaneous idea, etc.

A Dream. Recent, past, recurrent, important, etc. "Enact the objects in the picture to integrate the experience of the dream." (See Chapters 16, 17, and 19).

Past, Present, and Future. Three separate pictures which then may be compared for mood and outlook.

Self-Portrait.

Idealized Self. This may be compared with the self-portrait.

A Significant Event or Situation. Useful when such is brought up verbally in a session. (See Chapter 18).

An Important Relationship. With spouse, parent, child, friend, lover, therapist, boss, another group member, etc. As above, especially useful when the relationship comes up verbally in a session.

Shadow. "Draw someone you hate in all his or her most vile manifestations." After completing, "Recognize that this is a self-portrait." A way to discover and own unacceptable, disowned portions of the self which are projected onto another.

Group and Family Exercises

All the above techniques may be used in a group setting with the processing including the group reactions. The following techniques, however, are designed specifically for more than one person.

Self-Introduction. What you want to convey about yourself on first meeting the group. This task makes explicit what happens anyway in a first picture produced in group art therapy.

Mural. Planned or spontaneous. Territory, leadership, subgrouping and tone of the group are important issues here. (See Chapter 10.)

Feelings about Common Experience. (See Chapter 19.)

Gift. "Draw a gift you would like to give to someone in the group, or draw a gift you would like to receive from someone in the group, or from the group as a whole."

Picture of the Group. (See Chapter 19.)

Picture of Particular Person in the Group. Valuable feedback. (See Chapter 19.)

Joint Scribble. After each has drawn a scribble, one is selected and developed by the group. Similar results as mural with the addition that more fantasy material may be evoked.

Pass Around Picture. Each person works on a picture for three minutes and passes it to the next person. Each picture is worked on by all group members. Useful when group members are fearful of taking responsibility for a pictorial expression. Strength of influence of each member can be noted.

Joint Picture. Draw one well-integrated picture together without talking (two people—husband and wife, a pair with unfinished business, etc.) Territoriality, leadership, competition, cooperation, etc., may be explored. (See Chapter 20.)

Family Portrait. Include self. (See Chapter 20.)

Abstract Family Portrait. (See Chapter 20.)

Family of Origin.

Ideal Family.

Partners Exchange Portraits. "Draw a realistic self-portrait of yourself using the full paper. (When finished) Give 'yourself' (portrait) to your partner (spouse). Now you have your spouse. You can do anything you want with him or her." In this exercise, partners can make changes in one another and express their feelings about the changes the other has made in oneself. (See Chapter 20.)

References

Abraham, K. 1927. *Selected papers on psychoanalysis,* New York, Basic Books.

American Psychiatric Association 1968. *Diagnostic and statistical manual of mental disorders, second ed.,* Washington, D. C., Amer. Psychiat. Assoc.

Arieti, S. 1976. *Creativity the magic synthesis,* New York, Basic Books.

Arlow, J. and Brenner, C., 1964. *Psychoanalytic concepts and the structured theory.* New York, International Universities Press.

Barron, F. 1968a. *Creativity and personal freedom.* Florence, Ky, Van Nostrand Reinhold.

Barron, F. 1968b. The dream of art and poetry, *Psychology Today 2:*7.

Bateman, J. F., Agoston, T., Kovitz, B., and McCullough, M., 1954. The manic state as an emergency defense reaction, *J. Nerv. Ment. Dis. 119:* 349–357.

Beck, A., 1967. *Depression: clinical, experimental, and theoretical aspects,* New York, Harper & Row.

Bunney, W. and Fawcett, J. 1965a. Possibility of a biochemical test for suicide potential: an analysis of endocrine findings prior to three suicides, *Arch. Gen. Psychiat. 13:*232–239.

Bunney, W. and Hartman, E. and Mason, J. 1965b. A study of a patient with 48-hour manic-depressive cycles: II. strong positive correlation between endocrine factors and manic-depressive patterns. *Arch. Gen. Psychiat. 12:*619.

Bunney, W., Mason, J., Roatch, J., and Hamburg, D. 1965c. A psychoendocrine study of severe psychotic depressive crises. *Amer. J. Psychiat. 122:* 72.

Castenada, C. 1972. *Journey to Ixtlan.* New York, Simon & Schuster.

Chesler, P. 1972. *Women and madness.* New York, Avon Books,

Cohen, M., Baker, G., Cohen, R., Fromm-Reichmann, F., and Weigert, E. 1954. An intensive study of 12 cases of manic-depressive psychosis. *Psychiatry 17:* 103–138.

Dax, E. 1953. *Experimental studies in psychiatric art.* London, Faber & Faber.

Dax, E. 1965. The pictorial representation of depression. (Basel) Sandoz, (4) p. 12 plates (in portfolio) (*Psychopathology and pictorial expression,* series 8).

Enachescu, C. 1967. Psychopathologic analysis of symbolic content of drawings by schizophrenics. *Ann. Med. Psychol. 125:* 37–65.

Enachescu, C. 1971. Aspects of pictorial creation in manic-depressive psychosis. *Confin. Psychiatr., 14:* 133–142.

Erikson, E. 1950. *Childhood and society.* New York, Norton.

Faraday, A. 1974. *The dream game.* New York, Harper & Row.

Freud, S. 1925. *Collected papers,* Vol. IV. London, Hogarth Press.

Freud, S. 1963. *New introductory lectures on psychoanalysis* (ed. James Strachey). Part II: *dreams.*, Vol. XV London, Hogarth Press.

Goffman, E. 1969. The insanity of place. *Psychiatry 32:* 357–388.

Green, H. 1964. *I never promised you a rose garden.* New York, Signet.

Janowsky, D., Leff, M., and Epstein, R. 1970. Playing the manic game: interpersonal maneuvers of the acutely manic patient. *Arch. Gen. Psychiat. 22:* 252–261.

Johnson, N. 1967. *How to talk back to your television set.* Boston, Little, Brown.

Jung, C. 1964. *Man and his symbols.* Garden City, New York, Doubleday.

Keyes, M. 1974. *The inward journey, art as therapy for you.* Millbrae, Calif., Celestial Arts.

Klein, M. 1934. A contribution to the psychogenesis of manic-depressive states. *Contributions to Psycho-Analysis 1921–1945.* London, Hogarth Press, pp. 282–310.

Koestler, A. 1964. *The act of creation.* London, Hutchison.

Kramer, E. 1971. *Art as therapy with children.* New York, Schocken Books.

Kris, E. 1952. *Psychoanalytic exploration in art.* New York, International Universities Press.

Kwiatkowska, H. 1962. Family art therapy: experiments with a new technique. *Bull. Art. Ther. 1:* 3–15.

Kwiatkowska, H. 1967a. Family art therapy. *Fam. Proc. 6:* 37–55.

Kwiatkowska, H. 1967b. The use of families' art productions for psychiatric evaluation. *Bull. Art. Ther. 6:* 52–69.

Kwiatkowska, H. 1978 *Family therapy and evaluation through art.* Springfield, Ill., Thomas.

Laing, R. 1969. *The divided self.* New York, Random House.

Lehman, H. and Risques, F. 1953. The use of finger paintings in the clinical evaluation of psychotic conditions: a quantitative and qualitative approach. *J. Ment. Science. 99:* 763–777.

Levy, B. and Ulman, E. 1967. Judging psychopathology from paintings. *J. Abnorm. Psychol. 72:* 182–187.

Levy, S., McGlashan, T., and Carpenter, W. 1975. Integration and sealing-over as recovery styles from acute psychosis: metapsychological and dynamic concepts. *J. Nerv. Ment. Dis. 161:* 307–312.

Lewin, B. 1950. *The psychoanalysis of elation.* New York, Norton.

McGlashan, T., Levy, S., and Carpenter, W. 1975. Integration and sealing-over: clinically distinct recovery styles from schizophrenia. *Arch. Gen. Psychiat. 32:* 1265–1272.

McGlashan, T., Docherty, J., and Siris, S. 1976. Integration and sealing-over recoveries from schizophrenia: distinguishing case studies. *Psychiatry 39:* 325–338.

McGlashan, T., Wadeson, H., Carpenter, W., and Levy, S. 1977. Art and recovery style from psychosis. *J. Nerv. Ment. Dis. 164:* 182–190.

Naumburg, M., and Caldwell, J. 1959. The use of spontaneous art in analytically oriented group therapy of obese women. *Internatl. J. Group Psychth., Psychosomatics, Spec. Educ.*

Naumburg, M. 1966. *Dynamically oriented art therapy: Its principles and practice.* New York, Grune and Statton.

Perls, F. 1969. *Gestalt therapy verbatim*. Lafayette, Calif., Real People Press.

Perry, J. 1976. *Roots of renewal in myth and madness*. San Francisco, Jossey-Bass Publishers.

Phillips, L. 1953. Case history data and prognosis in schizophrenia. *J. Nerv. Ment. Dis. 117:* 515–525.

Plath, S. 1971. *The bell jar*. New York, Harper and Row.

Plokker, J. 1965. *Art from the mentally disturbed, the shattered vision of schizophrenics*. Boston, Little, Brown.

Prinzhorn, H. 1972. *Artistry of the mentally ill*. New York, Springer-Verlag.

Ram Dass. 1974. *The only dance there is*. Garden City, N.Y., Anchor Press.

Redlich, F., and Freedman, D. 1966. *The theory and practice of psychiatry*. New York, Basic Books.

Reitman, F. 1939. Facial expression in schizophrenic drawings. *J. Ment. Science 85:* 264–272.

Reitman, F. 1950. *Psychotic art*. London, Rutledge and Kegan Paul, pp. 22–25, 36, 40.

Reitman, F. 1954. *Insanity, art, and culture*. Bristol, Eng., John Wright and Sons.

Rhyne, J. 1973. *The gestalt art experience*. Monterey, Calif., Brooks/Cole.

Schube, P. and Cowell J. 1939. Art of psychotic persons. *Arch. Neurol. Psychiat. 41:* 707–728.

Shaffer, Peter. 1974. *Equus and Shrivings: two plays*. New York, Atheneum.

Sinrod (Wadeson), H. 1964. Communication through painting in a therapy group. *Bull. Art. Ther. 3:* 133–147.

Szasz, T. 1970. *Ideology and insanity*. Garden City, N.Y., Anchor Books.

Wadeson, H. and Bunney, W. Jr. 1969. Manic-depressive art: Tested graphic characteristics and psychodynamic implications. *Psychiatry and Art*. Basel: S. Karger, 249–252.

Wadeson, H., and Bunney, W. Jr. 1970. Manic-depressive art: a systematic study of differences in a 48-hour cyclic patient. *J. Nerv. Ment. Dis. 150:* 215–231.

Wadeson, H. 1971a. Characteristics of art expression in depression. *J. Nerv. Ment. Dis. 153:* 197–204.

Wadeson, H. 1971b. *Portraits of suicide*. Publication of exhibit, annual meeting, Amer. Psychiat. Assoc., Washington, D. C.

Wadeson, H., and Fitzgerald, R. 1971. Marital relationship in manic-depressive illness: conjoint psychiatric art evaluations. *J. Nerv. Ment. Dis. 153:* 180–196.

Wadeson, H. 1972. Conjoint marital art therapy techniques. *Psychiatry:* 89–98.

Wadeson, H. 1973a. *Art therapy and the anxiety/depression syndrome*. Merck & Co.

Wadeson, H. 1973b. Art therapy techniques used in conjoint marital therapy. *Amer. J. Art Therapy 12:* 147–164.

Wadeson, H. 1973c. Separateness. *Art Psychotherapy 1:* 131–133.

Wadeson, H. and Carpenter, W. 1973. *Hallucinations and delusions*. Publication of exhibit, annual meeting, Amer. Psychiat. Assoc., Honolulu.

Wadeson, H. and Carpenter, W. 1974. Pictorial presentation of hallucinations and delusions. *Jap. Bull. Art Therapy 5:* 97–104.

Wadeson, H. 1975a. Combining expressive therapies. *Amer. J. Art Therapy 15:* 43–46.

Wadeson, H. 1975b. Is interpretation of sexual symbolism necessary? *Art Psychotherapy 2:* 3/4.

Wadeson, H. 1975c. Suicide: expression in images. *Amer. J. Art Therapy 14:* 75–82.

Wadeson, H. 1976. The fluid family in multi-family art therapy. *Amer. J. Art Therapy 15:* 115–118.

Wadeson, H. and Carpenter, W. 1976a. A comparison of art expression in schizophrenic, manic-depressive bipolar, and depressive unipolar patients. *J. Nerv. Ment. Dis. 162:* 334–344.

Wadeson, H. and Carpenter, W. 1976b. Impact of the seclusion room experience. *J. Nerv. Ment. Dis. 163:* 318–328.

Wadeson, H. and Carpenter, W. 1976c. Subjective experience of acute schizophrehnia. *Schiz. Bull. 2:* 302–316.

Wadeson, H. and Carpenter, W. 1976d. TV in the hospital: programming delusions. *Amer. J. Orthopsych. 46:* 434–438.

Wadeson, H. and Epstein, R. 1976. Intrapsychic effect of amphetamine in hyperkinesis. In *Mental health in children* Vol. III, Westbury, N. Y., PJD Publications, 35–60.

Whitehorn, J. and Betz, B. 1954. A study of psychotherapeutic relationship between physicians and schizophrenic patients. *Amer. J. Psychiat. 111:* 321–331.

Whitehorn, J. and Betz, B. 1960. Further studies of the doctor as a crucial variable in the outcome of treatment with schizophrenic patients. *Amer. J. Psychiat. 117:* 214–223.

Wilson, J. 1964. *The mind.* New York, Life Science Library Series, Time Inc.

Wolin, S., Bennett, L., and Noonan, D., 1979. Family rituals, and the recurrence of alcoholism over generations, *Am. J. Psychiatry, 136:* 589–593.

Wynne, L., Cromwell, R., and Matthysse, L., 1978. *The nature of schizophrenia,* New York, John Wiley.

Yalom, I. 1975. *The theory and practice of group psychotherapy.* New York, Basic Books.

Zimmerman, J. and Garfinkel, L. 1942. Preliminary study of the art productions of the adult psychotic. *Psychiat. Q. 16:* 313–318.

UNPUBLISHED SOURCES

Humiston, K. *Manic patients and their families.* Presented at 9th Western Divisional Meeting, Amer. Psychiat. Assoc., Seattle, 1969.

Kafka, J. *Psychological concomitants of ego functioning in creativity.* Presented at Washington Psychoanalytic Society, 1967.

McGlashan, T. and Carpenter, W. *An investigation of the postpsychotic depressive syndrome.* Presented at annual meeting, Amer. Psychiat. Assoc., Anaheim, Calif., 1975.

Wadeson, H. and Carpenter, W. *Prevalence of universal themes and motifs in psychotic delusions.* Presented at Internat'l. Congress of Social Psychiat., Athens, 1974..

Weissman, P. *Theoretical considerations of ego regression and ego functions in creativity.* Presented at NIMH and Washington Psychoanalytic Society, Washington, D. C., 1967.

Author Index

Abraham, K., 47
Arieti, S., 5, 186
Arlow, J., 170

Barron, F., 4, 5, 186
Bateman, J., 301
Beck, A., 47, 93
Bennett, L., 224, 232
Betz, B., 187
Bleuler, E., 113
Bowen, M., 280
Brenner, C., 170
Bunney, W., 30, 46

Carpenter, W., 112, 129, 186, 320, 321, 322, 327
Castenada, C., 3
Chesler, P., 4
Cohen, M., 77, 308
Cowell, J., 61, 80
Cromwell, R., 113

Dax, E., 61, 63, 80, 301
Docherty, J., 187

Enachescu, C., 61, 80
Epstein, R., 324
Erikson, E., 8

Faraday, A., 212
Fitzgerald, R., 232
Freedman, D., 200
Freud, S., 9, 13, 29, 47, 210, 212

Garfinkle, L., 80
Goffman, E., 307
Green, H., 117

Humiston, K., 307

Jackson, D., 280

Janowsky, D., 307
Jung, C., 13, 210

Kafka, J., 186
Klein, M., 47
Koestler, A., 6
Kraeplin, E., 113
Kramer, E., 6, 13
Kris, E., 5, 186
Kwiatkowska, H., 14, 29, 241, 280, 298

Laing, R., 113
Lehman, H., 61
Levy, S., 186, 320, 327

McGlashan, T., 129, 176, 186, 187, 320
Mamas and The Papas, The, 39
Matthysse, S., 113

Naumburg, M., 13, 23, 61, 75, 327
Noonan, D., 224

Perls, F., 210, 211
Perry, J., 9
Plath, S., 117
Plokker, J., 61, 64, 80, 81
Prinzhorn, H., 13

Ram Dass, 3
Redlich, F., 200
Reitman, F., 61, 63, 80
Risques, F., 61

Schube, P., 61, 80
Sinrod, H., 14
Siris, S., 187
Strauss, J., 112
Szasz, T., 4, 113

Wadeson, H., 232, 320, 321, 322, 324, 327
Weissman, P., 5, 186
Whitehorn, J., 187
Wilson, J., 177
Wolin, S., 224, 232

Wynne, L., 29, 113, 241, 280

Yalom, I., 236

Zimmerman, J., 80

Subject Index

Abstract of the marital relationship, 285, 290-291, 301, 305
Acting out, 79, 82
Addiction, alcohol, 220-233
Adolescence, 280, 281
  adjustment reaction to, 241
  anxiety in, 242, 243, 248, 277
  communication, 242-255, 271
  schizophrenia, 241-255
  school difficulties, 242-255
  suicide, 247
Advocacy, 21-22
Affect, depressive, 61-67
  as determine of pictorial style, 126
  expression of, 118, 176, 225, 285, 298, 304, 305
  manic-depressive, 80, 308
  in seclusion, 163-170, 321, 322
Affective disorders, 45-110, 189
Alcoholics Anonymous, 220-221, 226, 229, 230
Alcoholism, 14, 220-233
  delusions and hallucinations in, 112
  as form of suicide, 82, 220
  impotency in, 229
  treatment of, 220
Alcohol Safety Action Programs, 221
Ambivalence, 82, 83, 90, 223
American Art Therapy Association, 14, 23
American Journal of Art Therapy, 14
Amorphousness, 190, 191, 239
Amphetamine, 219, 324, 330
Anger, 17, 19, 34, 108, 228, 230, 231, 249, 258, 266, 268, 271, 273, 282, 287, 309
  in depression, 47, 51, 59, 104
  infantile rage, 47-257
  in manic-depressive psychosis, 68, 72, 77, 78, 80
  in neurosis, 201, 202, 205, 264
  in schizophrenia, 114, 121-122, 152, 166, 168, 180, 246, 250, 252, 322

in suicide, 83, 84, 85, 87, 88-90, 91, 95, 96, 101
Antabuse, 220
Approval, in therapeutic relationship, 35, 240, 282
  by therapist, 41, 258
Art, 3-7
  comparison in schizophrenia, depression and manic-depressive psychosis, 188-198
  communication, 170, 177, 186, 237, 318, 330
  depression characteristics, 49-67
  education, 15
  as energizer, 11
  enriched expression in, 176-187
  evaluation of schizophrenics, 118, 119, 129, 187, 188-198, 328
  expression, 4-7, 9, 11-12, 13-14, 38-40, 61-66, 176-187, 236, 239, 281, 299
  as gift for therapist, 40-41
  improverished expression in, 176-187
  insane asylum, 13
  insight in, 13
  manic-depressive psychosis characteristics, 80-81
  media, 18, 225, 237, 241, 285, 324
  murals, 107
  objectification through, 10
  pre-historic, 13
  as process, 40-43, 289
  product as extension of self, 38-39, 42, 255
  schizophrenic, 61, 130, 324
  with schizophrenics, 117-162
  sculpture, 70
  spatial matrix in, 11
  storing of, 283-284
  style, 189, 308
  subjective experience of psychosis, 16, 118-130, 177, 321-328
  suicidal, collection of, 85

television in, 170-175
use of, 5-6, 8-13
Artist, 4, 5
  awareness, 186
  control of media, 9
  identifying with, 70
  in therapy, 9, 256-279
  training of, 6
Art therapist, as advocate, 21-22
  anger, 202
  approach of, 15
  changes in therapeutic style, 43
  communication process, 186
  confidentiality, 15, 35, 41, 277
  contract with client, 33-34, 83, 236
  creativity of, 6-7, 20, 104, 219
  empathy, 114, 186, 239
  expressive therapies, 102-111
  failures, 37, 82, 87, 103-104, 109, 131
  idealization by client, 35-36, 272, 273
  institutional politics, 19-22
  institutional team, 19, 33, 85, 239
  integrity of client, 38-39, 116
  internship, 23
  interpretation, 39
  intuition, 38, 39, 40, 82-83
  leadership, 104, 239
  as model, 35, 239, 269, 276-277
  negative feelings, 37, 39, 82, 84, 103, 116
  nurturance, 34-36
  participation in art work, 42-43, 240
  philosophy, 23-24, 37-38
  in private practice, 14, 33, 83, 201, 256-279, 284, 285
  public relations, 21
  research of, 317-331
  response to mood of picture, 39, 71, 289
  self disclosure, 37-38, 211-214, 240, 282
  testing of, 78
  use of power, 35, 38, 84, 114, 202, 240, 276
Art therapy, admission evaluation, 118
  advantages of, 8-12, 298
  and alcoholism, 14, 198, 220-233
  application of, 13-18
  beneficial effects of, 6-7, 85-87, 88, 96-97, 101, 219, 283, 316

catharsis, 101, 219, 297-298
communication, 116, 164, 186, 245, 287, 316, 318, 330
couples, 283-308
creativity, 6-7
crisis intervention, 14, 42, 85-88, 101
diagnostic evaluation, 14, 141, 164, 189, 198, 232, 282, 284, 300, 306, 319, 328
  with drug abusers, 14, 84, 88
education, 23
educational institutions, 14, 23
with the elderly, 10, 14, 48
family, 14, 82, 224-233, 242, 280-316
field of, 5, 30, 318
free picture, 119, 320, 327
group, 16, 83, 221, 236-279
history of, 13-14
individual sessions, 16, 119, 218
inservice, 8, 21
joint picture making, 284, 285-290
literature, 193, 329
with mentally handicapped, 14
multi-family, 308-316
murals, 107, 314
permanence of object, 10-11, 119, 284
playfulness, 12
polarity in field of, 13
predictive, 58, 76, 101
research, 317-331
resistance, 48, 93, 135
self-expression, 70, 101, 298, 329
short term, 13, 130, 310, 320
structure of sessions, 15-17, 79, 119, 237, 238, 319
suicidal expression, 85-87, 96-97
tension relief, 59-60, 297-298
therapeutic relationship in, 141, 176, 282
training, 23-31, 201, 241, 256-279, 318
uniqueness of individual, 81, 256, 319, 328
Awareness, 200, 201, 209

Bipolar depression, see Manic-depressive psychosis
Brain, disordered, 128
  effect of alcoholism, 220
  minimally damaged, 218

in schizophrenic art, 119, 121, 124-125, 142, 179, 323
Bulletin of Art Therapy, 14

Case studies, 10-11, 188
delusions, 152-162
depression, 49-60
family therapy, 286-298
manic-depressive psychosis, 68-75
neurosis, 201-209
schizophrenia, 152-162
student of art therapy, 24-28
suicide, 83-84
Center for Family Research, Department of Psychiatry and Behavorial Sciences, George Washington University Medical Center, 224
Child, 212-214
depression, 47, 99
development of, early, 8, 215-217
experiences in youth, 256, 257, 261, 277
loss, 95, 245
regression to, 246
work with, 13, 18, 218-219, 240, 281, 282, 309, 310-316, 324-326
Chlorpromazine, 114, 117, 135, 187
Color, 62, 63, 64-65, 74, 77, 80, 87, 120, 121, 123, 126, 165, 178, 181, 182, 183, 190, 193, 228, 230, 239, 266, 269, 286, 289, 301, 303-305, 308, 319, 327, 328, 329
Confidentiality, 11, 15, 33, 41, 277
Confusion, in alcoholism, 220, 230
in families, 309, 314
in schizophrenia, 120-121, 122, 124, 129, 149, 152, 166, 170, 179, 243, 247, 323
of therapist, 282
Consciousness, 4, 7, 137, 138
Contract, clarification of, 33-34
oral, 16-17, 83
Co-therapists, 239, 241
Countertransference, 36, 282
negative feelings toward client, 37
Couples, dynamics of, 306-307
similarity in, 301-305, 308
in therapy, 283-308
Creativity, 4-7, 186
alleviation of pain, 6
in art therapy, 6-7, 219, 331

of client, 6, 107, 186
in dreams, 210
energy in, 11-12
expression of, 5-7, 110, 255
healing properties of, 13
integration through, 6, 9, 13
process of, 3-7, 13
synthesizing force of, 6-7, 9

Death, 25, 26, 50-57, 59-60, 89, 90, 95, 104, 201, 205, 236, 248, 258, 269, 279
from alcoholism, 220
in dreams, 27
in hallucinations, 136, 143, 151, 165, 173, 175, 179, 182
mask, 83
murder, 252
Defenses, 9, 36, 68, 182, 187, 255
acting out, 79, 82
denial, 68, 75, 177, 186, 220, 221, 223, 230
projection, 74, 186
repression, 176
resistance, 10, 36, 48, 63, 65, 77, 101, 103, 109, 114, 176-221, 254, 266, 281
sublimation, 6-7
withdrawal, 85, 96, 101, 107, 219, 221, 223, 230, 231, 238, 255, 287
Delusions, certainty, 135
chlorpromazine, 114, 117
about current societal concerns, 149-151
in conquest of evil, 142
of devil, 134, 142-151, 156
doubt, 135, 142-151, 156
of God, 134, 142-151, 165
of persecution, 142, 144, 150-152
of power, 142, 144, 150-152
psychotic depression, 46-49
about recent history, 141
recurrent motifs, 141-162, 321
schizophrenic, 82, 112, 115, 119, 125, 131-141, 165, 182, 320
somatization, 128
systematized, 137, 139, 152
television, 170-175
Denial, 68, 79, 177, 186, 220, 221, 223, 230

Depression, 10, 30, 38, 41, 42, 46-47,
    68, 69, 74, 123, 223, 231, 257, 284
  affect, 62, 63, 66, 182, 285
  agitated, 48, 105
  anger, 88-90, 103, 205
  biological studies, 46, 68
  characteristics of art expression, 61-66,
    74-75, 85, 120, 303
  cognitive model, 47
  comparison of art expression, 188-198,
    324-325
  delusions, 46-49
  dynamic precursors of, 47
  endogenous, 46
  etiology of, 47
  guilt, 46, 58, 69, 93
  inertia in, 47, 88, 98-99, 102
  literature, 61
  neurotic, 46, 289, 296
  postpsychotic in schizophrenia, 120,
    324
  psychomotor retardation, 46, 48, 66,
    88, 98
  psychopathology of, 46, 61
  psychotic, 46, 84, 123, 323
  ratings of, 63
  reactive, 46
  research, 46-47, 61
  resistance, 48, 63, 65, 101, 103
  in schizophrenia, 120, 128
  suicide, 30, 42, 49, 59, 63, 82, 85-87,
    88, 97, 98-99, 120, 201, 247, 290, 323
  unipolar, 191, 197
  vegetative state of, 46
Devil, 4, 115
  in paranoid delusions and hallucinations,
    134, 136, 142-144
Dexedrine, 218-219, 324-326
Diagnosis, 188, 189, 197-198, 200
Dreams, 3, 27, 58-59, 210-219, 335
  Freud, 9, 29, 210
  Jungian analysis, 9
  Perls, Gestalt, 210-214, 217-218
  road to unconscious, 9
  symbolic imagery, 13, 202, 205, 273, 277
Drug, abuse, 14
  alcohol abuse, 220-233
  delusions and hallucinations, 112, 126,
    142, 149, 154, 165

  as form of suicide, 82, 84, 88, 97
  as management therapy, 170, 186-187,
    205, 207, 218, 220, 299, 300, 320,
    324-326, 330
  placebo, 324-326, 330

Education, about alcohol abuse, 220
  in art therapy, 23-31
Educational institutions, 14
Elderly, art materials, 18
  death, 25
  depressed, 49, 105, 107
  hopelessness, 93
  life review, 14
  nursing home, 29
  resistance, 10
  senility, 112
Energy, 11-12
  in depression, 48, 61
  levels of, 11, 48, 68, 82, 102, 106, 123,
    153, 190
  in manic-depressive psychosis, 68, 75
  pranic, 137
Environment for art therapy session, 15-
  16
Exhibits of patients' art work, 41
Expressive therapies, 102-111
  combining, 102-111
  communication, 105
  drama, 107-108, 109
  fantasy, 108
  movement to music, 104-105, 109
  poetry, 107, 109
  relaxation, 105-106

Failures, 34, 82, 91, 109
  of students, 37
  of suicide attempts, 82-83, 84
Family, art therapy, 14, 232-233, 235,
    280-316, 335-336
  communication, 18, 131, 281, 287, 291
  couples, 283-308
  crisis, 17, 82
  evaluations of, 224-233
  joint scribble, 298
  matrix, 280, 281, 284
  multi-family art therapy, 308-316
  myths, 280, 281, 308
  network, 280

of origin, 240, 256, 336
portrait, 298, 301, 306, 307, 310-316,
    336
primary, 236
roles, 281
separation from, 123, 130
studies of, 77, 113, 241
systems, 224, 280
territoriality, 289
therapy, 114, 118, 242
Fantasy, 7, 9, 40, 83, 218, 281, 299,
    314, 325, 335
distortion, 169
of self-destruction, 201-209, 205
of suicide, 88
Fear, 72, 83, 102, 104, 116, 205, 207,
    218-219, 257, 262, 272, 273, 292,
    304, 332, 335
in schizophrenics, 114, 132, 133, 135,
    138, 148, 152, 164, 165, 169, 170,
    243, 246, 250, 322
Feeling states, 119, 120-123, 131, 224,
    225, 233, 234-235, 248-255, 256,
    258, 276, 285
anger, 121-122, 128, 268-271
confusion, 120-121, 128, 166, 202,
    282, 289, 298, 323
depression, 120
negative, 231, 239, 257, 269, 277, 328
positive, 129, 164-165, 181, 277, 279
present, 126, 163
Free association, 13, 18, 108, 119, 121,
    132, 141, 164, 170, 171. 256, 285,
    296, 306

George Washington University Medical
    Center, Center for Family Research,
    224
Gestalt, 30, 202
Perls, Fritz, 210-211
therapy, 210-211, 212, 217-218
Gift of art product, 40-41
Goals, of psychotherapy, 42, 237, 238,
    239, 242
of self-acceptance, 34
setting of, 16, 34
God, 3, 4, 115, 306
delusions and hallucinations of, 134,
    137, 144-145, 151, 154, 165
Groups, 17

adolescent, 241-255
alcoholic, 221
alliances in, 83
art materials, 237
art therapy, 236-279, 282, 335-336
attention seeking in, 106
Bion-type, 30
cohesiveness in, 237, 257
communication, 102, 105, 107, 256
corrective emotional experiences in,
    241
co-therapists in, 239
couples, 283-308
curative factors in, 236
dramatic expression in, 107-108
experience, 103-111, 201
fantasy in, 108
goals, 237, 238
leadership in, 103, 104, 105, 106, 109
mural-making in, 107, 314, 335
network, 241
participation in art work in, 42-43
physical distance in, 16
private practice, 16, 237, 254
research about, 110
role of art therapist in, 236, 239-241
rules, 237
self-expression in, 102
sexuality, 261
shared experiences in, 256, 257-267
spontaneity in, 104, 108, 109
techniques in, 237
therapy in, 38, 102, 118, 236, 279, 281
time of, 238-239, 256
trust in, 237, 256
of women, 256-279
Guilt, 262, 311
in delusions of persecution, 151, 172
in depression, 60, 69, 93
in rage, 90, 249

Hallucinations, amorphous, 137, 335
certainty of, 135
chlorpromazine, 114, 117, 135
of devil, 134
doubt, 134
of God, 119, 131-141
schizophrenic, 112, 189, 320
in seclusion room, 164-165, 321
sensory deprivation, 169

transformations, 136
Handicapped, 18
  mentally, 14, 15
  physically, 14
Harmfulness, 60, 85, 90
Heidelberg Collection, 13
Heritage dominance in alcoholic families,
  224-233
Hopelessness, 73, 81, 83, 85, 88, 93-96,
  99
Human Potential Movement, 14, 15, 30
  personal growth, 15
Hyperkenesis, 218

Idealization of therapist, 35-36, 272, 273
Identification, 225, 226-228, 232
Illness, chronicity of, 303
  delusions of, 128
  literature on art expression, 177
  locus of, 125-126, 128, 179
  physical, 125-126
  positive experience of, 122-123
Illusion, 4
Imagery, 4, 6, 8-9, 13, 39, 102, 257, 268,
  294, 328, 332
  dreams, 13, 210-219, 273, 277
  language of, 39, 98
  processing of, 18, 239, 240
  reflection of, 9, 122, 152
  transference, 271-279
  visual, 7, 9
Insane asylum art, 13
Insight, 108
  from art, 14, 18, 289
  Gestalt therapy, 211
Institution, impact of, 163-170
  medication, 19
  personality of, 20
  politics of, 19
  students in, 22
  treatment team, 19
Integration, 126, 138, 176-187, 211,
  327-328
Interpretation, by art therapist, 119
  client's responsibility, 39, 62
Intuition, 38-40, 82-83
Isolation, 130, 131, 152, 163, 166, 169,
  170, 202, 230, 254, 255, 257, 309

Joint picture, 284, 285-290, 297

Joint scribble, 298, 301, 305
Jungian psychology, 14, 25
  dreams in, 210

Lithium carbonate, 300
Loss, 95, 158, 173, 221, 245

Mandalas, 39
Manic-depressive psychosis, 68, 80
  acting out, 79
  anger, 68, 72, 73, 88, 95
  attention seeking behavior, 106
  case study, 68-75
  characteristics of art expression, 191
  comparison of art expression, 188-198
  denial, 68
  dependency, 294, 306, 307, 308
  diagnosis, 189, 300
  energy, 232
  literature, 232
  mania, 284, 292, 328
  medication, 78
  mood disorder, 68
  mood swings, 68, 107
  pictorial themes, 70-75, 80
  research, 299-308
  session structure, 17
  spouses, 299-308
  suicide, 82, 88, 93
  use of seclusion room, 69, 102, 104,
    106, 191
  use of spiral symbol, 75
  therapeutic relationship, 79
  violence, 79, 102
Manipulation by patient, 37
Marital counseling, 283-308
Meaning, in art, 4, 55
  for art therapist, 4
  of client's symbolism, 126, 151, 256,
    329
  through communication, 83
  consensual, 4
  efforts to establish, 128
  of existence, 256
  idiosyncratic, 115
  as illusion, 3
  in psychotherapy, 4, 115
  in relationships, 49
  shared, 131
  values of, 4

Media, art, 18, 225, 237, 241, 285, 324
   clay, 48, 60; 84
   kinds of, 18, 225, 237, 241, 285, 324
Medical model, 200
   institution, 19
Medication, 19, 114, 117
Megavitamin therapy (orthomolecular
   therapy), 114
Mentally handicapped, 218, 237
Monster, 202, 218, 325
Mood, change, 76
   disorder, 68-69
   of group, 104, 105
   of picture, 71, 80, 289
   swings, 68, 69-70, 75
Movement, with drama, 107, 108
   to music, 104, 105
   in pictures, 303
Myths, 151, 225, 232, 280, 281, 308

National Institute of Mental Health
   (NIMA), 176, 280, 284, 285, 290,
   292, 300, 320
National Institutes of Health (NIH),
   152, 158, 189, 218, 241, 246, 280,
   285, 319, 320
Neurosis, 199-233
   self-destruction, 201-209
Nonjudgmentalness, 200, 240, 256
Nurturance in therapeutic relationship,
   34, 35, 38

Objectification, 10
Objectivity, 16
Organic mental disorders, 112, 117
Outpatient settings, 14
Ownership of art product, 41

Paradox, 36
Paranoia, 132-162, 169, 170-175
Perceptions, attitudes, 119, 285, 290,
   309
   shared, 299, 307
   visual, 131, 284
Permanence of art object, 10, 74
Personality, development of, 8
   growth of, 15
Pharmacology, in depression, 46
   in schizophrenia, 114
Pharmacotherapy, 164, 186, 187, 189

Physical environment, 15-16
Physically handicapped, 14
Pictorial characteristics, 61, 62, 63
   of anger, 121
   of confusion, 120
   of depression, 120
   development of, 67
   of mania, 80
   of psychiatric illness, 118, 119, 120,
      171, 181, 183, 320
Pictorial content, 120, 126, 177, 255
Pictorial themes, bursting out, 72
   death, 70
   in dreams, 210-219
   incarceration, 70, 75, 115
   in marital therapy, 283-308
   in schizophrenia, 119
   in suicide, 85, 97
Poetry, 158-162, 212-214, 332-333
Polarity, in art expression, 177
   in art therapy profession, 13
   in dreams, 213
   in family, 201
Politics of institution, 19-20
Primary process, 8
Prison, 70-71, 115
   dungeon, 205
   guard, 168
   incarceration, 71
   jail, 165, 182, 221, 321
Private practice, 14, 16, 30
   fee, 237
   groups, 241, 254, 256-279, 271, 284,
      285
   neuroses, 201, 215
   structure of, 16
   suicidal patients in, 82
Privileged communication, 41
Professional communication, confidentiality, 41
Projection, 186, 256, 262, 271
Psychiatric wards, 123, 141, 163, 242,
   247, 255
Psychiatry, assessments, 141
   psychiatrists, 5, 29, 63, 85, 112, 114,
      116, 122, 239
   psychoanalysis, 284, 297, 307
   research, 29, 46
   terms of, 8
   use in art expression, 13

Psychomotor retardation in depression,
   45, 48, 63, 64, 88
Psychotherapy, 332
   and alcoholism, 220
   as an art form, 6, 29
   challenge of, 39
   empathy, 33
   intensive, 17
   process of, 6, 9, 32, 41, 113
   progress in, 10
   psychoanalytic, 285
   reflection, 33
   responsibilities of, 35
   self-awareness, 24, 41
   training, 23
Public relations, 21

Raters in research, 178, 188, 301, 303,
   304, 320, 327, 329
Relaxation, 105
Repression, 176, 177, 205
Research, alcoholism, 224-233
   art tasks to elicit specific data, 320,
      322-324
   blind methodology, 324, 326, 329, 330
   confidentiality, 41
   control, 62
   data of, 119, 131, 188, 284, 285
   depression, 62, 64, 93
   double blind procedure, 330
   judgments, 320, 324-326
   manic-depressive psychosis, 299-308
   observations of emerging data, 320, 321-
      322, 331
   ownership of art product, 42
   population, 141
   predictive hypotheses, 320, 326-328
   problems in art therapy research, 328-
      329
   projects of, 317-331
   protocol, 164
   psychological, 46
   raters, 178, 188, 301, 303, 304, 320,
      327, 329
   schizophrenia, 126, 128, 131
   scientific methodology, 319, 329, 330
   structure of, 320
Resistance, 176, 221, 266, 281
   acting out, 33
   depression, 48, 63, 65, 78, 98, 103, 109

   schizophrenia, 135, 254
Role, in family, 281
   in therapeutic relationship, 239-241,
      271

Schizophrenia, acute reactive, 118, 120,
   129, 130, 132, 141, 151, 320
   adolescent, 241-255
   biological research, 133
   catatonic, 174
   chronic, process, 112-113, 118
   communication, 117
   comparison of art expression, 188-198,
      327
   comprehensibility, 130
   delusions, 119, 125, 128, 131-141, 165
   "dementia praecox", 112-113
   depression in, 120, 122, 123, 128, 247
   diagnosis, 188
   disorganization, 120, 123, 131, 132,
      138, 139, 148, 193, 242
   disorganized (heberphrenic), 113
   environment, 113
   etiology of, 176
   euphoria, 129
   families of, 280
   fear, 132, 133, 135, 246
   feeling states, 120-123, 323
   general characteristics, 112, 113
   genetic transmission of, 113
   hallucinations, 119, 131-141, 164-165
   idiosyncratic meaning, 115
   integration, 176, 327-328
   isolation, 130, 131, 152, 255
   megavitamin therapy (orthomolecular
      psychiatry), 114
   mixed undifferentiated, 113
   nature-nurture, 113
   paranoid, 132-162
   pharmocology, 114
   phenomenology of, 320
   positive feelings in, 129, 164-165, 323
   postpsychotic depression, 120, 129,
      139, 324
   recovery style, 176-187, 327-328, 329
   research, 176, 320-328
   resistance, 114
   schizoaffective, 189
   sealing-over, 176, 327-328
   seclusion room, 129, 133, 148, 321-322

sociology, 113
subjective experience of, 16, 118-130,
    321-328, 324
subtypes, 112-113
symptoms, 130
therapeutic relationship in, 114
thought disorder, 112
treatment goals, 118
variety, 112
Sculpture, 70
Sealing-over in schizophrenic recovery,
    176-187, 327-328
Seclusion room, 129, 133, 136, 148,
    321-322, 329
  impact of, 163-170
Self, acceptance, 36, 38, 39, 58
Self-awareness, 177
Self-concept, 324
Self-disclosure of therapist, 282
Self-expression, 211, 239, 255
Self-portrait, 119, 120, 126, 143, 180,
    181, 242, 262, 285, 320, 324, 325-
    326, 327, 335
  given to spouse, 285, 292-299, 301,
    304, 305, 306, 336
Self-revelation, 240-250
Sessions, art, 130
  experience, group, 103
  late, 202
  missed, 33
  structure of, 119, 221, 236, 237, 239
Sexuality, 261-267, 292, 297, 304
Sleep as avoidance, 73
Socialization, objective of, 17
  process of, 3
Spatial matrix in art, 11
Spiral, 75
  as suicide symbol, 85, 101, 120
Spouses, of manic-depressives, 299-308
  in therapy, 283-308
Staff, confidentiality, 41
  hostility, 33
  inservice training, 8, 21
  management of patients, 115, 116, 164
  meetings of, 11, 103
  patients' reactions to, 17, 19, 73, 79,
    103, 122, 168, 170, 321, 322
  psychiatric, 20, 30, 61-62, 85, 93, 168,
    239, 304
  relations, 20, 34, 103

response, 130
tensions in, 69, 102
Structure, of research, 319-328, 330
  of sessions, 17, 18, 189, 236, 237-239,
    310, 319, 324
Students, 22
  experiencing art therapy, 23, 24, 25
  failures, 37
Sublimation, 6
Suicide, 30, 42, 48, 59, 63, 82-101, 104,
    120, 247, 290
  ambivalence in, 82, 90
  anger, 85, 88
  communication, 83, 87, 96, 175
  deception, 84
  harmfulness feelings, 85, 90
  hopelessness, 93, 95, 96, 98, 323
  isolation, 83, 85, 96, 101
  message of, 83, 87, 144, 200
  rating of, 83, 84, 93
  research, 93
  self-hate, 85, 120, 201
  spiral symbol, 49, 85, 98
  therapeutic relationship, 83-84, 101
Symbolization, 124, 151, 169, 225-226,
    232, 297, 332
Symbols, 74-75
  of client, 39, 74, 142, 145, 185, 189,
    202-209, 225, 239, 292, 303, 329
  concordance of, 232
  cultural, 13
  sexual, 80, 152-162, 261-267, 297
  spiral, 85, 98, 120
Systems theory in family therapy, 280

Techniques, art therapy, 24, 284-308,
    appendix, 334-336
Television, 163, 170-175
Territoriality in pictures, 107, 289
Themes in pictures, 190
  adolescent, 242
  brains, 119, 121, 124-125
  bursting out, 73
  of client's work, 39
  college anxiety, 242-255
  death, 85
  in dreams, 210-219
  euphoric, 98
  incarceration, 71, 75, 115
  paranoia, 132-134

in psychotic delusions, 143-162, 189, 221, 225, 239, 310, 319
relationship with symbols, 75
schizophrenic, 119, 189, 321
seclusion room, 163-170, 321-322
suicide, 82-101, 201
war, 245-246
Therapeutic relationship, 32-43
alliance, 33, 35, 38, 41, 49, 78
approval of therapist, 35, 40-41, 240, 258, 282
becoming stuck, 36-37
change in style, 334
in depression, 47-48
empathy, 33, 36, 79
in groups, 240
in mania, 78-79
nurturance, 34, 35, 38
primary curative agent, 34, 92-93, 126, 186
reflection, 33, 200
relationship to art project, 39, 70
role in, 33, 42
in schizophrenia, 114-116, 132
in suicide, 83-84
therapeutic gain, 114, 115, 116
transference, 36, 271-279
trust in, 36, 37, 202
Therapeutic style, changes in, 42
Therapy, and drugs, medication, 78, 186
failures, 34, 82
as goal, 41
as laboratory, 34
in schizophrenia, 118
use of time, 42
Thought disorder, 131, 141
Training, in art therapy, 23-24
Bachelor's degree, 24
continuous growth, 24-31
group therapy, 256-279
improvisation, 24
Master's degree, 23-24
Ph.D. program, 24
Transference, 35, 122, 240, 256, 268, 271-279

Treatment, goals of, 17, 114-115
program, 20
team, 33
Trust in therapeutic relationship, 35, 37
Twin studies in schizophrenia, 113

Unconscious, 4, 6-7, 9, 26
blockage of, 186
dreams, 9, 207, 210-219
identifications, 225, 226-228, 232
phenomena of, 8-9, 328
universal, 13
Unipolar depression, see Depression

Verbalization, 9, 11, 238
Violence, feelings of, 101, 214, 250, 252
of manic patient, 79, 102, 104
on television, 175

Wain, Louis, 177
Wisdom, in client, 34-35
in therapist, 34-35, 85, 240
Witch, 143-144, 182, 257, 323
Withdrawal, 73, 85, 97, 98, 107, 221, 223, 230, 231, 238, 255, 281, 287
Women, anatomy, 74-75
assertiveness in, 83-84
group therapy, 241, 256-279
journey into self, 5, 6
as mother, 5, 158, 218
power issue, 268-269, 273, 276
proving competency, 20, 218, 257
role in society, 4
sexuality, 261-267
symbolism of, 154
therapist as model, 36, 239, 269, 276-277
trust, 277
Workshops, 21, 30
in expressive therapies, 102
as quasi-therapy, 33